Environmental Law in Colombia

Environmental Law in Colombia

Fourth Edition

Daniel Rincón Rubiano

This book was originally published as a monograph in the International Encyclopaedia of Laws/Environmental Law.

Founding Editor: Roger Blanpain
General Editor: Frank Hendrickx
Volume Editor: Kurt Deketelaere

Wolters Kluwer

Published by:
Kluwer Law International B.V.
PO Box 316
2400 AH Alphen aan den Rijn
The Netherlands
E-mail: lrs-sales@wolterskluwer.com
Website: www.wolterskluwer.com/en/solutions/kluwerlawinternational

Sold and distributed by:
Wolters Kluwer Legal & Regulatory U.S.
920 Links Avenue
Landisville, PA 17538
United States of America
E-mail: customer.service@wolterskluwer.com

ISBN 978-94-035-1218-1

e-Book: ISBN 978-94-035-1228-0
web-PDF: ISBN 978-94-035-1238-9

This title is available on www.kluwerlawonline.com

The Author

Mr Daniel Rincón Rubiano was born in Bogotá, Colombia, in 1984. He currently works as Senior Legal Counsel at the DEME Group in Belgium. Prior to that, Mr Rincón worked for the Schréder Group and for Enhesa in Brussels, Belgium, and for Dentons-Cárdenas y Cárdenas and Deloitte in Bogota, Colombia. Mr Rincón obtained his law degree at Universidad del Rosario, Colombia, in 2006 and completed a postgraduate specialization in Corporate Law at the same university. Mr Rincón has an LLM in Energy and Environmental Law from the University of Leuven. Daniel is a fellow member of the Sustainability College of Bruges, a member of the Ibero-American Association of Energy Law – (ASIDE) and carries out investigations on international topics for the Department of Mining-Energy Law of the Universidad Externado de Colombia.

The Author

Table of Contents

List of Abbreviations

ANH	National Agency of Hydrocarbons
ANLA	National Authority of Environmental Licences
CAR	Autonomous Regional Corporation
CBD	Convention on Biological Diversity
CDM	Clean Development Mechanism
CFC	Chlorofluorocarbon
CIF	Certificate of Forest Incentive
CITES	Convention on International Trade in Endangered Species of Wild Fauna and Flora
CIURE	Commission for the Rational and Efficient Use of Energy and Non-conventional Sources of Energy
CONPES	National Council of Economic and Social Policy
CRTL	Agreement of Conversion to Clean Technology
DDA	Declaration of Environmental Alternatives
EIA	Environmental Impact Assessment
FAO	Fish and Agriculture Organization of the United Nations
GDP	Gross Domestic Product
IAEA	International Atomic Energy Agency
ICJ	International Court of Justice
IDEAM	Institute of Hydrology, Meteorology and Environmental Studies
INCODER	Colombian Institute of Rural Development
INDERENA	Institute of Renewable Natural Resources and Environment
INVIMA	National Institute of Surveillance of Medicines and Food
ITU	International Telecommunication Union
IUCN	International Union for Conservation of Nature
MASD	Ministry of Environment and Sustainable Development
NCRNR	National Code of Renewable Natural Resources
NDP	National Department of Planning
NFS	National Forest Service

List of Abbreviations

NPFD	National Plan of Forest Development
NTC	Colombian Technical Standard
ODS	Ozone Depleting Substances
PGIRS	Plan for the Integrated Management of Solid Waste
PIC	Prior Informed Consent
POP	Persistent Organic Pollutant
POT	Territorial Zoning Plan
PROURE	National Program for the Promotion of Energy Efficiency
PRTL	Plan of Reconversion to Clean Technologies
RUIA	Registry of Environmental Offenders
SDA	District Secretariat of Environment
SIAC	Environmental Information System of Colombia
SINA	Environmental National System
SINAP	System of Protected Areas
SPNN	System of National Nature Parks
UAE	Special Administrative Unit
UAESPNN	Special Administrative Unit of the System of National Nature Parks
UN	United Nations
UNCCD	United Nations Convention to Combat Desertification
UNESCO	United Nations Educational, Scientific and Cultural Organization
UNFCCC	United Nations Framework Convention on Climate Change
UTO	Ozone Technical Unit
WHC	World Heritage Convention

General Introduction

Chapter 1. General Information

§1. Geography and Population

I. Geography

1. The Republic of Colombia is situated at the north-western corner of South America, on the Equatorial line, between the Tropics, with geographical coordinates 400 north and 72 west.[1] Its territory is crossed by powerful mountain chains that head to the north and are separated by valleys and broad rivers; to the south-east, the territory spreads out over an immense plain, forming the Orinoquia region and the Amazon jungle. Three-quarters of the country is located in the northern hemisphere.

Colombia is the only country in South America with coastlines on both oceans. The border at the north with the Caribbean Sea, between Panama and Venezuela, covers 1,600 km; north-east with Venezuela, 2,219 km; south-east with Brazil, 1,645 km; south-west with Peru, 1,626 km, and Ecuador, 586 km; west with the Pacific Ocean, between Panama and Ecuador, 1,300 km; and north-west with Panama, 266 km. Colombian borders were established by different treaties, including the Suarez-Muñoz Vernaza of 1916 with Ecuador; Lozano–Salomon of 1922, and the Protocol of Rio of 1934 with Peru; Vasquez Cobo-Martins of 1907, and Garcia Ortiz-Mangabeira of 1928 with Brazil; Spanish Arbitration of 1891, Swiss Arbitration of 1922, and Lopes de Mesa–Gil Borges of 1941 with Venezuela; and the Liévano-Boyd of 1976, with Panama.

2. The total area of the territory comprises 1,138,910 km^2, including 1,038,700 km^2 of land, equivalent to twice the size of Texas, and 100,210 km^2 of water. Colombian territorial sea extends to 12 nautical miles (nm), the exclusive economic zone is 200 nm, and the continental shelf is 200 miles deep. Colombian territory includes the archipelago of San Andres and Providencia in the Caribbean Sea and the islands of Malpelo, Gorgona and Gorgonilla in the Pacific Ocean. In November 2012, the International Court of Justice (ICJ) ruled on the territorial dispute between Nicaragua and Colombia, allocating sovereignty over certain islands to Colombia

1. The World Fact Book, 'Colombia', https://www.cia.gov/the-world-factbook/countries/colombia/, 29 Sep. 2020.

and establishing a new maritime boundary delimitation of the exclusive economic zones and continental shelf of both nations.

3. South American terrain presents a variety of geographical areas that shape different reliefs in the continent, such as the Amazon watershed, the Orinoco region, the Marabina space, the Caribbean Sea, the Pacific Ocean, the Guyana region, the Brazilian region, the trapezium of Chaco-Paraná, the Pampa and the Patagonian cone. As part of South America, Colombia participates from five geographical areas that give birth to the country's geographical and climatic conditions and are known in Colombia as regions. Colombian regions include the Amazon, Caribbean, Pacific, Orinoco and Andean, and exhibit different characteristics as to topography, hydrography, climate, natural resources and people, which shape a regional identity, ethnicity, economy and culture. The regional division is only taken into account for geographical and, to a certain extent, environmental management purposes, as the main administrative division of Colombia consists of departments and municipalities.

4. Being the least populated, the Colombian Amazon region concentrates 30% of the national territory and is wealthy in biodiversity, being home to more than 50,000 indigenous people dispersed in numerous communities and a multiplicity of species of fauna and flora amid a vast jungle. The Amazon territory is mainly flat, with variations of hills and low plateaus. The main economic activities taking place in this region include forestry, wild species trading and research for pharmaceutical products. Further up in the northeast and bordering Venezuela, the Orinoco River marks the beginning of the Orinoco region. It has an extensive, flat and warm savanna landscape which forms a beautiful contrast between the greens of the grassland and the blue of the horizon, covering the surface of low-populated departments such as Arauca, Casanare, Meta and Vichada. Cattle breeding is the main economic activity of the region and is carried out in the area known as Oriental Plains. In recent years, the discovery of oil fields in Arauca and Casanare has attracted settlers to this region.

5. The Andean region is the industrial region of Colombia, occupying 27% of the territory and hosting the main and most populated cities, including Bogota, Medellin, Cali and Bucaramanga. As the region covers the three mountain ranges, it offers different landscapes like *paramos*, high plateaus, snowy mountains, volcanoes, valleys, lacunas, springs and mountainous sources of water. In the northern part of the country, we find the Caribbean region with its varied array of ecosystems, like dry forests in the Guajira peninsula, humid jungle in the gulf of Uraba or the archipelagos and islands in the Caribbean Sea. Although the terrain of the Caribbean region is mainly plain, the highest peaks of the country, Colon y Bolivar, are found in this region at the Sierra Nevada de Santa Marta, where indigenous communities dwell together with endemic species of flora and fauna. Finally, the Pacific region located on the west side of the country, with its wild coastal trip covered with jungle and mangrove swamps, gives origin to one of the most humid climates with annual precipitations of 9,000 millimetres in areas like Choco, as well as high temperatures in the whole region. Due to its biodiversity, this area is known as the Choco-bio and is home to four natural national parks.

6. In general, the Colombian climate is tropical and rather homogeneous throughout the year. Given its location, there is no spring, summer, autumn or winter, but rather a rainy and dry season that marks changes in weather and ecology. Climatologic conditions also vary according to latitude and altitude factors, resulting in temperatures that exceed 23°C in the coastal zone, the Amazon, Orinoco and the Pacific region, as well as temperatures between 0°C on top of the Andean Mountains and 14°C, which is the case of the capital city, Bogota. In mountainous regions, the temperature drops 6°C every 1,000 metres.

7. Three mountain ranges, known as '*cordilleras*', dominate the Colombian relief. As the Andes enters Colombia at the border with Ecuador at the Nudo de los Pastos, it splits further up north into two branches: the Western and Central cordilleras. From the Central cordillera, a third separates: the Eastern cordillera. The combination of these ridges with the valleys and rivers that travel along the mountains gives rise to ecosystems like *paramos*, the Amazon jungle, herbaceous vegetation in Amazon hills, plain savannas, low forests, deserts, wet forests, mangrove swamps, Andean forests, Caribbean savannas, swamps, tropical forests and intervened areas.[2]

8. The hydrographic system of Colombia is formed by five large basins (*vertientes*), which include the Caribbean, Pacific, Orinoco, Amazon and Catatumbo areas. The main rivers rise in the Colombian Massif: the Magdalena, Cauca, Caquetá and Patía, and it is estimated that 1,800 rivers exist in the national territory. Some lacunas located above 2,700 metres are considered sacred and magical, thanks to the legends and myths that former cultures created to explain the origins of the universe prior to the arrival of the Spanish.

II. Population

9. Colombian population is a mixture of indigenous ancestors, Spaniard colonizers and African tribes. According to Worldometer's elaboration of the latest United Nations (UN) data[3] in 2022, Colombia had a population of 52,118,053. With respect to the world, Colombia is 29th among the most populated countries and the 3rd most populated country in Latin America after Brazil and Mexico. The birth rate is estimated to be 14.89 births per 1,000 inhabitants, and the death rate is 5.56 per 1,000 inhabitants. Urban population represents 82% of the population, concentrated in three major cities: Bogota, Medellin and Cali. The increasing migration rate has

2. Germán Márquez Calle, 'Ecosistemas Estratégicos de Colombia', www.sogeocol.edu.co/documentos/07ecos.pdf, 15 Jul. 2003.
3. Worldometer. Colombia Population, https://www.worldometers.info/world-population/colombia-population/.

left half of the Colombian territory with less than 3% of the population. Only 1% of Colombian people are considered indigenous people according to their traditions and languages.

10. The existing ethnic groups are classified as mixed blood or mestizo (53.5%), white European Colombian (30.7%), African Colombian, Mulatto, Palenquero, or Raizal (10.5%), Native South American (3.4%) and other ethnicities (1.9%).[4] Concerning economic activities: 48% of the population engages in trade and services; 26% in agriculture, forestry and fishing; 18% in industrial activities; and 8% in other occupations. In terms of age structure, the majority of Colombians are comprised between 15 and 64 years of age, representing 68% of the population, 16,932,143 being male and 17,607,445 female. The annual population growth rate is estimated at 1.517%.

§2. Legal and Political Structure

11. Constitutional tradition in Colombia dates back to 1810 with the first declaration of independence from the Spanish Crown. After a long process of defining the federal and republican nature of the Colombian State, reflected in the adoption of different State constitutions, in 1886, Colombia defined itself as a national state and adopted the 1886 Constitution, which lasted until 1991. In 1991, amid a bloody national conflict fuelled by drug trafficking, guerrillas, emerging paramilitary groups, proposals to adopt extradition in Colombia, and a growing trend to open internal markets towards globalization, the national Political Constitution of 1991 was enacted.

12. The 1991 Constitution defines Colombia as a social democratic State governed by the rule of law. The political form of Colombia is a unitary republic, decentralized, with autonomy of its territorial entities, such as departments, municipalities, districts and indigenous territories, and with separation of powers in executive, legislative and judicial branches. Colombia is a central State territorially divided into departments, municipalities and/or districts. Departments are considered the main political-administrative unit, and they are responsible before the national government for issues concerning the department's jurisdiction and the municipalities/districts. Departments can only exercise the executive and legislative powers expressly granted by the Constitution or Law and must not exceed those powers.

13. The Colombian executive branch is represented by the President, who represents the chief of the State, the government and the Army. The President is democratically elected by direct vote for a four-year period. The President has the supreme executive power to adopt and promulgate national laws and regulations.

4. World Atlas, 'Ethnic Groups of Colombia', https://www.worldatlas.com/articles/ethnic-groups-of-colombia.html July 2019.

The executive branch is integrated by the President, the Vice President, the Ministries and the directors of the Administrative Department. At departmental level, the executive branch is represented by the Governor, and at the municipal or district level by the Mayor.

14. The legislative branch is represented by the Congress of the Republic. The Congress is democratically elected by direct vote for a four-year period and is integrated by two chambers: the Senate and the House of Representatives. The Congress is responsible for approving any amendments to the Constitution, passing and enacting laws, and enforcing political control on governmental and administrative authorities. The Constitution establishes the cases where the Senate or the Chamber of Representatives has the exclusive competence on a specific matter; for example, the approval of international treaties is an exclusive competence of the Senate, whereas the presentation of draft laws concerning taxes belongs exclusively to the Chamber of Representatives. At the departmental level, the legislative branch is represented by the Departmental Assembly, and at the municipal or district level by the Local Council.

15. The judicial branch of power is represented by the four high courts: the Supreme Court of Justice, the Council of State, the Constitutional Court and the Supreme Council of the Judicature. The Supreme Court of Justice is the court of last resort for settling differences arising from criminal, labour, civil, procedural and commercial litigations, as well as for validating sentences adopted in foreign countries. The Council of State is competent to rule on controversies arising between citizens and the Colombian State, including matters of public procurement, licences, concessions, administrative sanctions, intellectual property, taxes, elections and State liability. The Council of State also serves as an advisory body to the executive branch. The Constitutional Court is the highest court on constitutional matters and is responsible for ensuring that laws and regulatory instruments do not contravene the Constitution. The Supreme Council of the Judicature is the entity in charge of justice administration in the country and settlement of jurisdiction conflicts.

§3. Economic Characteristics

16. Colombian economy is focused on service activities, accounting for 63%; industry, 18.9%, including textiles, coal, emeralds, cement, food processing, and clothing and footwear; and agriculture, 18%, comprising coffee, cut flowers, bananas, sugar cane and oilseed. The main Colombian exports are petroleum, coffee, coal, nickel, emeralds, apparel, bananas and cut flowers.

17. The official currency in Colombia is the Colombian Peso (COP). The Gross Domestic Product (GDP) is estimated at USD 323 billion, with purchasing power per capita of USD 14,565 and an unemployment rate of 14.4%, according to official statistics.[5] The Average Annual Income is USD 1,470, and the estimated population living below poverty line is 46.8%. In comparison with Latin American countries, Colombia is the 4th economy in the region.[6]

§4. Social and Cultural Characteristics

18. According to the Constitution, Spanish is the official language of Colombia, accounting for 80% Spanish speakers. Languages and dialects spoken by ethnic groups include more than sixty-nine tongues and are enshrined in the Constitution. The Constitution establishes that languages different from Spanish are deemed as official languages in the territories in which they are spoken; however, the education provided thereof has to be bilingual. The various Spanish expressions, idioms and dialects spoken in different regions of Colombia mark relevant cultural differences among Colombians, which are evident in their traditions, behaviour, ethnicity, political orientation and relationship with the environment.

19. Pursuant to the Constitution, the education system is free in primary school and to some extent in secondary and high school. In terms of higher education, Colombia has a wide range of universities, colleges and institutions that are mainly located in Bogota and the main cities. The prices of higher education are considerably different for private and public institutions, which, in some cases, limits the access of low-income families to high-quality education. The literacy rate is 95.093%.

20. The former Constitution of 1886 established the Catholic, Apostolic and Roman religions as the official religions of the whole nation. The adoption of the National Constitution of 1991 brought along the protection of the right to free beliefs and practice of one's own religions, ensuring non-discrimination for religious reasons. It is estimated that 81% of the Colombian population is Roman Catholic, although only 25% are practising Catholics. The second largest religion is Protestantism with 13.5%, followed by other faiths with 3.4%. Although the separation between the State and the Catholic Church is a principle of Colombian Constitutional Law, the church still plays an important role in shaping laws involving fundamental rights and has influence over national security issues.

§5. Main Environmental Problems

21. The main environmental problems of Colombia are attributed to its natural and geographical situation, the negative impacts that human activities in developing economies entail and the overexploitation of natural resources. The decrease in

5. Departamento Administrativo Nacional de Estadística (DANE). Indicadores económicos, https://www.dane.gov.co/index.php/indicadores-economicos.
6. Proexport. 'Invierta en Colombia', www.inviertaencolombia.com.co/images/Adjuntos/Presentacion_Colombia_Espanol_Marzo_2019.pdf.

availability and offer of environmental services and the diagnosis of deadly diseases in human beings caused by polluting conditions reflect the noxious effects that contamination has had in Colombia. Although proposing a closed list of environmental problems may serve to illustrate the environmental situation of the country, it may also exclude some current factors perceived as small-scale problems that can prompt serious environmental issues in the future. Hence, this chapter will present an overview of the main environmental problems by describing their natural and man-made causes, as well as the gaps and challenges facing governmental institutions when tackling environmental problems.

I. Illegal Mining

22. Illegal mining has become a major environmental, social and political issue in Colombia. According to Article 159 of Law 685/2001, illegal mining consists of all exploratory or extractive activities carried out in public or private property without a valid mining title or prior authorization granted by the owner of the property. The lack of a strong presence and coordination from national, regional and local governments, effective regulation and the deployment of armed forces; the growing price of gold in times of economic uncertainty; and the lack of formal employment are all important factors that have contributed to an increase of illegal mining activities within recent years.

23. In accordance with the EVOA report (evidence of alluvial gold exploitation) issued by the Ministry of Mines and Energy, the United Nations Office on Drugs and Crime (UNODOC) and the United States Embassy, Colombia recorded 92,046 hectares being used for the extraction of alluvial gold, with approximately 53% of the activities being undertaken in territories with restrictions to mining (i.e., national parks, forest reserves). Approximately 53,000 hectares of protected areas are being used for illegal mining activities. The two departments that are most affected by the illegal extraction of gold in the country are Antioquia and Chocó; it is worth noting that out of the 125 municipalities of Antioquia, 53 of them are affected by illegal mining.

24. Criminal bands have become important actors in this problem, as 43% of the areas affected by unlicensed exploitation of gold coincide with territories that are used for the harvest of illegal crops such as coca leaves. These forces use illegal mining as a way of funding their operations, showing a strong presence in departments such as Norte de Santander, Antioquia Tolima, Valle del Cauca, Nariño, Cauca, Meta, Guaviare, Guainía and Vaupés.

25. The lack of a valid mining title in the development of mining activities derives from an absence of the corresponding environmental permits. The negative effects on the environment derived from illegal mining account for the loss of nearly

200,000 hectares of rivers and jungle areas. Another grave effect of this activity consists of water contamination as a result of the use of mercury in the extraction of gold, which has become a major health issue for fauna and people surrounding illicit mining territories.

26. The region most affected by the use of mercury in Colombia is the Caquetá River Basin. In a recent study made by the Instituto Nacional de Salud de Colombia, there were findings that 80% of the indigenous population of said region had mercury poisoning, exhibiting effects such as loss of memory, irritability, involuntary limb movement and kidney failure.

II. Atmospheric Pollution

27. Atmospheric pollution is perceived by Colombians as the main environmental problem of the country. This appreciation is due to the fact that most of the population dwells in metropolitan and urban areas, where about 80% of the industry is settled. The causes of atmospheric pollution can be traced back to the release of particulate matter, Sulphur Dioxide (SO_2), Nitrogen Oxide (NO_2) and Dioxins and Furans from industrial activities; open-air incinerations and extractive activities; combustion of fossil fuels in power plants; and the emission of Carbon Monoxide and fine particles from vehicles. At the residential level, households using wood, coal and other fuels for food cooking contribute to worsening indoor air quality, leading to respiratory diseases.

28. The cities with higher levels of atmospheric contamination include Bogota, Barranquilla, Cali, Medellin and Sogamoso, Bogota being the city where 50% of the harmful effects of air pollution take place. Colombia has a legal framework for air pollution aimed at controlling emissions from fixed and mobile sources, as well as the combustion of certain fuels. However, coordinated and efficient action from local and sector authorities, as well as better-articulated monitoring stations, is required to provide truthful information on air quality in the cities.

III. Water Pollution

29. The inappropriate management of water resources has led to contamination of surface, ground and maritime water, evidenced by aquatic biodiversity loss and high concentrations of pollutants. Furthermore, water pollution has triggered a problem of public health due to the scarce offer of drinking water and the consequent proliferation of diarrheic diseases in minors. The main sources of water pollution are found in wastewater which is discharged into water bodies without any treatment and into the sewerage system, exceeding the maximum allowable pollutant thresholds. These wastewater discharges are produced as a result of waste generation from industrial, mining and agricultural activities.

30. Water pollution, insufficient provision of hygiene and sanitation services, and the lack of drinking water generate significant annual costs. In terms of environmental damage, the aquatic ecosystems of Cartagena have suffered considerable loss; the rivers of Bogota, Cali, Otun and Oro require costly and complex decontamination processes to re-establish their quality levels; and other strategic ecosystems such as wetlands, lagoons and lacunas are continuously exposed to high environmental pressure. Some administrative problems preventing water pollution from being adequately approached include the inefficient coordination between the Ministry of Environment and Sustainable Development (MASDS for its initials in Spanish) and the Ministry of Agriculture and the issuance of concession and abstraction permits without certainty on the actual offer of water resources and their availability.

IV. Deforestation

31. Colombia's biodiversity wealth is increasingly threatened by deforestation. Deforestation is one of the problems that best reflect the environmental effects of internal conflict, including displacement of farmers and rural communities to urban centres, growing of illegal crops, land colonization and expansion of agricultural borders. These factors represent 70% of deforestation causes, while timber production, wood consumption and wildfires account for 30%. Although soil degradation requires a special analysis, it is important to note that 45% of Colombian soil is used for purposes different from those for which soil is suitable, and 8% of the total soil inventory presents some degree of erosion. Deforestation in Colombia jeopardizes the existence of endemic species, flora and fauna biodiversity, and the availability of basic environmental services, such as wetlands, tropical forests and appropriate soil.

V. Natural Disasters

32. Due to its geographical situation and the conditions of its terrain, Colombia is often exposed to natural disasters. Natural disasters are mainly caused by earthquakes, landslides and floods, which trigger devastating consequences. The lack of strategic ecosystem protection, appropriate drainage systems and poor management of municipal waste intensify the magnitude of natural disasters and impede natural barriers to activating and countering the disastrous effects of floods and landslides.

VI. Other Problems

33. The economic growth of Colombia boosted characteristic environmental problems of developing economics like solid and hazardous waste generation, residues from mining and industrial activities, and the uncontrolled use and disposal of chemical substances. The main industrial cities of Colombia produce an average of

24.85 million tonnes of solid waste per year, mainly composed of vegetable and animal products and paper. Five departments account for 89% of the total amount of hazardous waste generated in Colombia. These numbers contrast with the absence of hazardous waste treatment installations or safe landfills in Colombia and raise concerns about the sound disposal of hazardous waste. Furthermore, Colombia does not have an information network on waste generation, handling, transport, treatment, recovery and/or final disposal. These facts, which amounted to the lagging enforcement of waste management plans, labelling of hazardous goods and safety data sheet requirements, may be the first symptoms of potential environmental problems in Colombia.

Chapter 2. Basic Principles of Environmental Law

§1. Introduction

34. Basic principles of environmental law are contained in the Constitution of 1991, Law 99/1993 and the National Code of Renewable Natural Resources (NCRNR). The 1991 Constitution is referred to as the 'green' or 'ecologic' Constitution due to the number of provisions addressing environmental issues, as it will be further detailed in the upcoming lines. In addition, Law 99/1993 develops environmental constitutional postulates and establishes a set of environmental principles that guide environmental policy in Colombia. Law 99/1993 integrates international environmental principles by expressly referring to the Rio Declaration of 1992 and providing them with full normative value. The NCRNR establishes environmental principles that have guided national policy for almost twenty years and which are mainly inserted in Law 99/1993. Therefore, this chapter will deal with constitutional provisions and environmental principles guiding the development and implementation of environmental policy and law in Colombia.

§2. Constitutional Provisions

35. The making process of the 1991 Constitution was surrounded by an international desire to turn good ecological intentions into effective environmental protection. The incorporation of environmental protection into the Colombian political agenda was certainly achieved by consecrating the various provisions on the conservation and protection of natural resources, the establishment of the right to a healthy environment and the inclusion of environmental considerations as a matter of public policy.[7] According to the Constitutional Court, the 1991 Constitution has a threefold environmental dimension: the protection of the environment, which configures the environmental legal framework; the right of every person to enjoy a healthy environment; and the range of obligations imposed on public authorities and citizens. The number of environmental provisions established in the Constitution, the fundamental connotation that the right to a healthy environment bears, and the close relationship between the right to a healthy environment and the rights to public health, decent life and personal integrity attribute the Constitution an ecologic nature that has been acknowledged by the Constitutional Court.

36. The following provisions of the 1991 Constitution set the basis for environmental regulation: Article 8, on the obligation to protect nation's cultural and natural wealth; Article 49, on healthcare and environmental sanitation; Article 58, establishing the ecologic purpose of the property; Article 66, on agricultural credits for environmental calamities; Article 67, on education for environmental protection; Article 79, establishing the right to a healthy environment and participation in environmental decision-making; Article 80, on the management and exploitation

7. Constitutional Court, Sentence No. T-092 of 19 Feb. 1993, Magistrate, Simon Rodriguez.

planning of natural resources; Article 81, on the prohibition of chemical, biological and nuclear weapons; Article 82, establishing the duty to protect cultural and natural resources; Article 215, establishing situations of emergency for the perturbation or threat to ecological order; Article 226, on the internationalization of ecological affairs; Article 268 number 7, on the surveillance of natural resources and the environment; Article 277 number 4, establishing environmental protection as one of the functions of the Public Attorney; Article 282 number 5, establishing the People Ombudsman and popular actions as mechanisms for environmental protection; Article 289, on cooperation and integration programmes for environmental preservation in bordering areas; Article 300 number 2, on Departmental Assemblies and the environment; Article 301, on fiscal and administrative management according to the department's natural resources and ecological circumstances; Article 310, on the population density control in San Andres and Providencia to preserve the environment and natural resources; Article 313 number 9, on Municipal Councils and ecological heritage; Articles 317 and 294 on land appreciation tax for environmental and natural resources conservation; Article 330 number 5, on Councils of Indigenous Territories and preservation of the environment; Article 332, on the State ownership over the subsoil and non-renewable resources; Article 333, on limitations to economic activities for environmental reasons; Article 334, on State intervention to preserve natural resources and a healthy environment; Article 339, on environmental policy in the National Plan of Development; Article 340, on the representation of ecological sectors in the National Council of Planning; and Article 344 on the provision of environmental sanitation and potable water as part of the aims of the State. These provisions and the right to a healthy environment are regarded as the legal basis for environmental legislation in Colombia. The Constitutional Court allocates special value to the ecologic character of the 1991 Constitution by using an environmental-protective interpretation criterion when testing the hierarchy of constitutional rights and values.

§3. Principles of Environmental Law

37. Law 99/1993 establishes fourteen environmental principles that guide environmental policy and law in Colombia. Law 99/1993 states that the economic and social development of Colombia should be guided by the principles and the sustainable development concept established in Rio de Janeiro in 1992. The legal remission that Law 99/1993 makes to the Rio de Janeiro principles has been challenged before the Constitutional Court, arguing that such remission requires a law of higher hierarchy than the one of an ordinary law, such as Law 99/1993. The Constitutional Court has found that the remission of Law 99/1993 to the Rio Declaration is part of the lawmaker's autonomy; the application of the principles must be indirect and shall serve as interpretation criteria for same-hierarchy provisions. Hence, the full application of the Rio principles requires the concurrence of other normative elements in order to provide these principles with full normative value.[8]

8. Constitutional Court, Sentence No. C-528 of 24 Nov. 1994, Magistrate, Alejandro Martinez Caballero.

38. At national level, environmental principles established in Law 99/1993 include: protection and sustainable use of national biodiversity; the policies related to population have to take into account the right of human beings to a healthy and productive life in harmony with the nature; the zones of *paramos*, *subparamos*, water sources and aquifer recharge zones must be subject to special protection; the use of water resources has to give priority to water for human consumption; the development of environmental policies must be the result of scientific investigation, and the lack of scientific certainty must not be used to postpone the adoption of effective measures to impede the degradation of the environment, meaning precautionary principle; the State must promote the incorporation of environmental externalities, and the use of economic instruments for the prevention, correction and restoration of environmental deterioration, and the conservation of renewable natural resources; the landscape must be protected; disaster prevention must be a matter of collective interest, as well as enforcement measures to avoid non-compliance; protective and recovery actions must be shared and coordinated tasks between the State, community, non-governmental organizations and the private sector; Environmental Impact Assessments (EIAs) must be the basic instruments for the adoption of decisions regarding activities negatively affecting the environment; environmental management must be decentralized, democratic and participative; the national environmental system must be established for the environmental management of Colombia; and governmental institutions must be structured by taking into account the integrated management of the environment, and their interaction with economic, social and land planning.

39. From the list of principles consecrated in Law 99/1993, one of the principles that has had the attention of the Constitutional Court is the precautionary principle. The Constitutional Court describes how the different conceptions of the application of the precautionary principle share basic elements: first, it is applied whenever there is a threat of serious hazard to human health or the environment from which no scientific certainty exists; second, there exists a certainty principle; and third, the authorities must adopt protective measures without conditioning the adoption of such measures to the obtaining of conclusive proofs. Pursuant to the Constitutional Court, the adoption of protective measures based on the precautionary principle and the lack of scientific certainty must be conditioned to the existing environmental policies adopted by law, duly motivated and far from any arbitrariness. Likewise, the Constitutional Court has delimited the application of the precautionary principle to the following conditions: the existence of a hazard likely to cause environmental damage; the irreversibleness of the damage the hazard can cause; the existence of a certainty principle about the hazard, even though there is no conclusive proof of its hazardousness; that the decision of the authority is addressed towards impeding environmental degradation; and that the authority's decision is motivated and exceptional.[9]

9. Constitutional Court, Sentence No. C-293 of 23 Apr. 2002, Magistrate, Alfredo Beltran Sierra.

Chapter 3. Historical Background

40. Colombian environmental law developed, as in many other countries, as a set of different provisions intended to protect and preserve natural resources. The evolution of Colombian environmental law certainly coincides with international developments, including the Stockholm Declaration of the United Nations Conference on the Human Environment in 1972, the Rio Declaration on Environment and Development in 1992, and the growing number of treaties regulating environmental issues. With the adoption of the NCRNR in 1974, three moments can be distinguished in the development of environmental law: prior to the adoption of the NCRNR, between the adoption of the NCRNR and the enactment of Law 99 in 1993, and from 1993 onwards, when the national environmental law-making process is influenced by the ratification of international treaties, the adoption of foreign regulatory developments from industrialized countries, and the increase of national projects involving the exploitation of natural and non-natural resources.

41. Prior to the adoption of the NCRNR, Colombian environmental legislation was fragmented into different regulations, partially addressing the management of natural resources. Some examples of this trend are reflected in the laws adopted by the Liberator Simon Bolivar in 1825 and 1829 concerning the conservation of forests and water; other legislation during the republican period of Colombia, like Decree 1279/1908 establishing the Department of Waste Land and National Forests that implemented the payment of works and projects with forests; the National Fiscal Code of 1912, containing provisions on the use of forests in the wasteland; Decree 376/1957 on marine fishing; and Decree 1975/1959 regulating fishing in fresh water. Notably, Decree 1975/1959 also created the National Institute of Renewable Natural Resources and Environment (INDERENA) as part of the Ministry of Agriculture, which is responsible for the management of natural resources, conservation and environmental protection. The creation of the INDERENA could arguably be the most important legacy of the period before 1974, as the INDERENA undertook the task of preparing a law empowering the President to adopt a code of natural resources and the task of drafting and debating the proposed code. Since its birth in 1959, the INDERENA has taken care of citizens' participation in environmental decision-making, the creation of the national system of nature parks, natural resources and biodiversity investigation, preparation of an environmental permitting system, and meaningful ecologic awareness programmes for more than twenty years until its liquidation in 1993, and the subsequent creation of the Ministry of Environment.[10]

42. In 1973, by means of Law 23/1973, the Congress of Colombia granted the President the power to adopt an NCRNR and Environmental Protection with the purpose of achieving a rational exploitation and conservation of natural resources. Law 23/1973 also establishes the basis of what the NCRNR would later develop, meaning the prevention of environmental pollution; the acknowledgement of air,

---

10. Manuel Rodriguez Becerra, 'Inderena, el gran pionero de la gestión ambiental en Colombia', www.manuelrodriguezbecerra.org/bajar/inderena.pdf, 6 Aug. 1994.

water and soil as goods prone to suffer from contamination; environmental policy, economic incentives, education programmes; environmental quality, maximum emission limits and sanctions. The project of drafting the new code was led by the Advisory Commission established in Law 23/1973 and backed by the technical bodies of the INDERENA. The Legal Office of the Colombian Presidency of Mr Alfonso Lopez Michelsen reviewed the text of the proposed Code and corrected procedural and regulatory aspects. The NCRNR and Environmental Protection were finally adopted by Decree-Law 2811/1974 as the central piece of environmental legislation in Colombia.

43. The code of 1974 was issued in response to the Stockholm Declaration of 1972 as the first attempt in Colombia to regulate the relationship between society and the environment, which incorporates the ongoing philosophical trends of conservationism and environmentalism. The NCRNR's provisions reflect a whole-like conception of the environment, demanding integrated protection and an environmental-media approach that looks at each natural resource. The NCRNR establishes coherent, coordinated and harmonious regulatory provisions aimed at protecting the environment and regulating the sustainable use of renewable natural resources in two books and an additional third part. The first book deals with the definition and provisions of environmental policy, international environmental matters, means for the development of environmental policy, and provisions on environmental preservation from elements other than natural resources, such as noise, solid waste, and human and animal health, among other subjects. The second book addresses, on the one hand, the ownership, use and formalities of renewable natural resources and, on the other hand, the atmosphere and aerial space, non-maritime water, the sea and the seabed, primary energy resources, geothermal resources, the land and soil, ground flora, ground fauna, hydro-biological resources, sanitary protection of fauna and flora, the landscape and its protection, and the management of renewable natural resources.

44. The enactment of the Political Constitution in 1991 marks the start of a new environmental legal framework in Colombia by upgrading environmental issues to constitutional provisions and thus providing them with constitutional protection. The 1991 Constitution is said to be an ecologic constitution due to the number of provisions containing environmental aspects, including the right to a healthy environment; the duty to protect the environment, conserve special areas, promote education on environmental issues, prevent and control polluting factors, provide the means to ensure community's participation, and control the entry and exit of genetic resources. The 1991 Constitution integrates the environmental dimension into national planning, gives environmental policy the same hierarchy as other matters of national policy, introduces the concept of sustainable development, grants environmental competences to territorial entities and establishes that the property has an inner ecological purpose which has to be fulfilled. On top of that, the 1991 Constitution provides citizens and groups with expedite and accessible mechanisms to protect environmental rights.

45. The adoption of the Political Constitution in 1991 and the forthcoming meeting in Rio de Janeiro in 1992 gave momentum to rethinking a new institutional environmental framework in Colombia, leading to the proposal for the creation of the Ministry of Environment. The attempt to switch environmental competences from the INDERENA to fresher environmental institutions was not new in the political agenda; however, it was the historical circumstances of 1992 and the wilfulness of the existing government that led to the second most important piece of environmental legislation, Law 99/1993. The Colombian President Mr Cesar Gaviria commended the development of a proposal to create new environmental institutions so that the environmental aims of the 1991 Constitution could be reached. In addition, Colombia wanted to have a Ministry of Environment in place for the Earth Summit of 1992 in Rio in order to show the compromise of the country with environmental protection to the international community.

46. As a result, in 1993, Law 99 was enacted, creating the Ministry of Environment, reorganizing the public sector responsible for the management and conservation of the environment and renewable natural resources, creating the Environmental National System (SINA), and regulating environmental licences, among others. Law 99/1993 updates the provisions established in the NCRNR, harmonizes the NCRNR with international environmental law and articulates its regulation with the Rio Declaration's environmental principles. Moreover, Law 99/1993 defines sustainable development as the integrator element for environmental management and establishes biodiversity protection as a national priority. Law 99/1993 also prompts knowledge on environmental and natural resources topics by creating more than five research institutes and technical agencies responsible for advising the Ministry in policymaking. Since the adoption of Law 99/1993, environmental legislation has focused on the development of topics regulated in the NCRNR, like solid waste regulation or atmospheric pollution.

47. International environmental law has also played a key role in shaping Colombian environmental law. The signature and later ratification of international conventions on environmental aspects, such as Ozone Depleting Substances (ODS), climate change, transboundary movement of hazardous waste, *in situ* and *ex situ* protection of biodiversity, prior consent for hazardous chemicals, import and export of drug precursors, development of threatened species books, or Persistent Organic Pollutants (POPs) are some examples of international environmental law being transposed in the national legal framework and enforced by governmental institutions. This international influence is observed in Colombia in laws ratifying international treaties, decrees providing for the general framework and regulation on the matter, and resolutions establishing the technicalities to make international environmental legislation a tangible reality. Furthermore, the influence of international law is also observed in the environmental regulatory trend of Colombia, which responds to new regulatory developments in industrialized countries, negotiation of free trade agreements, response to endemic contamination problems and development of specific economic activities.

Chapter 4. Role of Government Institutions in the Shaping and Administration of Environmental Law and Policy

§1. Introduction

48. Law 99/1993 establishes two main environmental authorities, the Ministry of Environment and the Autonomous Regional Corporations (CARs), and grants territorial entities (departments, municipalities and districts) specific competences on environmental matters. The CARs date back to 1959 with the creation of the Valle del Cauca Corporation under the auspices of the Tennessee Valley Authority of the United States and the subsequent establishment of eighteen autonomous corporations, whereas the Ministry of Environment has its main antecedent in the creation of the INDERENA. Law 99/1993 creates sixteen additional CARs for a total of thirty-three CARs and empowers them to be the maximum environmental authority within their jurisdiction. Concerning the Ministry of Environment, Law 99/1993 vests it with the highest powers on nationwide environmental matters and makes it responsible for environmental management in Colombia.

49. Environmental competences and authorities created by Law 99/1993 do not follow the territorial and administrative decentralization of Colombia. As illustrated in Chapter 1 on the legal and political structure, Colombia has a territorial division integrated by the national state, departments, and municipalities and/or districts, in which departments and municipalities are subject to national regulations and have exclusive powers within their jurisdictions on the matters that the law expressly provides so. This territorial division differs from the approach of the CARs to environmental matters, for the CARs are regional authorities which have been created by taking into account geographical and environmental criteria, such as river basins, strategic ecosystems or nature parks. The jurisdiction of one CAR can comprise more than one department and can also lead to situations where two municipalities of the same department are subject to the environmental competence of two different CARs. In this context, the system of governmental institutions in environmental matters requires quite a harmonious coordination between the national state, the CARs, departments, municipalities and/or districts.

50. The role that governmental institutions have played in shaping and implementing environmental policy has been complemented by the rulings of the high courts, the research bodies of the Ministry of Environment and the community. Concerning environmental investigation, Law 99/1993 creates five research bodies responsible for providing technical advice to the Ministry and contributing towards the consolidation of the national system of environmental information. The participation of the community has also helped shape the administration of environmental law by taking part in the environmental permitting system and raising issues that may have a negative environmental impact on the community. In order to determine how national, regional, departmental and municipal governmental institutions have added up to existing environmental law, the following lines will elaborate on the competences of the existing governmental institutions and how those competences are actually exercised.

§2. THE GOVERNMENTAL INSTITUTIONS AND THEIR COMPETENCES

I. National Level

51. The Ministry of Environment is the main environmental authority at the national level. The structure, functions and aims of the ministry have been amended on different occasions due to the planning and administrative policies of each government. By means of Law 1444/2011, the former Ministry of Environment, Housing and Territorial Development was split into the current Ministry of Environment and Sustainable Development (MASD) and the Ministry of Housing, City and Territory. The main aim of the MASD is to protect Colombia's national natural resources and general environmental health.

52. Decree 3570/2011 further develops Law 1444/2011 by establishing the internal organization and responsibilities of the MASD. The MASD manages the environmental sector through its subordinate entities (*entidades adscritas*), which include the National Fund for the Environment and the Institute of Hydrology, Meteorology and Environmental Studies (IDEAM); and through linked entities (*entidades vinculadas*), including the Institute of Marine and Coastal Research José Benito Vives de Andreis (INVEMAR), Institute of Biological Resource Research 'Alexander von Humboldt', Amazon Institute of Scientific Research 'Sinchi', and the Environmental Research Institute of the Pacific 'John von Neumann'.

53. The general structure of the Ministry (Article 5) includes:

- the Minister's office: seven offices (international affairs, green businesses, coordination of the national environmental system, etc.);
- the office of the Vice-minister: four directorates (climate change, environmental and urban affairs, water resource management, etc.);
- the general secretary; and
- the organs, committees and councils of consultation and advice: seven agencies (management, administrative development, National Environmental Council, etc.).

54. The former power of the Ministry to grant or deny certain environmental licences, permits and authorizations has been undertaken by the National Authority of Environmental Licences (ANLA), as provided for in Decree 3573/2011. Therefore, the functions of the MASD focus on the drafting, design and establishment of environmental and natural resource policies and regulations. Some of the main functions of the Ministry include:

- proposing and establishing the national policy on the environment and natural resources, and establishing the regulation on land use and sea zoning so as to ensure their conservation and sustainable use;

- designing and regulating the general conditions on environmental sanitation; and use, management, exploitation, conservation and recovery of natural resources in order to impede, restrict, eliminate or mitigate the negative impacts of polluting activities;
- supporting other government agencies in the formulation of public policies that may involve environmental issues;
- participating along with the Ministry of Foreign Affairs in the design of the international environmental policy;
- establishing and administering the environmental information system; and
- establishing areas within the System of Protected Areas (SINAP), among others (Article 2).

55. In addition, the MASD draws the regulatory trend of the country by transposing international environmental conventions into national legislation and by establishing environmental regulations covering almost all the technical and practical aspects of their implementation. The CARs and environmental authorities of Great Urban Centres have residual regulatory powers, yet they are limited to the parameters established by the MASD and can only establish stricter threshold values or parameters.

56. The ANLA is set to ensure that projects or activities subject to any kind of environmental licence, permit or authorization comply with the applicable environmental legislation. The ANLA is part of the MASD, and among its functions, it can grant or deny environmental licences, permits or authorizations; follow up on licences, permits and procedures; ensure that public participation mechanisms are duly implemented; and start and conclude investigations on cases of environmental offences.

57. Some of the main powers entrusted to the ANLA that have an impact on the private sector include:

- granting or denying environmental licences, permits or authorizations that are part of the competences of the MASD. For example, the environmental licence for the exploration and use of alternative energy sources with an installed capacity greater than 3MW initially corresponds to the Ministry. However, as of the adoption of Decree 3573/2011, the ANLA is responsible for issuing the environmental licence to these projects; and
- following up on the environmental licences, permits and authorizations. This competence translates into verifying compliance with the obligations established in the environmental licences, permits or authorizations, among others.

II. Regional and Local Levels

58. According to Law 99/1993, the CARs are the entities in charge of creating regional policies of environmental protection within their jurisdiction. The CARs are defined as regional institutions integrated by territorial entities that due to their features constitute a geopolitical, biogeographical or hydro-geographical unit. The entities in charge of the Colombian Amazon, San Andres, Uraba, the Mojana and the Macarena have been named as Corporations of Sustainable Development due to the eco-systemic importance they have. The CARs and the Corporations of Sustainable Development cover thirty-three specific regions of the national territory, which are different from the existing departments, municipalities and districts and which respond to strategic ecosystems criteria. The legal competences of the CARs exclusively concern environmental matters.

59. The CARs are administratively and financially autonomous, have their own budget, and have their own legal standing for accountability purposes. The autonomy of the CARs allows them to act independently from the public power branches, although they remain linked to the MASD by being part of the SINA. The CARs are responsible for administrating natural resources and issues concerning the environment within the area of their jurisdiction. For such purposes, the CARs have to ensure the sustainable development of the region by following the policies and regulations of the MASD. The competences of the CARs include environmental planning, environmental education, management of environmental information and the authorization of projects carried out in the CAR's jurisdiction. Colombian geographical conditions, as well as the regional development of economic activities, have given the CARs a relevant role in the shaping and administration of environmental policy and law, which will be analysed in the following paragraphs.

60. The actual role of the CARs consists of being the maximum environmental authority in the region, responsible for the administration of natural resources and the execution of environmental policies, plans and programmes from the MASD. The CARs' inspection and surveillance powers are executed through follow-up and control activities aimed at ensuring environmental protection. Follow-up and control activities focus on the use of water, soil, air and other renewable natural resources, as well as the movement and trade of such resources. The CARs have enforcement powers to ensure the sound disposal of waste and the appropriate performance of activities involving exploration, exploitation, transport or deposit of non-renewable natural resources.

61. The CARs are the entities in charge of approving or rejecting projects entailing significant negative impacts. Decree 2041/2014, which is compiled in Decree 1076/2015, empowers the CARs to issue environmental licences for projects listed in Article 9 (Article 2.2.2.3.2.3.) of Decree 1076/2015. This important role allows the CARs to authorize the development of activities and projects and the consequent use or affection to natural resources through concessions, permits, authorizations or environmental licences. The CARs also develop biodiversity conservation and protection plans and provide technical advice to territorial entities in disaster planning and prevention.

III. Departmental Level

62. Law 99/1993 gives departments certain and very specific competences on environmental issues. These competences are additional to the ones delegated by the MASD and the CARs. Departments are mainly executors of national, regional and sector programmes, policies and plans on the environment and renewable natural resources. Departments are called to give technical, administrative, financial and budgetary support to the CARs and municipalities for the conservation of the environmental and national resources. In addition, departments enforce environmental law with the coordination of the town hall of each municipality; develop cooperation and integration programmes with other departments and foreign institutions; promote, finance and coordinate projects of irrigation, drainage, land recovery, flood prevention, water flow regulation and protection of river basins; and establish standards on municipal land use and planning programmes, among others.

IV. Local Level

63. Municipalities, districts and the Capital District of Bogota have specific competences on environmental issues, according to Law 99/1993. These competences are the ones delegated by the MASD or the CARs and the ones established in Article 65 of Law 99/1993. The competences on environmental matters at the local level include the promotion and execution of environmental policies, plans and programmes; the adoption of regulations on the control, preservation and defence of the municipal ecological heritage; participation in the plans, programmes and projects of environmental development and natural resources at departmental level; helping the CARs in enforcing environmental legislation in the municipality on issues related with the movement, processing, use, exploitation and trade of renewable natural resources; and control of polluting activities and preservation of water, soil and air. Municipalities and districts have the same environmental powers that departments do in their own jurisdiction.

64. Law 99/1993 refers to Great Urban Centres as municipalities or metropolitan areas with a population higher than 1,000,000 inhabitants. In these areas, local environmental authorities take over the environmental powers that the CARs have in the regions. Law 768/2002 creates other municipal environmental authorities provided with the same environmental powers as the CARs, which include the Districts of Cartagena, Barranquilla and Santa Marta. The environmental powers given to Great Urban Centres and the aforementioned districts concern the issuance of licences, concessions, permits and authorizations for the works and projects taking place within their jurisdiction; the follow-up and control of wastewater discharges, disposal of solid, toxic and hazardous waste; and the adoption of the necessary mitigation, decontamination, sanitation and correction measures to tackle environmental degradation.

65. At the local level, environmental authorities play an important role in the authorization of economic activities, enforcement of environmental law, participation mechanisms and environmental awareness of citizens. This role is comparable to the one played by the CARs at the regional level, with the difference that authorities of Great Urban Centres are often subject to the political wilfulness of local administrations. A good example of these authorities is the District Secretariat of Environment (SDA) in Bogota, which decides on requests for groundwater exploitation, concessions, surface water, occupation of water flows, wastewater discharges and atmospheric permits. The SDA also imposes sanctions for environmental infringements.

Chapter 5. Sources of Environmental Law

66. Colombia has a legal system based on the Roman-Germanic tradition of civil law and establishes a written hierarchical scheme of laws where the constitutional law is the highest source of law. International treaties, laws and any other regulatory instruments must be in accordance with constitutional provisions so they can be part of the Colombian legal framework. The principles and aims of the State are embedded in the Constitution and have a normative value that must be regarded by laws. Concerning environmental law, the Political Constitution establishes the rights, duties, competences and instruments for environmental protection.

67. International treaties are part of the sources of environmental law and are considered constitutional norms. In general, the incorporation of international treaties in national legislation involves the approval of its text by the government; the submission of the Law Proposal approving the treaty before the Congress of the Republic; the enactment of the Law approving the treaty; a mandatory review of the law's constitutionality by the Constitutional Court; and the issuance of a Decree from the President of the Republic promulgating the treaty.

68. Below the Constitution and International Treaties, the first and broadest regulatory instrument is the Law. Laws are adopted by the Congress of the Republic after completing the corresponding legislative procedures. Laws can have different hierarchies due to the matters they regulate, such as organic laws, frame laws and laws vesting the President with legislative faculties. Concerning environmental matters, they are mostly regulated by ordinary laws, such as Law 99/1993, creating the Ministry of Environment, Law 1333/2009 on the enforcement procedure for environmental infractions, Law 1124/2007 regulating the profession of environmental manager or Law 1159/2007 approving the Rotterdam Convention for application of the Prior Informed Consent (PIC) Procedure on the export and import of pesticides and hazardous chemicals. Whenever the President asks the Congress to grant special legislative faculties, the laws to be adopted under these circumstances are known as Decree-Laws. For example, Law 23/1973 empowered the President to adopt the regulation on natural resources and environmental protection, which was finally adopted through Decree-Law 2811/1974 establishing the NCRNR and Environmental Protection.

69. Going lower in the pyramidal legal system, Decrees are found after Laws. As part of the regulatory powers given to the President in the Constitution, Decrees are adopted by the President of the Republic and have the signature of the Ministry involved in the matter regulated by the Decree. In some cases, the Decrees can involve the signature of more than one minister, such as Decree 1609/2002 regulating the handling and transport of dangerous goods by road, which is signed by the MASD and the Ministry of Transport. Decrees regulate and develop the content of Laws. In Colombia, most of the regulations on environmental matters are developed through decrees provided that the NCRNR and Law 99/1993 set the general legal basis to regulate issues like water abstraction, atmospheric emissions, regulation of hunting and fishing, environmental licences and protected areas.

70. Decrees may also be used to compile an existing body of laws, such as Decree 1076/2015, which compiles all environmental-related regulations issued by the national government, in accordance with the President's legislative powers established by Article 189 of the Constitution. This decree was created with the sole purpose of adopting a unified document that provides easy access to all environmental-related regulations. It contains approximately 1,650 articles pertaining to 84 decrees. The Decree contains provisions pertaining to governmental institutions and their competences and regulatory provisions of the environmental sector, such as biodiversity, environmental management, water treatment, air treatment, hazardous waste, institutional management, financial, economic and tax instruments, administrative measures and environmental fees and taxes.

71. Resolutions are another source of environmental regulation. They are regulatory instruments whereby the corresponding Ministry provides for technical or practical issues contained in the Decree. For example, Decree 4741/2005 on hazardous waste provides that some types of hazardous waste are subject to the presentation and approval of take-back management plans, such as used acid-lead batteries. As a result, the MASD adopts Resolution 372/2009, establishing the elements that Take-Back Management Plans for Used Acid-Lead Batteries must contain. By means of Resolutions, the governmental institution can establish the deadlines and forms to be used when reporting environmental emissions or the criteria that environmental authorities must use when imposing sanctions.

Part I. Pollution Control

Chapter 1. General Law

§1. The Right to a Healthy Environment

I. Political Constitution

72. The Colombian Constitution of 1991 repealed the former Constitution of 1886 and established the protection of the environment. The right to a healthy environment is developed in the Constitution through State principles (Article 8), a duty of care applicable to the State and its nationals (Articles 79, 80, 81 and 95), and other instruments implementing environmental protection (Articles 215, 289, 361, 366).

73. Title I of the Constitution sets out the fundamental principles guiding State acts. Article 8 establishes that it is an obligation of the State and the people to protect the nation's cultural and natural wealth. The 1991 Constitution provides the State with tangible instruments to achieve this purpose, including: Article 215, empowering the President to adopt urgent measures where there is a threat to ecology; Article 361, providing for a National Fund of Royalties aimed at sourcing environmental protection; and Article 289, promoting international cooperation among the environmental authorities of bordering countries.

74. Constitutional rights are developed further in three chapters: fundamental rights; social, economic and cultural rights; and collective and environmental rights. The right to a healthy environment is regulated in Chapter III on 'Collective and Environmental Rights', more specifically in Articles 79, 80 and 81. Article 79 establishes the right to a healthy environment and the duty of the State to protect and preserve the environment; Article 80 requires the State to plan and administer the use of natural resources in order to ensure its sustainable development, conservation and restoration; what is more, the State must also control and prevent environmental contamination factors. Finally, Article 81 restricts the introduction into Colombian territory of nuclear and toxic waste; the manufacture, import, distribution and possession of nuclear, biological or chemical weapons; and the use, entry and exit of genetic resources.

II. Legislation

A. NCRNR and Protection to the Environment

75. The NCRNR was adopted on 18 December 1974 with the aim to provide a legal framework for renewable natural resources, including the atmosphere and the national aerial space, water, land, soil, subsoil, flora, fauna, renewable sources of energy, slopes with energy potential and geothermal resources. The NCRNR is divided into two books regulating the environment, and the use, ownership and environmental impacts of renewable natural resources. Its main aim is to preserve and restore the environment by encouraging the conservation of renewable natural resources and the remediation of environmentally degraded sites, as well as to control the noxious effects of non-renewable natural resources exploitation over renewable natural resources.

76. The right to a healthy environment is established in Article 7 of the NCRNR, and it is protected through the creation of environmental principles and regulation of polluting factors. The environmental principles elaborate on the general duty of care to carry out activities without compromising the state of the natural environment, public cleanliness and health. Article 8 lists the following contamination factors: inflicting damage to the environment or contaminating air, water, soil and other renewable natural resources; soil erosion and degradation; harmful alterations to the topography and the natural flow of water; sedimentation in water courses and reservoirs; harmful changes in the bed of water bodies and courses; noise; introduction and propagation of diseases and plagues; the inappropriate accumulation or disposal of waste, trash, rubbish and discarded materials; and dangerous substances; among others.

77. Although new regulations provide for different instruments of environmental protection, the NCRNR provisions on the right to a healthy environment remain fully applicable and enforceable.

B. Law 99 of 1993

78. Law 99/1993 lays down the basis for environmental policy in Colombia and enables public authorities to exercise environmental powers. Law 99/1993 creates an environmental regulatory system involving competent authorities, permitting requirements, public participation, infractions and environmental funds. The harmonization of such elements under the national environmental system allows for effectively guaranteeing the right to a healthy environment.

§2. Environmental Licence

I. Background

79. The NCRNR provided for an instrument whereby individuals and companies were required to declare the likely hazards of their undertakings. The purpose of this instrument was to inform the authorities on the possible effects or harmful effects that activities, projects or works could cause to the environment. The evolution of international environmental law drove lawmakers towards requiring such developers to carry out impact assessments and obtain environmental licences before the starting of the desired activities. As a result, Law 99/1993 established the Environmental Licence in Colombia and Decree 2041/2014 provided for its regulation.

II. Concept

80. Law 99/1993 conceives the environmental licence as a policy instrument of environmental management. The environmental licence allows for assessing the environmental performance of proposed activities at their planning, execution and follow-up stages. The approach to new activities and project licensing is preventive, provided that studies like the EIA anticipate the likely negative impacts the project may have and the alternatives to tackle those impacts.

81. Decree 2041/2014 regulates Law 99/1993 on environmental licences. According to Decree 2041/2014, the environmental licence is the authorization that a competent environmental authority issues for the construction and execution of a work or activity that is likely to cause significant negative impacts on natural resources, the environment or the landscape. The environmental licence covers the whole life cycle of the project, work or activity, including construction, assembly, operation, maintenance, dismantling, final restoration, abandonment and site closure.

82. The environmental licence comprises all the authorizations or concessions for the use or exploitation of renewable natural resources which are needed to carry out the proposed activity, work or project. In order to obtain such authorization, project developers have to assess the extent, likelihood and prevention of negative environmental impacts by carrying out impact studies.

III. Environmental Licence and EIA

83. Any projects, works or activities listed in Article 2.2.2.3.2.2 and 2.2.2.3.2.3 of Decree 1076/2015 require an environmental licence before starting construction works or operations and, therefore, must undergo environmental assessments. Activities or projects requiring environmental licence are divided into two big groups: the ones that fall under the ANLA's exclusive competence (centralized) and the ones that fall under other environmental authorities' competence (decentralized). The competent authority assesses the environmental viability of the proposed activity/project and approves or rejects the licence request.

84. Activities and projects requiring environmental licences are typically classified by sectors, including hydrocarbons, mining, hydropower, electricity, nuclear energy, maritime and port infrastructure, airports, public works, irrigation projects, pesticides, hazardous substances, projects affecting natural protected areas, watershed management and introduction of new species of flora and fauna. Depending on the size, location and complexity of the project, the competent authority will be the ANLA or the decentralized authorities. For example, projects falling under the exclusive competence of the ANLA include the following:

- Hydrocarbon sector: seismic exploration activities that require construction of roads for vehicle traffic; seismic exploration activities in maritime areas, when they are carried out at less than 200 metres of depth; exploratory perforation projects in new oil wells; transport of liquid and gaseous hydrocarbons; storage associated to the transport of oil by ducts; and construction and operation of petroleum refineries.
- Mining sector: exploitation of construction materials or non-metallic industrial minerals when the projected production is greater than or equal to 800,000 t/year.
- Electric sector: projects for development and use of alternative energy sources with an installed capacity greater or equal to 100MW.
- Irrigation: construction and operation of irrigation/drainage districts with coverage equal to or greater than 20,000 hectares.
- Pesticides: the import and production of pesticides in one of the five cases detailed in number 10 of 2.2.2.3.2.2. For example, pesticides for agricultural use (active ingredient and/or formulated product), with the exception of pesticides of biological origin made from plant extracts.
- Hazardous substances: the import and/or production of substances, materials or products subject to controls established in international environmental conventions, treaties or protocols, unless such instruments provide for a special authorization.

For example, in August 2021, the ANLA issued an environmental licence for a 500kV transmission line between the departments of Atlántico and Bolívar. The licensing process, including EIA, took ninety business days.

85. Projects falling under the exclusive competence of decentralized authorities, namely the CARs, Great Urban Centres (*Grandes Centros Urbanos*) and the environmental authorities created by Law 768/2002, include: (i) activities of the sectors covered by the ANLA with lower thresholds, and (ii) activities belonging to other sectors. Below are some examples:

- Mining sector: coal mining, when the projected exploitation is less than 800,000 tonnes per year; precious materials, when the projected exploitation is less than 2,000,000 tonnes per year, etc.

- Construction of dams or reservoirs with a capacity of less than 200 million water cubic metres.
- Electric sector: construction of overhead electrical power lines with a voltage equal to 50KV and less than 220 KV, etc.
- Maritime and port sector: construction and operation of canals, beaches, hydraulic fills, etc.
- Construction and operation of national airports and runways.
- Construction and operation of facilities for the storage, treatment and reuse of electric and electronic waste.
- Construction and operation of landfills.
- Construction and operation of wastewater treatment facilities.
- Manufacture Industry: chemical substances, alcohols, inorganic acids, etc.
- Projects for the storage of hazardous substances, excluding hydrocarbons.
- Projects requiring transfer of water between river basins, where water currents exceed 2 cubic metres per second during periods of normal water flow.
- Commercial hunting and captive breeding facilities for commercial purposes.
- Steel, cement and concrete fixed plants with production greater than 10,000 m^3/month.
- Construction and operation of plants for the treatment of biodegradable organic solid waste greater than or equal to 20,000 tons/year.
- Any activities/works/projects to be carried out in regional systems of protected areas.
- Projects/works/activities performed on submerged national heritage sites within 12 nautical miles.

IV. Environmental Studies

A. *Declaration of Environmental Alternatives (Diagnóstico de Alternativas Ambientales)*

86. Developers of projects listed in Article 2.2.2.3.4.2 of Decree 1076/2015 must request the authority to establish whether they need to carry out a Declaration of Environmental Alternatives (DDA). Some of the projects requiring a DDA include activities related to hydrocarbon exploration, production and distribution; dams, reservoirs and hydropower stations; projects on renewable energies that derive from biomass products with an installed capacity of more than 10MW, excluding activities related to solar, wind, geothermic and tidal energy; and the construction of ports, airports, highways and other infrastructure activities.

87. If the project or activity requires a DDA, the authority will issue the terms of reference and decide on the best environmental alternatives to carry out the project. The developer will have to undergo an EIA for the chosen alternative.

88. The DAA must include at least the following information:

- aim, scope and description of the project, work or activity;

- information on the land use of the project and its conformity with Decree 2201/2003;
- project location and information on its geographical, environmental and social surroundings;
- a comparative analysis of the project effects and risk posed to the environment, as well as the use of natural resources for each alternative;
- identification of communities and mechanisms to inform them about the project; and
- selection and justification of the best alternative.

B. Environmental Impact Assessment (Estudio de Impacto Ambiental)

89. An EIA is defined as the basic decision-making instrument for projects, works or activities requiring an environmental licence, as established in Article 2.2.2.3.5.1 of Decree 1076/2015. Different from the DAA, the EIA is mandatory for all activities requiring an environmental licence. The EIA contains information such as the location of the planned development/project, a description of the environmental abiotic, biotic and socio-economic factors which may be impacted by the proposed project and other data that the environmental licence petitioner must submit to the environmental authority. The EIA must also address environmental impact prevention, correction and compensation measures, as well as a proposed environmental management plan.

90. The EIA must be submitted to the corresponding environmental authority along with the licence request. According to the information submitted and the evaluation criteria of the authority, the project's licence may be granted, denied or revoked. The authority may request the petitioner to present additional information within a maximum period of thirty days. The authority verifies that the EIA accomplishes its aim (Article 2.2.2.3.5.1) and the terms of reference (Article 2.2.2.3.3.2); that the EIA has relevant and sufficient information on environmental impact identification and assessment, specifying which one of the impacts cannot be mitigated or avoided; and the establishment of environmental management measures. The terms of reference are drafted and adopted by the MASD as a general, non-exclusive guide for the preparation of the EIS for specific activities. For example, Resolution 1060 of 2021 establishes the terms of reference for the preparation of the EIS for biomass energy projects, while Resolution 0561 of 2022 sets them out for geothermal energy projects. Applicants may include information not foreseen in the terms of reference when, in their opinion, such information is considered essential for the competent environmental authority to make the respective decision.

V. Environmental Licence

91. Colombian legislation establishes two types of environmental licence: the global environmental licence and the environmental licence as such. The global environmental licence applies to works and activities related to mining and hydrocarbon projects. Developers of those activities must put in place an environmental management plan which must be implemented as soon as they start operations. Regular environmental licences apply to all other activities.

VI. Content of the Environmental Licence

92. The environmental licence is issued through an Administrative Act from the competent authority: the ANLA or the decentralized environmental authority. The main elements of the licence are the following:

- Identification of the individual or legal entity, public or private, authorized to develop the project, work or activity, indicating the company name, number of identification and address.
- The general purpose and location of the project, work or activity.
- A detailed account of the environmental motivations that have been taken into account for granting the licence.
- A list of the different activities and works authorized by the environmental licence.
- The natural resources authorized for use and exploitation, as well as the conditions, prohibition and requisites of use.
- Additional requirements, conditions and obligations in a Plan of Environmental Management that must be complied with during the construction, operation, maintenance, dismantling, abandonment or finalization of the project, work or activity.
- Publication of the administrative authorization notice as required under Article 71 of Law 99/1993.
- Any other information that the authority deems relevant.

93. Licence holders must request the modification of the environmental licence in any of the events listed under Article 28 of Decree 2041 of 2014. These events include when the licence holder intends to modify the project, construction, or activity in a way that generates additional environmental impacts beyond those already identified in the environmental licence; when, during monitoring activities, the licensing authority identifies additional environmental impacts beyond those already stated in the environmental studies, requiring the licensee to make adjustments; or for existing hydrocarbon exploration and/or exploitation projects in conventional deposits, which are also intended for activities in non-conventional deposits, provided that the project is planned within the same licensed area and under the same title holder; as otherwise, it will require a separate environmental licensing process.

94. Certain modifications to projects covered under an environmental licence are considered minor changes and, therefore, do not require a formal application to modify the environmental licence. Resolution 0855 of 2022 establishes the list of adjustments to activities in the hydrocarbon sector considered 'minor changes' or adjustments within the regular scope of hydrocarbon projects and sets out the procedure to verify and validate such adjustments. Minor changes may take place in (i) seismic exploration, (ii) design, drilling and operation of wells, (iii) transport of liquid and gaseous hydrocarbons, (iv) offshore exploration and exploitation activities, (v) delivery terminals, and (vi) oil installations.

95. For example, for oil installations, the implementation of new facilities for fluid collection, storage and treatment systems, rainwater and oily water facilities, operation rooms, buildings, facilities for the removal of contaminated products, and fire control systems within the specifically designated areas are considered minor changes.

96. Minor changes must be communicated to the authority prior to their implementation. The holder of the environmental licence must submit a report to the ANLA, providing a detailed description of the activities to be executed, including a description of the activity with location plans or maps and their respective georeferencing and a justification that the activity conforms to one of the minor changes listed in Resolution 0855 of 2022. For activities requiring an update to the Contingency Plan, such as the example of the oil installations listed above, the updated Contingency Plan must be submitted along with the required report.

97. If during inspection, monitoring or enforcement activities, the ANLA determines that the conducted activities do not align with those described in the submitted report on minor changes, the ANLA will take the necessary preventive measures and initiate an environmental sanctioning investigation.

98. For those licence holders that believe the intended activity qualifies as minor changes or normal adjustments in hydrocarbon sector projects, they will have to formally request, through written communication and accompanied by supporting information, a decision from the competent environmental authority regarding the necessity of initiating the environmental licence modification process.

§3. Environmental Management Within Companies

I. Departments of Environmental Management

99. Law 1124/2007 creates the departments of environmental management (*departamentos de gestión ambiental*) for companies. According to Law 1124/2007, companies with industries listed in the Uniform International Industrial Classification *(Clasificación Internacional Industrial Uniforme* – CIIU) must set up and have an environmental management department in place. Decree 1299/2008 regulates Law 1124/2007, which are both compiled in Decree 1076/2015 and establishes that companies required to hold an environmental licence, environmental management plan, environmental permits, concessions or any other type of environmental authorization must have an environmental management department in place.

100. The purpose of the environmental management department includes the following:

- establishing policies to control environmental management within companies;
- assuring compliance with environmental regulations;
- taking measures to prevent, minimize and control generations of pollutants;
- promoting clean production and rational use of natural resources;
- improving energy efficiency and cleaner fuels;
- implementing activities to reduce greenhouse emissions; and
- fostering and preserving ecosystems.

101. According to Decree 1299/2008, the environmental management department is mandatory for micro, small, medium and big industries, pursuant to the number of employees (i.e., micro, no more than ten employees; small, between ten and fifty employees; medium, between 50 and 200 employees; and large, more than 200 employees (Law 590/2000)).

II. Environmental Fees and Taxes

102. Activities and projects requiring environmental licence or environmental permits are subject to the payment of administrative fees. For environmental licences, the payment corresponds to the costs involved in the evaluation of environmental studies, such as the EIA and the DDA. This payment is done prior to submitting the EIA or DDA. In addition, a number of environmental permits are granted prior to payment of the corresponding fee, such as the air emissions permit or the wastewater discharges permit.

103. Tax contributions are levied on the direct or indirect use of the atmosphere, land, soil, rivers, lakes or underground water courses for disposal of agricultural, mining or industrial waste and discharge of wastewater, smoke, vapours and noxious substances from economic activities. These taxes are also justified for the costs involved in the maintenance of renewable natural resources. When setting the tax, the authority takes into account the depreciation and regeneration values associated with renewable natural resources. This assessment is done by taking into account factors such as the impact on public health, public and private goods, social welfare, and environmental damage to ecosystems. The CARs are responsible for enforcing environmental pollution tax payments.

III. Record-Keeping

104. Developers of activities requiring environmental licence must keep information on the release of pollutants and further report their emissions to the authorities, as established in the NCRNR. Article 15 provides that any company using elements that could potentially pollute the environment is under the obligation to inform and notify the authorities, as well as the community, of the potential risks that the activity poses to human health and the environment. According to Law 99/1993, this information must be available on the SINA for public consultation and updated whenever there is a modification to the conditions established in the environmental licence. Environmental information comprises the quantity of natural resources and other environmental elements consumed. Although Colombia does not have legislation requiring companies to report on environmental performance, the information described in this section must always be available and, if required, submitted to the authority.

A. *Information on the Use of Renewable Natural Resources*

105. Resolution 941/2009 creates the Information Sub-System on the Use of Renewable Natural Resources (SIUR, for its initials in Spanish) as part of the SINA. This information subsystem seeks to standardize and consolidate all the information concerning the use of renewable natural resources. The SIUR gathers, analyses, stores and integrates data on renewable natural resources data from economic activities, including the production of goods and services. The SIUR administrates information regarding the use of renewable natural resources, discharges, energy consumption, atmospheric emissions, waste, fauna and other issues affecting water, soil, air, climate and biodiversity. The entity in charge of administrating the SIUR is the IDEAM.

B. *Official Environmental Registry*

106. The Official Environmental Registry (RUA) is created by Resolution 941/2009. Individuals and companies using renewable natural resources must be registered with the RUA. The RUA is to be gradually implemented by sectors, starting with manufacturing, hydrocarbons, agriculture, mining, energy and others.

§4. Enforcement

I. Administrative Measures

107. In Colombia, the executive and the judicial power are responsible for enforcing environmental law. The executive branch enforces environmental law through administrative sanctions, including fines, arrest or suspension of activities. The judicial branch does it through judgments on legal actions, torts or criminal procedures. This chapter will address enforcement through administrative sanctions.

108. Law 1333/2009 establishes the procedure to prevent, correct and sanction environmental infractions. For that purpose, Law 1333/2009 sets forth the list of conducts considered environmental infractions and the applicable preventive measures and sanctions to penalize such offences. In addition, it sets procedural rules, restitution of flora and fauna, competences on environmental surveillance and control, and a registry of polluters. Environmental infractions are defined in Article 5 of Law 1333/2009 as any breach of environmental legislation or any damage to the environment. Environmental infractions lead to administrative actions against the offender without prejudice of civil or criminal liability. Law 1333/2009 establishes aggravating factors (i.e., reiteration of the infraction) and factors to reduce responsibility (i.e., confessing the infraction to the authority prior to the start of the administrative procedure) that help authorities determine the applicable sanction. The time limit to prosecute environmental infractions is twenty years after the commission of the offence.

109. Preventive measures are enforcement instruments that seek to prevent, impede or avoid any fact, conduct or activity that can harm the environment, natural resources, landscape or human health. Preventive measures include written warnings; preventive confiscation of resources, products and equipment that have been used to infringe environmental law; confiscation of fauna and flora products or specimens; and temporary cancellation of the project or activity when its operation harms the environment, the natural resources, the landscape or human health.

110. Regarding sanctions, these are intended to correct or compensate environmental damages by guaranteeing the effectiveness of constitutional principles, international treaties, laws and regulations. Depending on the infraction magnitude, the following sanctions can be imposed on the offender: daily fines up to 5,000 Colombian legal monthly minimum wages (in 2020, the Colombian legal monthly minimum wage was COP 877.703, approximately USD 290); temporary or permanent closure of the facility; cancellation of the environmental licence; demolition of the whole project; confiscation of the resources, products, equipment, etc., used to infringe environmental law; restitution of fauna and flora specimens; and, community work.

111. The last enforcement measure provided for in Law 1333/2009 is the registry of environmental offenders (*Registro Unico de Infractores Ambientales* – RUIA), regulated in detail by Resolution 415/2010. The RUIA records data about environmental offenders and their identification, infractions, place of occurrence, type of sanction, date, environmental authority imposing the sanction, and offenders' representatives. This registry is administered by the ANLA.

112. As part of the enforcement procedure, Law 1333/2009 also regulates administrative liability for environmental damage. This topic will be dealt with in the Liability Questions part.

II. Environmental Insurance

113. Law 491/1999 establishes compulsory environmental insurance for those activities that are likely to cause negative environmental impacts (those requiring environmental licence). The environmental insurance policy covers any economic losses resulting from non-compliance with environmental protection regulations. If the developers of polluting activities have already purchased an insurance policy covering environmental damage, the authority evaluates whether the insurance policy meets the required coverage under Law 491/1999.

Chapter 2. Air Pollution

§1. Introduction

I. National Code of Renewable Natural Resources

114. Atmospheric pollution is identified in the 1974 NCRNR as one of the factors amounting to contamination in Colombia. Articles 73–76 of the NCRNR lay down the main provisions on outer space and the atmosphere, requiring the government to keep the atmosphere in good condition and to avoid harming or interfering with the normal development of human, animal or nature life or natural renewable resources. The NCRNR establishes a general prohibition on the release of any dust, vapour, gas or any other substance that may knowingly be a potential source of human illness or damage to the environment, including fauna and flora.

115. The NCRNR creates policy instruments to prevent atmospheric pollution. These instruments include regulating air quality standards, permissible concentration limits for harmful substances and the best methods to avoid atmospheric pollution. The State also regulates air contamination from mobile sources, including aeroplanes and vehicles; restrictions to the import, manufacture or marketing of transport means that may endanger air quality; and the establishment of sampling and monitoring network stations to locate sources of atmospheric pollution and detect existing or potential hazards.

II. Decree 948 of 1995

116. Decree 948/1995 regulates Part II of the NCRNR on atmospheric pollution and repeals former Decree 2/1982. Decree 948/1995 sets out the legal framework for air quality standards, polluting emissions, mobile sources, noise and odour emissions. It also determines the competent public authorities and their powers, requirements on atmospheric emission permits for fixed sources, certification mechanisms for mobile sources, contingency plans for contamination incidents, air contamination control and enforcement, and mechanisms for public participation in air-related matters.

A. *Air Pollutants*

117. Decree 948/1995 classifies air pollutants as primary and secondary pollutants. Pursuant to Article 2.2.5.1.2.1. of Decree 1076/2015, which includes Decree 948/1995, primary atmospheric pollutants are those affecting air quality, such as troposphere ozone or photochemical smog production and its precursors, Carbon Monoxide, particulate matter, Nitrogen Dioxide, Sulphur Dioxide and Lead. Primary atmospheric pollutants, either regularly or accidentally released, may cause cancer, acute illnesses or birth defects and genetic mutations. Secondary pollutants are those substances that, without affecting air quality standards, cause damage to the atmosphere, such as chemical compounds degrading the ozone layer or those pollutants leading to global climate change.

B. Controlled Activities

118. Controlled activities refer to those activities that are subject to prior control and inspection by environmental authorities. These activities include: burning of natural forest, protective vegetation, and forbidden open-air burnings; burning of fossil fuels used by vehicles and trucks; industrial or commercial burning of fossil fuels; controlled open-air burning in rural areas; incineration or burning of hazardous substances and waste; industrial activities generating, using or releasing substances covered under the Montreal Protocol; and construction material quarries and crushers.

C. Contamination Incidents

119. Regarding emergency incidents of air contamination, Decree 979/2006, amending Decree 948/1995, establishes three contamination levels: prevention, alert or emergency. Depending on the contamination level, environmental authorities will take appropriate measures to re-establish normal air conditions. If the authorities declare one of the three levels of contamination, they have to inform the public about the incident and allow the transit of ambulances, firemen and official vehicles, among others. Environmental authorities at national, regional or municipal level must have adopted contingency plans to be executed in case of air contamination incidents.

D. Conversion to Cleaner Technologies

120. Decree 948/1995 allows owners of existing polluting sources to adjust their facilities in accordance with the new provisions on emission limits and atmospheric pollution control. The purpose of this mechanism, named Clean Technologies Conversion Plan (*Planes de Reconversión a Tecnologías Limpias* – PRTL) (Article 2.2.5.1.10.5 of Decree 1076/2015), is to ensure that generators of atmospheric emissions from fixed sources are in full compliance with legal requirements. Since January 1996, a system of atmospheric pollution prevention applies between 'new' and 'existing' operators of fixed sources: new operators must guarantee that their atmospheric emissions are below the maximum permissible levels, whereas operators of existing sources must submit a PRTL to convert their facilities into clean technologies, pursuant to the latest standards.

121. The PRTL contains information relating to dates, measures and commitments assumed by the operator to achieve compliance with Decree 948/1995 and related regulations (i.e., emission limits, monitoring requirements, etc.). The environmental authority assesses the content of the PRTL, classifies the facility in a special category and signs a covenant with the operator: Agreement of Conversion to Clean Technology (*Convenio de Reconversión a Tecnología Limpia* – CRTL) establishing the duties to meet the PRTL commitments. The purpose of establishing special categories is to rank industries and activities according to the level of conversion into clean technologies and establish the dates for such conversion. For example, industries or activities classified under type IV are those requiring a high degree of conversion and are required to comply with the standards within five to ten years.

E. Zoning of Polluted Areas

122. Decree 948/1995 requires authorities to guarantee that no atmospheric emission permits are issued in areas where industrial activities are not permitted. In fact, Article 2.2.5.1.10.3 of Decree 1076/2015 establishes that fixed sources located in non-industrial areas must move to industrial-enabled zones within a ten-year term; otherwise, they risk losing the Atmospheric Emission Permit and the environmental licence. The MASD in coordination with environmental authorities can classify specific urban or rural zones as 'source-areas' *(area-fuente)* according to the quantity and concentration of atmospheric pollutants. Depending on the level of pollution, the source-area is classified as a high, average, moderate or marginal contamination area. Each type of area establishes whether contingency measures must be taken or not and the conditions for granting atmospheric emission permits. In source-areas categorized as type III, also known as Moderated Contamination Areas, the concentration of pollutants exceeds the air quality standard by more than 25% but less than 50%. In this case, prevention measures have to be taken, and settlement of new fixed sources is restricted for three years.

§2. Permit of Atmospheric Emissions

I. Definition

123. Article 2.2.5.1.7.1. of Decree 1076/2015 defines the Atmospheric Emission Permit (*Permiso de Emisión Atmosférica*) as the authorization given to a natural or legal person to release emissions into the air granted by the competent environmental authority. The permit is only granted to the owner of the project, undertaking, activity, industry or facility generating atmospheric emissions. The Atmospheric Emission Permit must be obtained to operate fixed sources, including pipes, chimney stacks, etc.

II. Activities Covered

124. Activities subject to the Atmospheric Emission Permit are established in Article 2.2.5.1.7.2. of Decree 1076/2015 and include the following:

- controlled open-air burnings in rural areas;
- release of smoke, gas, vapour, dust and particulate matter from industrial chimneys or ducts;
- dispersed emissions from open-pit mining activities;
- solid, liquid or gas waste incineration;
- storage, transport, loading and unloading operations causing air emissions;
- industrial or commercial operation of boilers or incinerators;
- fuel burning operations in oil and gas facilities;
- processes causing toxic air emissions;
- manufacture of lubricants and fuels;
- oil refineries;
- operation of thermoelectric plants;
- nuclear reactor operations;
- activities generating offensive odours; and
- any other activity stated in a technical report issued by the MASD.

125. Some of the activities subject to permitting have been further regulated by Resolution 619 of 1997. This resolution sets out rules for open-air burnings in rural and is applicable to certain harvest burnings, whereas the release of atmospheric pollutants is regulated for cement kilns, sodium carbonate production, nitric acid, sulphuric acid, chloride acid, etc., industrial activities that produce more than 20 tons/day of Carbonates, detergents manufacturers with spray and dry ovens with a capacity of up to 5 tons/day, among others.

III. Procedure

126. The procedure to obtain the Atmospheric Emissions Permit is detailed in Articles 2.2.5.1.7.4., 2.2.5.1.7.4. and 2.2.5.1.7.6. of Decree 1076/2015. The procedure starts with a formal petition from the interested party containing information on the facility's location, starting date of activities, blueprints, meteorological data, description of the project, soil use certificate, type of fuels, and a description of emission control devices or clean technologies. Once the petition is submitted, the authority assesses the viability of the application. At this point, the authority can return the petition to the developer in order to have it corrected or provide more information, and can also carry out inspections and gather additional evidence related to the activity. If all the requirements are met, the authority then issues the corresponding permit.

IV. Content of the Permit

127. According to Article 2.2.5.1.7.7. of Decree 1076/2015, the Atmospheric Emissions Permit is issued through an Administrative Act (*acto administrativo*) containing all the necessary information, including the operator's identification and description of the facility; permitted atmospheric emissions, its characteristics and technical conditions; permit validity term; the conditions to be fulfilled by the operator; obligations on monitoring devices, infrastructure or installations; guarantees; provisions on the permit modification; and the authority's powers regarding permit conditions.

128. The Atmospheric Emissions Permit must be updated in the event of any modification or extension to existing authorized installations and also in case of any changes to the type of fuels used in industrial processes.

§3. Air Quality Standards

129. Decree 948/1995 defines air quality standard as the legally permissible concentration of polluting substances in the air. Air quality standards are established by the MASD for annual, daily, eight-hour, three-hour and one-hour exposure periods. Resolution 601/2006 further develops Decree 948/1995 by approving the national air quality standards for atmospheric pollutants, non-conventional atmospheric pollutants with carcinogenic effects, substances generating offensive odours and different emergency levels of air pollution.

130. Resolution 651/2010 creates the Sub-system of Information on Air Quality (SISAIRE). The SISAIRE gathers and stores data on air quality and emissions and aims to be the main source of information for the design, assessment and implementation of national policies and strategies on air pollution prevention and control. Companies required to report on atmospheric emissions will have to obtain a number and password for carrying out such reports through the SISAIRE.

131. Air quality standards are established by taking into account the pollutant type, its unit of measurement, the maximum allowed concentration and the time of exposure. The maximum concentrations for general pollutants are detailed in Table 1 of Resolution 601/2006 and include Total Suspended Particles (TSP), Particulate Matter 10 (PM10), Sulphur Dioxide (SO_2), Nitrogen Dioxide (NO_2), Ozone (O_3) and Carbon Monoxide (CO). Concerning non-conventional pollutants with carcinogenic effects, Table 2 includes concentration limits for Benzene, Lead and related compounds, Cadmium, Mercury, Methane, Toluene and Vanadium. Finally, Table 3 provides for air quality standards of substances generating offensive odours, such as Acetaldehyde (C_2H_4O), Butyric Acid ($C_4H_8O_2$), Ammonia (NH_3), 2-Chloroethanol (C_2H_5ClO), Disulfur Dichloride (S_2Cl_2), Ethanethiol (C_2H_5SH), Tethanethiol (C_2H5SH), Ethyl Acrylate ($C_5H_8O_2$), Styrene (C_8H_8), Methylamine (CH_5N),

Methyl Mercaptan (CH_3SH), Nitrobenzene ($C_6H_5NO_2$), Ethyl Methyl Sulphide (C_3H_8S), Diethyl Sulphide ($C_4H_{10}S$), Dimethyl Sulphide (C_2H_6S) and Hydrogen Sulphide (H_2S).

§4. Release of Atmospheric Pollutants

I. Emission Limits

132. Article 2.2.5.1.2.11. of Decree 1076/2015 establishes that any release or emission of pollutants into the atmosphere must be conducted under the permissible limits and according to the conditions specified in the laws and regulations. In Colombia, the sources of atmospheric emissions are classified as mobile and fixed sources. Mobile sources are sub-classified as aerial, terrestrial, maritime or fluvial sources, whereas fixed sources are classified as punctual, dispersed and area-source units.

133. Decree 948/1995, embedded in Decree 1076/2015, establishes restrictions and limits to certain activities leading to air quality degradation. Those activities include the use of certain fuels exceeding the limits set out in regulations; the operation of facilities generating offensive odours in residential areas; the storage of waste in public areas that may release particles into the atmosphere; installation of devices to ensure the adequate dispersion of emissions; use of heavy oils; open-air burning of tyres, batteries or any other elements producing toxic emissions; incineration of pathological waste; burning of forests and vegetation; installation of protective nets in construction activities; special control on atmospheric emissions from operations in harbours; and special conditions on the storage of volatile toxic compounds.

134. Resolution 909/2008 develops Decree 948/1995 by approving the maximum permissible limits for air pollutants and also providing for measurement methods and agreements of conversion to clean technologies. Emission limits are set out for existing and new emission sources from the following activities:

- industrial activities: Resolution 909/2008 establishes threshold values for atmospheric pollutants associated with each type of industry, as well as for dioxins and furans;
- external combustion equipment;
- thermal power stations, establishing different limits for those generating more than, equal to or less than 20MW, as well as for the ones working with gas turbines;
- manufacture of textiles;
- refinery of oil products;
- manufacture of cement, concrete or similar products;
- refractory and non-refractory ceramics;
- thermal treatment of animal by-products;
- incinerators of hazardous and non-hazardous waste; and
- cremation ovens.

II. Reporting

135. Any existing or potential fixed source of atmospheric pollution must report its level of emissions to the competent authorities (Article 2.2.5.1.10.2. of Decree 948/1995). This report must be submitted to the authority by using the IE-1 Report on Emissions (*Informe de Estado de Emisiones*), which shall contain information on the location and type of activity and description of the facility; fuel and raw materials, their origin, amount and storage method; the facility's energy consumption per hour; the type and quantity of goods manufactured in the facility; technology used to ensure compliance with applicable air emission limits; the licences or authorizations of the facility (environmental licence, Atmospheric Emission Permit and other authorizations); pollutant emissions; and any other information that the MASD may request.

136. Decree 948/1995 provides that those developers that submit the IE-1 Emissions Report on time and with all the necessary information are entitled, for once, to obtain a 50% reduction in fines or sanctions for the lack of Atmospheric Emissions Permit or for exceeding the maximum limits. On the contrary, if operators of polluting sources fail to submit the emissions report, they are exposed to the temporary suspension of activities and works causing atmospheric pollution, the closure of the facility and daily fines. The IE-1 Report on Emissions must be available to the competent environmental authorities and must be updated every five years or during every new application for an emission permit, as required for those processes regulated under Article 2.2.5.1.7.2. of Decree 1076/2015 and Resolution 909/2008.

137. In order to have accurate information on the release of atmospheric pollutants, facilities must have in place equipment for the monitoring and measurement of their emissions. According to Article 2.2.5.1.10.10 of Decree 948/1995, the records on the control and maintenance operation systems installed in fixed sources are required to be kept on site so that governmental authorities can consult them. For such purpose, facilities must follow the Protocol for the Control and Surveillance of atmospheric pollution caused by fixed sources, which is a technical instrument that establishes the procedures to measure, assess and monitor atmospheric emissions. In addition, the Protocol establishes how to determine the height of chimneys and stack outlets.

III. Restrictions on Fuels

138. Resolution 898/1995, modified by different resolutions in 2001, 2003, 2004 and 2017, establishes the environmental criteria for the quality of liquid and solid fuels used in industrial and commercial ovens and boilers and vehicle internal combustion engines. The criteria provided for in Resolution 898/1995 apply to liquid fuels, including Colombian petrol, imported or new petrol, diesel and sulphur-content; quality standards for mineral coal; and atmospheric emissions from heavy fuels. Resolution 898/1995 includes a general obligation for any natural and legal persons using coal or fuel mixtures, consisting of carrying a monthly record of the fuel quantity and the total sulphur-content. Resolution 415/1998, modified by Resolution 1446/2005, regulates the conditions under which waste oils may be burnt for combustion and heating installations. Fuel or liquefied fuels from tetraethyl lead-containing petroleum are prohibited for use by both Decree 2622/2000 and Resolution 415/1998. Sanctions for violating this prohibition are regulated by Decree 1172/2016.

§5. Climate Change

I. The UNFCCC and the Kyoto Protocol

139. Colombia is a party to the United Nations Framework Convention on Climate Change (UNFCCC) as ratified by Law 164/1994, as well as to the Kyoto Protocol, ratified by Law 629/2000 and implemented through Decree 1546/2005 and is part of the Non-Annex I Parties so it does not have greenhouse gas (GHG) reduction targets. Colombia has nevertheless implemented voluntary measures to combat climate change, such as making inventories and sharing information on GHG emissions; developing national policies and best practices; launching national strategies to mitigate GHG emissions and searching for the appropriate financial and technological support from developed countries; and fostering cooperation on adaptation to the impacts of climate change.

II. Paris Agreement – UNFCCC (COP21)

140. Following the adoption of the Paris Agreement of 2015, ratified through Law 1844 of 2017, Colombia committed to reducing 20% of its emissions by 2030 with respect to the 2010 projected emissions. To achieve this, two measures have been adopted: the creation of a national system on climate change and the adoption of the climate change law in 2018.

141. Decree 298/2016 creates the National System for Climate Change (*Sistema Nacional de Cambio Climático – SISCLIMA*). This programme englobes the entities, including the private sector and entities at all government levels, as well as the policies that need to be articulated to reduce emissions and mitigate the impacts of climate change.

142. Law 1931/2018 establishes principles, institutional aspects, planning instruments, information systems and financial and economic instruments for climate change measures. It assigns the management of SISCLIMA to the Intersectoral Commission for Climate Change (*Comisión Intersectorial de Cambio Climático* – CICC) and creates the National Council of Climate Change (*Consejo Nacional de Cambio Climático*), which forms part of the CICC. Some of the planning instruments incorporated by this law are as follows:

- Comprehensive Sectorial Management Plans for Climate Change – (*Planes Integrales de Gestión del Cambio Climático – PIGCC*): Instrument used by each Ministry to identify, evaluate and guide the incorporation of measures regarding mitigation of GHGs and the adaptation to climate change. The plans incorporated by means of the National Development Plan 2014–2018 must be adjusted to the PIGCC requirements.
- Comprehensive Territorial Management Plans for Climate Change – (*Planes Integrales de Gestión de Cambio Climático Territoriales (PIGCCT)*): Instruments by which regional government and environmental authorities identify, evaluate, prioritize and define measures or actions of adaptation/mitigation of GHGs that must be implemented in their jurisdiction.
- Nationally Determined Contributions (NDC): Commitments made by Colombia regarding the reduction of GHG emissions by 2030.
- National Climate Change Policy (PNCC).
- *Information System for Climate Change* (SNICC): Linked to the SIAC. This system provides data and centralized information for decision-making. It includes a National Registry for Emission of Greenhouse Gases (RENARE). The RENARE system was regulated by means of Resolution 1447/2018.

III. Policy Instruments

143. The National Climate Change Policy (PNCC for its initials in Spanish) integrates climate change into the decision-making of public entities and private organizations. It began its formulation in 2014 and built on the past policy documents adopted in 2002, such as the Guidelines on the Policy of Climate Change and the National Council of Economic and Social Policy (CONPES) document, CONPES 3242. This policy attempts to articulate all the existing activities and agencies involved in the Colombian Low Carbon Development Strategy – ECDBC – the National Plan for Adaptation to Climate Change – PNACC – and the National REDD+ Strategy, which have existed since 2011 and seeks to give continuity to the actions undertaken under those initiatives. The PNCC adds new elements to strategically guide all efforts towards the fulfilment of the commitments under the Paris Agreement.

144. The PNCC draws on five strategic lines: rural, urban, mining and infrastructure development, and conservation of key ecosystems, all geared towards a low carbon and climate-resilient economy. The PNCC supports the development of these strategic objectives in four instrumental lines: climate change management planning; information, science, technology and innovation; education; and financing and economic instruments.

145. Law 2169 of 2021 established intersectorial goals and minimum measures for short, medium, and long-term carbon neutrality, climate resilience, and low-carbon development in Colombia. Article 20 of this law created the Study Commission tasked with analysing the state and potential of carbon markets in Colombia and instructed the MASD to regulate the Commission's functioning.

146. Resolution 522 of 2022 further regulated the Commission's objective, composition, membership and operation. The Commission's objective is to assess the state and potential of carbon markets in Colombia, offering recommendations to the national government on market regulation and the necessary restructuring of the Colombian state's organizational structure to propel the development of these markets as a new economic sector and an effective tool for greenhouse gas emission reduction. The Commission's composition, as outlined in Article 2, includes representatives from the Ministry of Finance and Public Credit, the MASD, and the National Planning Department. It is presided over by the Vice Minister of Environmental Planning of the MASD. Additionally, it includes representatives from the Senate and the House of Representatives, along with six national and international experts.

IV. Institutions

147. Decree 298/2016 creates the National System for Climate Change (Sístema Nacional de Cambio Climático – SISCLIMA) in order to coordinate, articulate, formulate and evaluate policies, regulations, strategies, plans, programmes and projects related to climate change and the mitigation of GHGs, by means of coordination of government authorities, at a national, department and municipal level, as well as private entities and non-profit organizations. Some of the entities created and integrated under this system include the: (i) Intersectoral Commission for Climate Change – *Comisión Intersectorial de Cambio Climático* (CICC) – tasked with coordinating actions for the implementation of the National Policy for Climate Change, and (ii) Regional Nodes for Climate Change – *Nodos Regionales de Cambio Climatico* – which promote, assist and support the implementation of policies, strategies, plans, programmes, projects and actions relating to climate change in Colombia's regions.

A. Territorial Comprehensive Climate Change Management Plans

148. According to Article 18 of Law 1931 of 2018, Territorial Comprehensive Climate Change Management Plans (PICGCCT) are instruments through which so-called territorial entities (*entidades teritoriales),* such as departments, regional environmental authorities, and National Natural Parks in Colombia identify, evaluate, prioritize, and define measures and actions for adaptation and mitigation of GHG emissions. These plans are drafted based on vulnerability analysis and GHG inventories specific to each territory.

149. Resolution 0849 of 2022 establishes a guide for the formulation and implementation of PIGCCT.

150. The guide is specifically designed for use by departments, regional environmental authorities, and National Natural Parks when such natural parks entity has jurisdiction over climate-related matters. PIGCCT involve the identification, assessment, prioritization, and definition of measures and actions for both adaptation and the mitigation of greenhouse gas emissions within their respective jurisdictions.

151. Furthermore, the guide is intended for use by districts and municipalities that are formulating more detailed territorial climate change plans. This is done in accordance with the guidelines issued by the Intersectoral Climate Change Commission (CICC), ensuring a comprehensive and detailed approach at a local scale. Entities that have already adopted their PIGCCT must make the necessary adjustments based on the guide within a maximum period of two years from the issuance of Resolution 0849 of 2022.

V. Clean Development Mechanisms

152. Resolution 2734/2010 of the MASD establishes the requirements, conditions and procedures that Clean Development Mechanisms (CDMs) must fulfil for approval by the national authority. Pursuant to Resolution 2734/2010, a CDM project may involve, for example, a rural electrification project using solar panels or the installation of several energy-efficient boilers in industrial facilities. Natural or legal persons interested in developing CDMs must submit a petition to the MASD in order to obtain national approval.

153. Decree 1076/ 2015 establishes the verification agencies and characteristics of GHG emission reductions and removals, including those reductions from CDMs. For verifications performed under international accreditation schemes, the verification body shall issue a verification statement indicating that the GHG emission reductions or removals were generated in accordance with the methodology defined in ISO 14064-2:2006 and the results obtained in the verification performed under standard 18014064-3.

The GHG emissions verification body shall be accredited by the National Accreditation Body of Colombia – ONAC – or by an accreditation body member signatory of the International Accreditation Forum, which shall issue a verification statement that responds to the methodology defined by the UNFCCC for the CDM.

VI. Carbon Tax

154. The national carbon tax was created by Article 221 of Law 1819 of 2016 (Structural Tax Reform) in response to the country's need for economic instruments to incentivize compliance with national GHG mitigation goals. This tax corresponds to a levy on the carbon content of all fossil fuels, including all petroleum derivatives and all types of fossil gas used for energy purposes, provided they are used for combustion (except coal).

155. The fuels that are taxed by this tax are gasoline, kerosene, jet fuel, ACPM, and fuel oil; natural gas is also taxed but only for use in hydrocarbon refining and petrochemical industry, and liquefied petroleum gas (LPG) only for sale to industrial users. The tax has a value of COP 15,000 per ton of CO_2. This rate will be adjusted every 1 February with the inflation of the previous year, plus one percentage point until it is equivalent to one tax value unit (UVT) per ton of CO_2.

156. In the same law that creates this tax, a mandate is given to the MADS, which is consolidated in Decree 926/2017, to establish a procedure to exempt certain activities from the Carbon Tax. The purpose of this is to stimulate the implementation of mitigation initiatives that generate GHG emission reductions or removals in exchange for the carbon tax exemption.

VII. Energy

157. Law 697/2001 promotes the rational and efficient use of energy and the use of alternative energies. This piece of legislation promotes the efficient use of energy by declaring it as a matter of public and social interest and creating a National Program for the Promotion of Energy Efficiency, named PROURE, which was later developed by Resolutions Nos 180919/2010 and 41286/2016 – *Plan de Acción Indicativo 2017–2022 para el Desarrollo del PROURE* – that consists of a programme that develops the PROURE, by defining objectives, and indicative goals of energy efficiency, in order to comply with COP21 commitments assumed by Colombia. The rational use of energy is defined as the use of energy in such a way that the greatest energy efficiency is obtained, either from an original form of energy or during any activity of production, transformation, transport, distribution or consumption of different energy forms, within the context of sustainable development, and in compliance with current environmental and renewable natural resource regulations. As part of the efficient and rational use of energy programmes, public service companies must include information in their bills prompting users to use energy in a rational and efficient manner.

158. The Ministry of Mines and Energy is responsible for the administration, organization, development and promotion of energy efficiency and rational use. In addition, the Ministry of Mines and Energy promotes the use of non-conventional sources of energy. In Colombia, non-conventional sources of energy are those globally available energy sources that are environmentally sustainable, but are not used or are only marginally used, and not widely commercialized in the national territory. In order to promote the use of these sources of energy, Law 697/2001 and Law 1715/2014 on renewable energies require the government to put in place programmes encouraging undertakings to import and produce equipment using non-conventional energies.

159. Decree 3683/2003 regulates Law 697/2001 and establishes the institutional framework, incentives, financial mechanisms, company's duties and consumers' rights regarding the rational and efficient use of energy. Concerning the institutional framework, Decree 3683/2003 creates the Inter-sector Commission for the Rational and Efficient Use of Energy and Non-conventional Sources of Energy (CIURE), aimed at developing and enhancing education and research on energy efficiency and rational use. The CIURE coordinates the national policy on the rational and efficient use of energy and non-conventional energy sources; supports the development of energy efficiency programmes regarding public transport in urban areas as well as transport of goods; coordinates a selection process of relevant candidates that can be awarded the Merit Order of the Rational Use of Energy (URE); and acts as an advisory committee to the government in case of energy crisis or whenever strategic measures are needed to be adopted.

160. Incentives on the rational and efficient use of energy are envisaged for research and education and for the URE award. The Merit Order of URE includes four categories: energy supply, energy demand, research and teaching-education. Finally, Decree 3683/2003 establishes that the Ministry of Mines and Energy must adopt technical regulations on energy efficiency in products and the conditions for energy efficiency labelling in order to protect the rights of consumers.

VIII. Carbon Neutrality, Climate Resilience and Low-Carbon Development

A. Context

161. The Climate Action Law, officially known as Law 2169 and sanctioned on 22 December 2021 by the National Government, was strategically crafted to align with commitments arising from the Paris Agreement. This legislation serves as a pivotal tool for addressing climate change by focusing on both carbon neutrality and mitigation strategies.

162. The primary objective of Law 2169 of 2021 is to establish comprehensive goals and essential measures to guide Colombia towards carbon neutrality, climate resilience, and low-carbon development. These objectives are set for the short, medium, and long term, in strict adherence to the international commitments undertaken by Colombia in the realm of climate action.

163. Structurally, the law comprises six titles and thirty-eight articles, delineating a detailed framework of goals and measures, which can be grouped into four main groups: targets on mitigation, adaptation and implementation; specific and concrete measures for public authorities; a comprehensive regulation on carbon markets; and two concluding chapters on implementation, financing and other measures. Most of the measures transcribed in the law are those presented by Colombia as part of its National Contributions to the UNFCCC.

B. Objectives

164. The agenda for transitioning towards carbon neutrality and climate resilience, set out in Law 2169, is expressed through sixteen pillars, including:

- Alignment of climate change actions with those of food safety, health and eradication of poverty.
- Adoption of measures on environmental protection for present and future generations.
- Recognition of the central role played by women and population groups with special constitutional protection with regard to knowledge, differentiated impact and actions for mitigation and adaptation to climate change.
- Sustainable employment creation through the establishment of green jobs.
- Shared responsibility and goals for governmental entities (central and territorial), including private sector stakeholders.
- Emphasis on transitioning towards carbon neutrality and climate resilience to advance the Sustainable Development Goals (SDGs).
- Educational campaigns.

C. Targets

165. The law sets sector-specific goals from 2020 to 2030, divided into mitigation, adaptation and implementation targets.

Mitigation

166. On the mitigation front, Law 2169 of 2021 sets the ambitious target of achieving carbon neutrality by the year 2050. Additionally, it aims to effect a significant reduction, specifically by 51%, in greenhouse gas emissions within the national territory by the year 2030, which represents a maximum of 169.44 million tCO2eq for the target year; establishing carbon budgets for the period 2020–2030; reducing black carbon emissions by 40% by 2030. Black carbon is defined as a fraction of particulate matter with a diameter of less than 2.5 microns, composed of elemental carbon with a high potential for absorption of visible light that contributes significantly to global warming and has negative effects on the health of humans and ecosystems; and achieving zero net deforestation of natural forests by 2030.

Adaptation

167. Law 2169 of 2023 introduces ambitious goals for adaptation and sets them out for every sector: housing, health, mining and energy, industry, transport, agriculture, environment and sustainability. These include the ecological restoration of a minimum of 1 million hectares, the reutilization of domestic wastewater, and the designation of continental and maritime areas under protection categories or with complementary conservation strategies.

168. For the mining and energy sector, for example, the following targets on adaptation are foreseen: (i) By the year 2025, integrate climate change guidelines into sectoral planning instruments dedicated to hydrocarbons, coal mining, and electric power. These guidelines should be designed to ensure the comprehensive operability under emerging scenarios of operational and environmental demand; (ii) formulating and updating climate risk analysis methodology by 2025, together with a strategy for regular updating at the national and company levels; and (iii) implementing by 2025 an ecosystem-based adaptation project for the electricity sector, which helps companies in the sector ensure compliance with their strategic objectives.

169. For the transport sector, measures include (i) by 2025 deploy three tools to enhance the geographic information systems of transportation infrastructure for effective risk management, (ii) developing two technical guideline documents by 2025 specifically designed to facilitate the conduct of risk studies for transportation infrastructure, and, notably, (iii) formulating the Policy for Disaster Risk Management (GRO) and Climate Change Adaptation (ACC) by 2025, among other.

170. For the environmental and sustainable development sector, adaptation targets are much more comprehensive: (i) updating and implementing 100% of the National Program for the Sustainable Use, Management and Conservation of Mangrove Ecosystems by 2030, (ii) adopting by 2030, 100% of the Integrated Management and Management Plans for Coastal Environmental Units (POMIUAC) with ecosystem-based adaptation actions on mangroves and seagrasses, coral reefs, and other coastal ecosystems, and (iii) incorporating ecosystem-based adaptation (EbA) in 100% of the Marine Protected Areas that are part of the SINAP Marine Protected Areas Subsystem by 2030, through climate change management measures.

Means of implementation

171. Targets on means of implementation of the aforementioned actions are also detailed in Colombia's NDCs and further reflected in Article 7 of Law 2169 of 2021, including planning instruments, science and technology, economic instruments and education and training.

172. In the planning scope, specific targets include the execution of nine pilot projects for Comprehensive Territorial Climate Change Management Plans (PIGCCT) by 2025, with a goal of formulating and implementing 100% of these plans by territorial entities by 2030. Additionally, the formulation of 100% of Sectoral Comprehensive Climate Change Management Plans (PIGCCS) is set to be achieved by 2025, with full implementation targeted for 2030.

173. The Information, Science, Technology, and Innovation section outlines objectives such as defining sub-lines of research aligned with climate change needs, executing projects within the National Strategic Plan for Environmental Research (PENIA), integrating Science, Technology, and Innovation (STeI) in climate actions nationwide, and conceptualizing and implementing the National Climate Change Information System (SNICC) by 2025 and 2030, respectively.

174. Economic instruments and financial mechanisms are addressed with targets for the National Climate Finance Strategy (ENFC), the National Program of Tradable Emission Quotas (PNCTE), and Colombia's green taxonomy, all aiming for full implementation by 2030. The Financial Management Committee of SISCLIMA will oversee and report on spending related to climate change for all entities of the National Government.

175. The Education, Training, and Awareness section emphasizes updating the National Environmental Education Policy by 2030, integrating climate change into formal education and education for work and human development, and incorporating training and awareness processes into climate change policies with a focus on human rights, differential, ethnic, gender, and intergenerational rights. Specific strategies are outlined for the integration of education, training, and awareness-raising processes in the PIGCCT and PIGCCS, as well as within the National School of Environmental Training (SAVIA) to empower citizens for effective participation in climate action.

D. Measures to Achieve Mitigation Targets

176. Law 216 of 2021 sets out measures for every sector to achieve the mitigation targets set out in Article 5. In the mining and energy sector, for example, the Ministry must put in place plans to implement energy efficiency measures in the electric power, hydrocarbons, and mining sectors, with specific goals and strategies to improve energy performance, reduce emissions, and quantify associated co-benefits. Second, efforts are directed toward proper management of fugitive emissions in the hydrocarbon chain, emphasizing leak reduction, recovery of associated gas, efficient flaring practices, and improved information tracking for fugitive emissions. Lastly, measures are proposed to narrow the gap in electricity consumption between peak and off-peak hours, intending to flatten the demand curve and minimize emissions from the SIN by prioritizing less polluting sources in electricity generation during peak periods.

177. In the agricultural sector, for example, measures are geared towards the reduction of GHG emissions generated in livestock production and increase of carbon removals from agroecosystems dedicated to this activity through the establishment of sustainable livestock production models and arrangements that guarantee the conservation or restoration of natural ecosystems. Also, deployment of actions to increase GHG removals through the promotion and consolidation of the production chain of forest plantations for commercial purposes in areas suitable for this purpose, in which sustainable technological packages are promoted. Finally, actions to increase GHG removals by crops that incorporate activities of efficient use of fertilizers, renovation and rehabilitation of crop areas, as well as the proper management of water resources and agroforestry systems, among other initiatives.

E. Carbon Markets

178. Law 2169 of 2023, Title IV, outlines measures designed to promote and develop carbon markets. These measures are organized into three key pillars:

facilitating information exchange, validation of effective biodiversity offsetting (referred to as 'compensaciones bióticas efectivas') and its migration to GHG mitigation initiatives, and establishing an institutional framework to support and regulate carbon markets.

Information related measures

179. Legal entities, whether public, private, or mixed, are required to report their direct and indirect greenhouse gas (GHG) emissions, as well as provide information and documentation for the preparation of GHG inventories. The reporting obligation applies to entities meeting criteria set by the MASD, considering factors such as GHG emission levels and company size. The Reporting Obligation (ROE) will be integrated into Environmental Information System of Colombia (SIAC), with the MASD determining methodologies for emission calculation, reporting methods, instruments, processes, and reporting frequency.

180. The information submitted through the ROE will be publicly accessible in accordance with Law 1712 of 2014, enabling the generation of reports aligned with regulations specified by the MASD. In addition, a mandatory GHG Emissions Reporting Platform will be established as part of Colombia's Environmental Information System (Article 16).

Validation and migration of biotic offsetting

181. Effective biotic offsetting may be constituted as GHG mitigation initiatives only when compliance with the legal terms of the obligation derived from environmental licensing by the competent environmental authority is completed and certified, taking into account the additionality criteria established by the MASD. Through this transition, the corresponding holder will be able to opt for payment for similar results or compensations.

F. Institutional Framework

182. Law 2169 of 2021 foresees the establishment of a study commission to analyse the status and potential of carbon markets in Colombia, with the purpose of generating recommendations to the National Government regarding the regulation of such markets and the reorganization of the organizational structure of the Colombian State required to promote the development of these markets as a new economic sector and an effective tool to reduce greenhouse gas emissions under the parameters of the carbon markets.

G. Enforcement

183. In case of identifying alleged irregularities or receiving well-substantiated complaints from any community regarding the development and implementation of regulations within GHG mitigation initiatives, the MASD has the authority to request additional information, visit the initiative's implementation site, and communicate findings to the relevant entities. This allows for necessary actions to be taken and communicated to the public as required.

H. International Commitments

184. As part of Colombia's international obligations, Law 2169 of 2021 establishes an Implementation and Monitoring Plan to oversee and fulfil all objectives and measures outlined in the UNFCCC. Its purpose is to advance low-carbon development, bolster the nation's climate resilience, and achieve carbon neutrality by 2050. Within six months of the enactment of Law 2169 of 2021, ministries, their affiliated entities, Special Administrative Units (UAEs), and other entities are mandated to formulate the plan. Approval within the same period will be sought from the Intersectoral Commission on Climate Change (CICC). The MASD will be responsible for the coordination of such initiatives.

I. Additional Measures

185. In addition to the measures outlined in Law 2169 of 2021, other initiatives include establishing the National System of Conservation Areas, designating Green Hydrogen projects as of public utility and social interest, and creating incentives like exempting the 30% quota of natural gas fleets for providers adopting electric and/or hydrogen vehicles. The law also introduces the National Registry of Deforested Areas, creates funds for the Technological Ascension of cargo transport, and proposes modifications to the Special Tax on Carbon, ensuring equal allocations for environmental degradation mitigation, prevention, and substitution of illicit crops.

Chapter 3. Water Pollution

§1. INTRODUCTION

186. Water pollution in Colombia is one of the main concerns at the national level. According to the IDEAM, the availability of water resources is gradually limited due to the alteration of water quality levels caused by industrial and economic activities, which materialize in the discharge of effluents into water bodies without any treatment. These practices have led to a reduction in oxygen levels, causing ecosystem, fauna and flora degradation. In addition, these water bodies receive large amounts of sediments from natural erosion processes. A national study on water management conducted by the IDEAM in 2022[11] identified some other problems related to water availability, including the lack of clear policies on water use systems and the increasing number of human settlements in places where water sources are scarce, among others.

I. Institutional Framework

187. With respect to water management authorities, Colombia has an institutional framework integrating the MASD, the CARs, the IDEAM and the Ministry of Housing, City and Territory. The Vice-Ministry of Water and Basic Sanitation adopts nationwide water resource policies. At the regional level, the CARs enforce water-related provisions, grant permits concerning water abstraction or wastewater discharges, and help in river basin planning. The IDEAM provides technical and scientific support to the CARs in the design and implementation of water management plans and establishes criteria for river basin planning.

II. Legal Framework

188. The legal framework for water protection and water pollution control is mainly embedded in the NCRNR and its complementary decrees, Law 99/1993 on the national environmental system and Law 1151/2007. The NCRNR provides for water resources classification, water property rights, water pollution control and prevention, and groundwater regulation. Decree 1541/1978 (Article 2.2.3.2.1.1 – Decree 1076/2015) develops the NCRNR by regulating water concessions, permits, authorizations and control of wastewater discharges, while Decree 3930/2010 (Article 2.2.3.3.1.1 & ss – Decree 1076/2015) sets water quality standards and maximum allowable limits on wastewater discharges. Decrees 1729/2002 and 1640/2012 regulate river basins. In addition to the NCRNR, the Sanitary Code (Law 9/1979) provides for certain measures on water pollution prevention, while Law 99/1993 establishes the environmental authorities empowered to manage water resources from an environmental point of view.

11. Institute of Hydrology, Meteorology and Environmental Studies (IDEAM), 'Estudio Nacional del Agua', https://www.andi.com.co/Uploads/ENA%202022_compressed.pdf.

189. Water is considered a public domain resource which cannot be transferred or changed over time. The NCRNR classifies non-marine hydric resources as: water contained in the atmosphere; rivers and water running on natural water beds; artificial water beds coming from natural water beds; lakes, lagoons and swamps; rain water; wastewater or black water; and groundwater.

190. The MASD sets out the provisions for zoning and planning of river basins in order to establish control measures on water use and pollution prevention. According to Decree 1729/2004, river basins must have a management plan containing a study of the basin, the objectives for its sustainable management and the strategies to achieve the goals contained in the plan. The river basin studies shall take into account geographic, hydro-climatic and biological aspects, ecosystems, threat identification, risks and vulnerability, and socio-economic characteristics of the surrounding communities. The concessions for the use of water are subject to the availability, planning and priorities of the river basins.

§2. Water Use

I. Concessions

191. The NCRNR establishes that any person has the right to use public domain water to satisfy their own needs insofar as no damage is caused to third parties. Any other use of water requires a concession title. In other jurisdictions, a concession title has the same meaning as a licence, lease or permit. According to Decree 1541/1978 (Article 2.2.3.2.5.1, Decree 1076/2015), concession titles are required for activities such as the supply of household water, irrigation activities, nuclear or power generation, mining, oil exploration, geothermal generation, hydroelectricity, transport of toxic materials and minerals, transport of wood logs, fishing and aquaculture, sport and recreation, medicinal use activities, and certain mining applications. In addition to the aforementioned authorizations, Decree 1541/1978 establishes special permits for the abstraction or use of sands, stones and gravels from waterbeds, streams or deposits. Notably, the competent authority must give priority to certain water uses when granting concessions. In order of preference, the priority refers to water for human consumption, individual domestic needs, community agricultural uses, generation of hydropower, industrial or manufacturing uses, mining activities, and recreational uses. The hierarchy of water uses may be changed by the authority in order to satisfy the special economic or social needs of the region.

192. Concession title holders must comply with all the conditions established in the title and the parameters on water quality; for example, title holders are not allowed to change or alter the uses for which the concession has been granted. In addition, hydraulic works required to abstract water must be approved by the authority and control devices must be installed so the amount of abstracted water can be measured. Pursuant to the NCRNR, water users are obliged to use water in an efficient way and according to the concession terms. In order to ensure the efficient use of water, users must construct and maintain installations and hydraulic works in good condition, avoid any water deviation, leaks or spills, or exceed water usage limits.

193. Decree 1541/1978 (Article 2.2.3.2.10.1 of Decree 1076/2015) regulates concessions for sewerage systems for household use; agricultural uses, drainage and irrigation; industrial uses; energy generation; water use for mining and oil-related activities; and wood floating. In particular, holders of water concessions for agricultural uses must construct and maintain appropriate drainage and drainpipe systems to avoid soil erosion, salinization and slump. Regarding industrial uses, concession holders have to put into operation wastewater treatment systems to ensure that waste effluents comply with quality standards; the authority may revoke or cancel the concession for failing to comply with this obligation. Finally, the fluvial transport of wood, oil or toxic substances is subject to special requirements, as well as the operation and cleaning of vessels for passengers and cargo transport.

194. Governmental authorities have different roles in water use and protection. The NCRNR requires authorities to classify water bodies and establish the quality criteria; set out technical parameters for water abstraction; enforce legislation on water abstraction, supply, transport and quality of water; establish criteria for wastewater treatment installations; and monitor water quality through periodic assessments. What is more, governmental authorities may restrict or even prohibit water use concessions in order to accomplish certain purposes, such as facilitating the provision of a public service or restoring the quality, flow or environment of the water body. For example, if an area of groundwater is at risk of being depleted, or there is a danger of contamination or a substantial decrease in the quantity or quality of the water resource, the competent authorities can temporarily or permanently suspend any operations that take place in the area.

195. Finally, Decree 1541/1978 (Article 2.2.3.2.20.5 of Decree 1076/2015) prohibits the introduction or incorporation into water bodies of solid, liquid or gaseous substances in quantities, concentrations or levels that may interfere with the welfare or health of people, or damage flora and fauna. Decree 1541/1978 (Article 2.2.3.2.24.1 of Decree 1076/2015) also forbids the harmful alteration of the natural water flow, sedimentation in streams and water bodies, the deposit of noxious substances that may alter the chemical and physical properties of water beds or channels, eutrophication, the extinction or decrease of aquatic flora or fauna species diversity and the decrease of water resource availability as a natural source of hydroelectric energy.

II. Water Use Fees

196. Fees for water use are provided for in Law 99/1993. The fee is levied on any activity involving water use, such as recreation, irrigation, industrial or agricultural activities. Decree 155/2004, modified by Decree 4742/2005, establishes the minimum fee, the way of calculating the amount, the water use fee in shared basins, collection methods and the future destination of the sums. The fee is established by the MASD on a yearly basis according to social and environmental damage and remediation costs that must be covered by the national budget. The CARs must collect water use fees from water users in their jurisdiction.

197. Any legal or natural, private or public person holding a concession must pay water use fees for the utilization of the resource. The fee is charged by taking into account the actual amount of abstracted or used water according to the terms of the concessions. The concerned regional authority, CAR, may collect water use fees by means of an invoice, a bill or any other instrument complying with accounting and tax provisions. Pursuant to Decree 155/2004, the period for collecting water use fees must not exceed one year. Law 1450/2011, Article 216 (PND) included a provision establishing that the fee for water use is charged to all water users, including those utilizing water by means of a concession title, but excluding those using water by means of a legal mandate.

III. Water Information System

198. Decree 1323/2007 (Article 2.2.3.5.1.1 of Decree 1076/2015) creates the Water Information System (*Sistema de Informacion de Recursos Hidricos* – SIRH) as part of the Environmental Information System of Colombia (Sistema de Informacion Ambiental de Colombia – SIAC). The SIRH gathers and integrates information concerning water uses, water abstraction, registers, statistics and related data with the purpose of having an integrated management of water resources. Natural or legal persons holding concessions or permits for water use must provide information to the authority about the use of water subject to concession or permit when needed. The SIRH seeks to support the decision-making process by providing water data, establishing a national inventory of water quantity and quality, and implementing a system to monitor water activities in order to prevent water pollution.

199. In addition, Decree 1324/2007 establishes the Register of Water Resources Users (*Registro de Usuarios del Recurso Hidrico*), which is regulated by Decree 303/2012 (Article 2.2.3.4.1.8 of Decree 1076/2015). This register serves as an information source for the SIRH and contains the inventory of natural and legal persons using water from river basins of high priority. Each CAR must create a registry for its own jurisdiction by using a protocol developed by the IDEAM. Concession or wastewater discharge permit holders shall register their authorizations with the corresponding authority. Information on the land owner and water source, quantity, injection and beneficiaries are some of the items included in this registry.

IV. Water Quality Standards

200. Decree 1594/1984, partially repealed by Decree 3930/2010 and modified by Decree 50/2008 (Article 2.2.3.3.1.1. of Decree 1076/2015), establishes water quality standards for human and domestic consumption, flora and fauna preservation, agricultural, livestock, recreational, industrial and transport. Water use for human and domestic consumption includes food manufacture or processing; direct preparation of food and beverages for human consumption; satisfaction of domestic needs, such as personal hygiene and cleaning of elements, materials or tools; and manufacture or processing of drugs, medicines, cosmetics and similar additives and products. Drinking water (human and domestic consumption) is regulated in Decree 1557/2007 and Resolution 2115/2007.

201. Decree 1575/2007 establishes a system to prevent and monitor the risks to human health caused by drinking water. Decree 1575/2007 provides for the physical, chemical and microbiological characteristics that drinking water must fulfil, which are further developed in Resolution 2115/2007. In addition, Decree 1575/2007 establishes the competent authorities for enforcing its provisions, the regulatory instruments to ensure drinking water quality and the basic process for water monitoring and control.

202. Water for flora and fauna preservation is that kind of water intended to maintain natural lives in aquatic and land ecosystems without causing alterations to these ecosystems. Flora and fauna water also refers to activities that allow the reproduction, survival, growth, extraction and utilization of hydro-biological species, such as fishing and aquaculture. Decree 1594/1984 (Decree 1076/2015) establishes quality standards for flora and fauna in cold or hot fresh water, marine and estuary water. Agricultural use of water concerns crop irrigation and related activities, and its quality standards are established in Article 40 (Article 2.2.3.3.9.5, Decree 1076/2015), whereas standards for livestock and related activities are established in Article 41 (Article 2.2.3.3.9.6, Decree 1076/2015).

203. Water for recreational activities refers to primary human-contact water, such as swimming and scuba diving; and secondary human-contact water, such as nautical sports and sportive fishing. Each recreational water contact type has its own quality standards in Article 42 (Article 2.2.3.3.9.7, Decree 1076/2015) and Article 43 (Article 2.2.3.3.9.8, Decree 1076/2015), respectively.

§3. WASTEWATER DISCHARGES

I. Water Protection

204. The NCRNR regulates the discharge of industrial and household wastewater into water bodies. The restrictions apply according to the receiving water body: water for domestic consumption of humans and animals and for food production; breeding places and habitats of crustaceous and species requiring special management; and into main water sources, falls, lakes and any other water deposits or water currents, either artificial or natural. Authorities are required to establish special zones where no discharges or introduction of waste, excretes, toxic substances, gases, agrochemical products, detergents and other similar waste is allowed. For example, pursuant to Decree 1541/1978 (Article 2.2.3.2.20.1, Decree 1076/2015), the following wastewater discharges into these areas are prohibited: high basin of rivers; groundwater; water bodies or coastal zones for recreational areas; an upriver sector of the water inlet established by the authority; and any other water body deemed by the authority as a protected area.

205. Due to the environmental impact of wastewater discharges, depending on the magnitude of the activity, the operator will be required to carry out an EIA or obtain a wastewater permit.

II. Wastewater Restrictions and Allowable Limits

A. *Restrictions*

206. Law 9/1979 and the NCRNR prohibit discharging wastewater directly into roads, canals or rainwater drainage systems unless appropriate pretreatment has been carried out. Other restrictions imposed by the regulation focus on the activity that generates wastewater in order to prevent their impact on the environment, such as domestic, industrial, agricultural, drainage or irrigation activities. For example, facilities carrying out industrial activities that are not able to guarantee the quality of their wastewater discharges may be required by the authority to relocate their premises or execute their activities in specially designated areas.

207. Decree 3930/2010 (Article 2.2.3.3.11, Decree 1076/2015) provides the regulatory framework for wastewater discharges. It establishes restrictions, activities requiring a permit and the procedure for non-compliant operations to catch up with the new requirements. Concerning restrictions, Decree 3930/2010 prohibits the injection of liquid waste into aquifers, with the exception of water from hydrocarbon activities and the use of water as wastewater solvent before it is discharged. Sediments, sludge and solid substances from water treatment facilities must not be discharged or placed into surface, ground, marine and estuary water or into the sewerage system. The discharge of visible oils and floating grease, floating materials originating from human activity and toxic substances or irritants whose action through contact, ingestion or inhalation produces adverse reactions to human health related to the use of channels, beaches and beds of water bodies, is prohibited.

B. *Standards and Concentration Limits*

208. Wastewater maximum concentration limits are established for discharges into water bodies and into the sewerage system. Decree 1594/1984 establishes in Article 72 (Article 2.2.3.3.9.14, Decree 1076/2015) the maximum permissible limits for wastewater discharges into water bodies for new and existing users. Maximum concentration limits apply to pH, temperature, floating material, greases and oils, and suspended solids (industrial and domestic); and parameters on the chemical demand of oxygen, including domestic and industrial waste. Regarding wastewater discharges into the sewerage system, Article 73 (Article 2.2.3.3.9.15, Decree 1076/2015) establishes limits to wastewater discharges on chemical demand of oxygen, specifying the maximum flow; and reference criteria, such as pH between 5 and 9; temperature below 40ºC; no acids, bases or acidic or basic solutions that can cause contamination; flammable or explosive substances contained in the effluents must be less than or equal to 10 mg/l of suspended solids, among others.

209. Additionally, although partially repealed by Decree 3930/2010, Decree 1594/1984, Article 2.2.3.3.9.16, Decree 1076/2015 remains applicable as to the maximum concentration limits for some substances that are present in wastewater discharges. Concentrations are expressed in milligrams per litre (mg/l) and include: Arsenic, 0.5; Barium, 5.0; Cadmium, 0.1; Copper, 3.0; Chromium 6, 0.5; Phenol compounds, 0.2; Mercury, 0.02; Nickel, 2.0; Silver, 0.5; Lead, 0.5; Selenium, 0.5; Cyanide, 1.0; Polychlorinated Biphenyls, not detectable; organic Mercury, not detectable; Trichloroethylene, 1.0; Chloroform, 1.0, Carbon Tetrachloride, 1.0; Dichloroethylene, 1.0; Carbon Sulphide, 1.0, other organic Chlorine compounds, each type 0.05; other organic Phosphorus compounds, each type 0.01; and Carbonates, 0.1. For the estimation of the maximum allowed concentration of the said substances in wastewater discharges, Articles 75–78 (2.2.3.3.9.17 – 2.2.3.3.9.20, Decree 1076/2015) provide for criteria, formulas and equations. The competent environmental authorities must establish the maximum allowable limits in their jurisdiction, like the SDA in Bogota.

210. Decree 3930/2010 allows the competent environmental authority to set out stricter limits to those wastewater generators that, even though they are compliant with existing limits, cause pollutant concentrations in water bodies above the quality parameters of such water bodies. For this purpose, the authority has to carry out a technical assessment justifying the measure imposed on the generator.

Discharge of treated domestic wastewater into the soil

211. Resolution 0699 of 2021 establishes the parameters and maximum permissible limit values for the punctual discharges of treated domestic wastewater (DWW) into the soil.

212. For the purpose of setting parameters and maximum permissible limits, legal or natural persons discharging DWW into the soil are categorized as (i) Users of Scattered Rural Housing, meaning those who makes use of infrastructure known as scattered rural housing, considered the housing unit located in rural soil in an isolated manner that is associated with the ways of life of the countryside and is not part of rural population centres or parcels intended for country housing; (ii) Users Comparable to Users of Scattered Rural Housing, meaning those using infrastructure associated with a productive activity or the use of country housing, whose generation of domestic wastewater is similar in quantity and quality (expressed in BOD5 load) to that produced by users of scattered rural housing, with values less than or equal to 1.0 Kg BOD5/d; and (iii) Users Different from Users Comparable and Users of Scattered Rural Housing, defined as those using locative infrastructure such as toilets and sanitary services, personal hygiene systems (showers and sinks), kitchens and kitchenettes, washbasins for cleaning hygiene items, performing cleaning of walls and floors of this locative infrastructure, and laundry (industrial laundry services are not included), whose generation of domestic wastewater is different in quantity and quality from that produced by the aforementioned type of users.[12]

213. Maximum permissible limits include physicochemical and microbiological parameters that DWW to the soil must comply with at the point source of discharges. Maximum allowable limits are categorized based on the type of users: Users of Scattered Rural Housing, Users Comparable to Users of Scattered Rural Housing (Table 1) and Users Different from Comparable Users and Users of Scattered Rural Housing (Table 2).

214. Parameters include temperature, pH, chemical oxygen demand (DQO), suspended solids (SST), sedimentable solids (SSED), fats and oils, active substances to Methylene Blue (SAAM), electrical conductivity, total phosphorus (P), nitrogen compounds, chlorides, among others. Depending on the infiltration rate, the limits will be higher or lower. The basic infiltration rate refers to the constant speed reached by infiltrating water during a three-hour minimum infiltration test conducted for every 2,500 m^2 or a fraction of the projected discharge area.

215. Users of Scattered Rural Housing whose individual sanitation solutions for domestic wastewater comply with the parameters defined in the technical regulations of the drinking water and basic sanitation sector do not require soil discharge permits. Competent environmental authorities are responsible for assessing, controlling, and monitoring compliance with these parameters.

216. Users covered under Resolution 0699 of 2021 must provide information on the analysis and quantification of specific parameters outlined in the resolution to the competent environmental authority. These authorities are then required to report this information in accordance with the established requirements of the Water Resource User Registration Format (RURH), as specified in Resolution MADS 955 of 2012 and incorporate it into the Water Resource Information System (SIRH). A monitoring frequency of biennial analysis is stipulated for Users Equivalent to Rural Scattered Housing, while Users Differing from Rural Scattered Housing must conduct annual parameter analysis, as per Article 7.

217. Compliance and management plans must adhere to the guidelines on the transition regime.[13]

12. Resolution 0699 of 2021, Art. 2.
13. Decree 1076 of 2015, Art. 2.2.3.3.11.2.

III. Wastewater Permit

218. Any discharge of effluents into surface, ground and/or marine water requires a wastewater discharge permit (*Permiso de Vertimientos*). Wastewater discharged to the sewerage system does not require this permit (Article 41, Decree 3930/2010 and Article 2.2.3.3.5.1, Decree 1076 of 2015). If the activity or project carried out by the company requires an environmental licence, the wastewater discharge permit is included in the environmental licence. Companies that have no wastewater discharge permit and exceed discharge concentration limits must submit a Compliance Plan for the authority's approval. Holders of permits obtained in accordance with now-repealed Decree 1594/1984 may voluntarily execute a Plan of Reconversion to Clean Technologies (PRTL) in wastewater management. The PRTL is part of the wastewater discharge permit, and therefore, it has to be authorized by the competent authority and must be updated by including the Plan in the permit.

219. In addition, developers of industrial, commercial or service activities, subject to an environmental licence and generating wastewater discharges to a water body or soil, must present a wastewater management plan (*Plan de Gestión del Riesgo para el Manejo de Vertimientos*). The Plan has to include a risk assessment, preventive and mitigation measures, emergency and contingency protocols, and remediation and rehabilitation plans for situations impeding or limiting wastewater treatment. The risk assessment for wastewater management has to be prepared according to the terms of reference adopted by Resolution 1514/2012.

IV. Wastewater Discharge Fees

220. Decree 2667/2012 establishes the minimum fee, the regional fee adjustment, the persons subject to the fee payment, the methods of fee collection and enforcement measures on wastewater discharge fees. The MASD adopts a resolution on a yearly basis, establishing the minimum wastewater discharge fee according to the direct costs of restoring and removing noxious substances from wastewater. The CARs must collect wastewater discharge fees from activities taking place in water bodies of their jurisdiction.

221. Wastewater discharge fees must be paid by any legal or natural person that discharges wastewater into water bodies. In case of wastewater discharge into the sewerage system, Decree 2667/2012 (Article 2.2.9.7.5.2, Decree 1076/2015) provides that the fee is paid by the public company that provides sewerage services. The fee amount depends on the pollutant substances contained in each user's wastewater discharges, as well as on the regional or sector targets established by the authority. This fee is calculated every month for the total amount of wastewater discharged and is charged by the CAR through an invoice, a bill or any other instrument complying with accounting and tax provisions.

V. Reuse of Wastewater

222. Law 1955 of 2019 stipulates that, based on the assessment of existing regulations, there is a need to amend the rules governing the use of treated wastewater. In addition, the National Circular Economy Strategy, developed by the National Government in 2019, incorporates wastewater reuse as a practice to enhance resource efficiency. As a result of the evaluation and monitoring process of existing regulation, Resolution 1256 of 2021 has been issued regulating the use of wastewater and repealing Resolution 1207 of 2014.

223. Resolution 1256 of 2021 sets out conditions for three main aspects of wastewater management: recirculation, reuse and prevention of water pollution.

224. Recirculation refers to the use of wastewater in unitary operations and processes within the same economic activity that generates it and by the same Generating User (further defined), without there being contact with the soil at the time of its use, except when it is infrastructure support soil. Generating User is the natural or legal person who generates wastewater, while Receiving User is the natural or legal person who uses such generated wastewater.[14]

225. Water users may implement recirculation of wastewater if it is both technically and economically feasible. No environmental authorization is required for this practice. However, for the monitoring and control of wastewater recirculation in infrastructure-supporting soils by the Environmental Authority, users must maintain the following information: (i) water balance of the recirculation system for economic activity; (ii) identification of potential risks to renewable natural resources arising from wastewater use; and (iii) preventive measures to be implemented to avoid the identified potential risks, along with corresponding follow-up activities. In the event of wastewater recirculation in infrastructure-supporting soils, runoff should not be generated.[15]

226. Reuse of wastewater is defined as the use of wastewater by a Receiving User for a use other than the one that generated it. For example, reusing wastewater from domestic activities for industrial purposes. To acquire the right to use wastewater as a public utility, interested parties must obtain a water concession unless stipulated otherwise in Article 148 of Decree-Law 2811 of 1974. The Generating User is responsible for defining the availability of the required quantities (volume or flow) of wastewater for reuse, while the Receiving User of Wastewater bears the responsibility for adhering to the provisions of Resolution 1256 of 2021.[16]

227. Wastewater can be reused for agricultural or industrial purposes to the extent they comply with the minimum quality criteria and additional regulatory

14. Resolution 1256 of 2021, Art. 2.
15. Resolution 1256 of 2021, Art. 3.
16. Resolution 1256 of 2021, Art. 4.

requirements.[17] Additional quality criteria for wastewater used in agriculture include limits for various parameters such as conductivity, total phenols, total hydrocarbons, free cyanide, chlorides, fluorides, sulfates, mercury, sodium, antimony, residual total chlorine, and nitrates. The Receiving User can request the exclusion of specific parameters from the Environmental Authority, providing support through material balances and the characterization of wastewater. For wastewater used in industrial processes, no environmental quality criteria are specified, but compliance with sanitary regulations and other relevant legislation is still required.

§4. Marine Water

228. The Second Book of the NCRNR includes Part IV on the sea and the seabed and imposes the duty on the Colombian State to protect the marine environment. The marine environment comprises marine water, soil, subsoil and aerial space of the territorial sea and the economic zone, as well as the beaches and renewable natural resources of the zone. The protection is focused on preventing pollution from substances that pose risks to human health, harm hydro-biological resources or hinder other legitimate uses of the sea. Measures must be adopted to establish marine water quality, limits and concentrations of waste dumped into the sea and regulate hydrocarbon-related activities in order to avoid contamination. Any activity that may lead to contamination or degradation of the marine environment requires a permit.

229. Decree 1875/1979 establishes the regulation on protection of the marine environment. Pursuant to its Article 2, the General Directorate of Marine and Harbours (*Direccion General Maritima y Portuaria*) is the competent authority on marine water protection and is in charge of authorizing wastewater discharges or waste dumping into the sea, subject to compliance with the maximum limits and concentrations. Notably, the discharge of Mercury, Cadmium, halogenated chemical compounds, materials from chemical or biological wars, and any other substances that the General Directorate of Marine and Harbours may consider hazardous is forbidden.

230. Decree 1875/1979 provides for insurance policies to be undertaken by ships and vessels transiting in Colombian territory in order to cover any environmental damage derived from their operation. Concerning facilities located at river banks or coastlines or performing hydrocarbon activities, Decree 1875/1979 requires them to be provided with pollution control devices and take out insurance policies for vessels and ships. Other pieces of environmental legislation on marine water refer to harbours' operation; handling, transport, unloading and storage of chemical substances at harbours; tourism activities; and regulations on the waste regenerated by piers, vessels, terminals and harbours.

17. Decree 1076 of 2015, Arts 2.2.3.3.2.5 and 2.2.3.3.2.8.

Chapter 4. Waste

§1. Introduction

I. Background

231. Title III (Articles 34–38) of the NCRNR lays down the basis for a regulatory framework on waste management aimed at preventing environmental damage. Municipalities must ensure the provision of adequate services of public waste collection, transportation and final disposal services. Furthermore, the Sanitary Code adopted by Law 9/1979 establishes general requirements to preserve, restore and improve sanitary conditions affecting human health. The Sanitary Code complements the NCRNR by including requirements on waste collection, transport, treatment and final disposal when such waste is generated in industrial operations.

II. Types of Waste in Colombia

232. There are two main classes of waste regulated in Colombia: solid waste and hazardous waste. Solid waste is regulated by Decree 2981/2013 which establishes provisions for companies rendering the public service of sanitation. Municipalities must ensure that all citizens are provided with sanitation services, including solid waste collection, transport, treatment, cleaning of public spaces and final disposal. Hazardous waste is regulated by Decree 4741/2005 (Article 2.2.6.1.1.1, Decree 1076/2015) which provides for an integrated waste management system for hazardous waste generators, including requirements on hazardous waste generation, storage, transport, treatment and final disposal. Although the two regulations refer to waste, they apply to different individuals and companies and, therefore, require a separate analysis.

§2. Solid Waste

I. Definition

233. Solid waste is defined as any object, material, substance or solid element resulting from the use or consumption of goods in household, industrial, commercial, institutional and service activities, that its generator abandons, rejects or hands over, and which is prone to be treated or transformed into another good. This definition covers public space waste, parks and garden waste, and ordinary solid waste, which can be recoverable or not.

II. Scope

234. Decree 2981/2013 regulates the public service of sanitation (*Servicio Publico de Aseo*) and the entities that provide this service. The sanitation service is classified as special and ordinary, understanding special sanitation as the service that cannot be provided under normal conditions due to the particular characteristics of the waste. The management of solid waste in Colombia is the responsibility of the authorized company that provides sanitation services, even though solid waste generators must comply with specific obligations on waste storage and presentation. Solid waste management comprises collection, transport, cleaning of public places, transference, treatment, reuse and final disposal.

III. Key Actors and Main Obligations

235. The management of solid waste involves three main actors: the municipality, responsible for guaranteeing the provision of sanitation services; the company providing sanitation services; and sanitation service users.

A. Municipalities and Special Districts

236. Solid waste management is guided by the principles established in Decree 2981/2013. These principles include guaranteeing the quality of sanitation services on a continuous basis, development and extension of services; developing methods in order to guarantee users' access to public services, its participation and control; minimizing the generation of waste and impact on natural resources; increasing the recovery of waste and guarantee an adequate final disposal of waste that may not be recovered; and enhancing waste and special waste processing systems and final disposal sites. In order to comply with these principles, the municipalities and districts must implement a Plan for the Integrated Management of Solid Waste (*Plan para la gestión integral de Residuos Sólidos* – PGIRS) (Article 88).

237. The PGIRS is a planning tool which sets out objectives, goals, programmes, and specific projects and activities to ensure sanitation services provision for the short (three years), medium (six years) and long (fifteen years) term. The PGIRS must include information on the assessment of existing technical, financial, institutional and environmental conditions of the entity (municipality, district, etc.) regarding solid waste generation and management; identification of alternatives for the integrated management of solid waste; assessment of proposed alternatives; programmes to implement the PGIRS at different management stages (i.e., promotion and training, segregation at source, collection, transport, treatment, recovery and final disposal); establishment of goals, objectives and targets; and contingency plans. The PGIRS must be regarded and complied with by public sanitation companies and implemented in their solid waste activities. Resolution 754/2014 provides further detail on the methods and implementation of PGIRS.

B. Public Sanitation Companies

238. Pursuant to Decree 2981/2013, companies providing public sanitation services are those in charge of one or more activities concerning waste management. Sanitation services are considered public services; therefore, companies providing these services must be registered as public service companies. Once solid waste is placed for further collection, public sanitation companies undertake the custody and management of such waste. The first phase is collection, where companies must comply with general and special conditions on collection systems, routes, schedules, frequencies, storage boxes and collection of solid waste from specific activities: industries and shops, markets, cemeteries, construction activities, public events, etc. For the transport of solid waste, Decree 2981/2013 establishes the conditions that public sanitation vehicles, vehicle equipment and accessories must fulfil.

239. Decree 2981/2013 also regulates activities of public space cleaning, transfer stations, facilities for waste recovery or treatment and final disposal sites. Waste transfer sites refer to installations for solid waste management and transfer from a collector vehicle to another vehicle with greater transport capacity that takes the waste to the processing site or final disposal. Waste transfer regulation includes requirements on the design and construction characteristics, special location conditions and operational provisions minimizing environmental impacts.

240. Final disposal is regulated in Decree 838/2005 that repeals the corresponding chapter of Decree 1713/2002 and provides for criteria, procedures, methodologies and prohibitions on the localization of waste final disposal facilities. In addition, Decree 2436/2008 establishes that landfill operators must not restrict the access of public sanitation companies to landfills, such as preventing the access of solid waste to landfills or transfer stations based on the region or municipality where the solid waste was generated; imposing different requirements, characteristics, or technical parameters for solid waste to the ones established in the regulations; or implementing special and discriminatory rates. When final disposal is carried out by incineration processes, the operator must comply with emission limits established in Resolution 58/2002, as amended by Resolution 886/2004 and Resolution 909/2008. Waste incinerators must also report the type of waste and quantity by indicating the toxic properties, halogenated compounds and their concentration, as well as implement an operation and maintenance manual which must have the authority's approval.

241. Finally, it is important to note that transfer stations, treatment plants and landfills are subject to EIAs prior to the start of activities.

C. Users

242. Users are defined as the legal or natural persons being provided with sanitation services, either as owners of the building where the service is provided or as direct users of the service. In case users are grouped in household units, buildings or any other unit, they are called 'Multi-users' (*Multiusiarios*) and are subject to special obligations. Pursuant to Chapter II of Decree 1713/2002 on solid waste storage and presentation, users are responsible for the adequate storage and presentation of solid waste and have to comply with obligations established in the PGIRS, in contracts with public sanitation companies and other pieces of legislation.

243. Solid waste presentation refers to the conditions in which solid waste must be handed over to the sanitation company or placed for further collection. Waste must be presented so as to avoid its contact with the environment or with people handling it, and must be placed during the established schedules (three hours before the collection time). Containers for solid waste presentation must be solid, constructed of impermeable material, resistant, easy to clean and lift, and with adequate conditions to mitigate negative impacts on the environment and people. Multi-users are required to be provided with storage units with flat surfaces for easy cleaning, ventilation, water supply, drainage and fire prevention systems, constructed to avoid rodents, insects or animals and to allow the collection of solid waste. If the PGIRS establishes any other provisions on waste storage and presentation, users have to ensure compliance with such provisions.

IV. Enforcement

244. Law 1259/2008, modified by Law 1466/2011 and partially repealed by Law 1801/2016, aims to promote the sound management of solid waste and establishes the procedures to punish infringers of solid waste provisions, in particular, of health, cleaning and waste collection provisions. Some of the conducts included in Law 1801/2016 consist of not using adequate containers for waste disposal, disposing of the garbage outside of prescribed schedules, and disposing of industrial waste in non-authorized sites. Decree 3695/2009 (Article 2.2.5.14.1.1, Decree 1076/2015) regulates Law 1259/2008 by inserting a definition of environmental sanctions, codifying the existing infractions on solid waste, providing municipal authorities with guidelines on how to apply environmental fines, and establishing a mandatory form to be used by national authorities when imposing the said environmental fine. Environmental sanctions consist of a formal notice requiring the offender to show up before the authority in order to be heard and receive the applicable sanction. The sanction for solid waste infractions does not preclude other sanitary or environmental sanctions.

§3. Hazardous Waste

I. General

A. Definition

245. Hazardous Waste is regulated in Decree 4741/2005 and partially developed by means of Resolution 1402/2006 and is defined as a waste that, given its corrosive, reactive, explosive, toxic, flammable, infectious or radioactive characteristics, may cause a risk or damage to human health or the environment. The packaging and wrapping that may have been in contact with the mentioned waste are also considered hazardous waste.

B. Hazardous Waste Management

246. In Colombia, hazardous waste management is contained in Decree 4741/2005 which regulates waste classification and identification; hazardous waste generators' obligations, registry and liability; waste packaging and products that become hazardous waste; competent authorities; and a list of prohibitions regarding hazardous waste. Decree 4741/2005 applies to natural or legal persons handling, generating and managing hazardous waste.

247. Regarding hazardous waste classification, Decree 4741/2005 establishes that waste listed in Annex I and Annex II (Article 2.2.6.2.3.5, Decree 1076/2015) are considered hazardous waste unless they do not exhibit the hazardous characteristics listed in Annex III. Annex I lists categories of waste to be controlled, and Annex II includes hazardous waste by waste stream. The three annexes are taken from the Basel Convention on the Control of Transboundary Movements of Hazardous Wastes and Their Disposal. The mixture of a non-hazardous waste with a hazardous one makes the former a hazardous waste. Nonetheless, waste generators can prove to the authority that their waste is not hazardous by undergoing a categorization procedure and supporting such procedure with sampling and analysis evidence from authorized laboratories.

248. Hazardous waste generators are classified as large (1,000 Kg/month), medium (100 and 1,000 Kg/month) and small (10 and 100 Kg/month) generators, according to the amount of waste generated per month and taking into account the average amount of waste generated in a six-month period. Decree 4741/2005 establishes different registration deadlines for each generator, although, by 2010, all types of generators should have been registered, except those generating less than 10 Kg/month. Resolution 1362/2007 regulates the Hazardous Waste Generators Registry by providing for registration timing, the registry purpose, application procedure, information update and related procedures.

C. Obligations

249. Hazardous waste generators are required to comply with specific obligations, such as implementing a waste management plan, identifying hazardous waste characteristics, and taking responsibility for any damages that hazardous waste management may cause. The waste management plan includes information on the objectives of the plan; a general description of the activities developed to manage hazardous waste; identification, classification and quantification of the waste generated; analysis of alternative waste minimization practices; internal waste management practices; identification of personnel responsible for waste minimization practices; and evaluation and improvement measures to enhance waste management and minimization. The waste management plan must be available at the workplace for consultation by the competent authorities.

250. The hazardous waste generator must identify hazardous waste characteristics; comply with standards on packaging and labelling; comply with Decree 1609/2002 on transport of hazardous materials, especially with Safety Data Sheets requirements, when consigning hazardous waste for its transport; be registered with the National Register, as specified above; train its staff and personnel in hazardous waste management; draft and implement a contingency plan; keep records for five years on certificates concerning waste storage, transport, reuse, treatment or final disposal; adopt the adequate measures for the permanent closure of the facility; and sign contracts with authorized companies for hazardous waste storage, treatment, transport and final disposal services.

251. Decree 4741/2005 also establishes a series of obligations for hazardous waste transporters and consignees. Regarding waste transporters, they have to comply with requirements on transport of hazardous materials, deliver the total amount of the received hazardous waste, have a contingency plan and clean their vehicles at authorized places. Transporters must not store or carry incompatible waste in their vehicles. In the case of consignees, which are those facilities providing services of storage, treatment, recovery or final disposal, the main obligations refer to having the necessary authorizations, giving a safe and environmentally sound management to hazardous waste, and issuing a certification to the generator indicating that the activity has concluded according to the contract agreed by the parties.

II. Liability

252. Regarding hazardous waste management liability, Colombian legislation distinguishes between hazardous waste generators and manufacturers, importers and distributors of products that become hazardous waste.

A. Generators

253. According to Decree 4741/2005, the hazardous waste generator is responsible for its waste and for its wastewater discharges, emissions, products and by-products, and the effects they cause to human health and the environment. Waste generator's liability extends up to the moment when hazardous waste is recovered or permanently disposed of. In addition, hazardous waste generators remain liable for the damages or noxious effects caused to human health or to the environment by the undisclosed chemical or biological content of their hazardous waste.

B. Producers

254. Producers and importers of products or chemical substances with hazardous properties are assimilated into hazardous waste generators. Therefore, they are required to comply with hazardous waste generators' obligations and to ensure a safe and responsible management of products or chemical substance packaging, containers and waste; inform consumers and end-users of the biological and chemical content of their products; and communicate any risks of their hazardous substances or products to consumers and end-users. The producer liability subsists until the waste is treated (recycled, recovered, etc.) or until it is finally disposed of.

255. Additionally, the packaging, waste and products listed in Article 20 of Decree 4741/2005 (Article 2.2.6.1.4.1, Decree 1076/2015) are subject to the implementation of take-back management plans *(Plan de Gestión de Devolución de Productos Posconsumo).* Producers and importers of the products listed therein must submit a Take-Back Management Plan to the authority for its approval within the deadlines established for such purpose. Furthermore, producers and importers are allowed to agree upon the take-back measures to be implemented in the take-back management plan; however, these plans must be individually submitted. Concerning distributors of products or chemical substances with hazardous properties, they must be part of the take-back management plans implemented by producers and importers.

C. Users

256. Decree 4741/2005 requires users and end-consumers to comply with certain obligations in order to ensure the sound management of hazardous waste. Users must follow and regard the safety handling instructions provided by the product manufacturer or distributor until the product has reached the end of its life cycle. In addition, users must hand over the hazardous residues or waste from products or chemical substances with hazardous properties, according to the take-back mechanism established by the manufacturer or distributor.

D. Contaminated Sites

257. Decree 4741/2005 establishes liability for the inadequate management of hazardous waste resulting in site contamination. Accordingly, those people responsible for wrongful hazardous waste management that led to soil contamination must diagnose, remedy and repair any damages caused to human health and the environment in accordance with existing regulations.

III. Transboundary Movement of Hazardous Waste

258. Colombia adopted the 1989 Basel Convention on the Control of Transboundary Movements of Hazardous Wastes and Their Disposal by means of Law 253/1996, which was later amended by Law 1623/2013. This international instrument aims to decrease and control the import and trade of hazardous waste and ensure its disposal in an environmentally sound manner. The Basel Convention elaborates on the principle of PIC, requiring the approval of importing countries before any hazardous waste enters its borders. Likewise, import and transit countries may refuse any request for hazardous waste transit or import within their territories unless they grant their PIC.

259. Regarding the adequate management of hazardous waste, the Basel Convention provides for the minimization of hazardous waste generation and the control of its storage, transport, treatment, reuse, recycling, recovery and final disposal. Furthermore, Law 253/1996 adopting the Basel Convention in Colombia establishes that hazardous waste must be managed from its generation source by appropriate waste elimination installations that prevent pollution from elimination processes.

IV. Products

260. Decree 4171/2005 includes a list of products and chemical substances that become hazardous waste and are subject to the implementation of take-back management plans. Nonetheless, the obligation to implement take-back plans becomes enforceable once the MASD issues a resolution regulating the content of such plans and the measures to be taken for specific listed products. The MASD has regulated take-back management plans for acid-lead automobile batteries and pharmaceutical products, which regulation is presented below, as well as for computers and peripherals (Resolution 1512/2010), light bulbs (Resolution 1511/2010) and batteries (Resolution 1297/2010). Finally, it is important to note that waste, electric and electronic products are regulated in Law 1672/2013.

A. Acid-Lead Batteries

261. Resolution 372/2009 establishes the elements that take-back management plans of used acid-lead automobile batteries must contain and the deadlines in which they must be submitted. Take-back management plans are mandatory for those legal or natural persons manufacturing acid-lead automobile batteries in Colombia or importing more than three hundred units per year. The take-back management plans shall include an executive summary, information on the product (characteristics, quantities and identification); the actors intervening in the product management, such as manufacturers, distributors and final disposal contractors; the product management actions and activities; and measures for hazardous waste planning and tracking.

262. Take-back management plans must be updated to comply with Resolution 0851 of 2021 on RAEE/WEEE collection and management systems.

B. Pharmaceutical Products

263. Resolution 371/2009 establishes the elements that take-back management plans of expired drugs and pharmaceutical products must contain and the deadlines in which they must be submitted. Take-Back Management Plans are mandatory for manufacturers and importers of drugs or pharmaceutical products. Manufacturers and importers of the said products are those holding a valid Sanitary Register issued by the National Institute of Surveillance of Medicines and Food (*Instituto Nacional de Vigilancia de Medicamentos y Alimentos* – INVIMA) to produce, import or package these medicines or pharmaceutical products. Pharmaceutical facilities, pharmacies and healthcare facilities must participate in the development of take-back management plans for expired drugs and pharmaceutical products. The content of those plans is the same as for used acid-lead automobile batteries.

§4. Other Special Waste

I. Radioactive Waste

264. Resolution 18005 of the Ministry of Mines and Energy, modified by Resolution 41178/2016, adopts the regulation on radioactive waste management and defines it as any material that contains a concentration of radionuclides greater than those deemed safe by the regulatory authority or that has been contaminated with such waste. Resolution 18005 establishes technical requirements for all phases of radioactive waste management so its whole life cycle is safe and kinder to the environment and people's health. The scope of Resolution 18005 covers legal and natural persons that generate, collect, segregate, classify, treat, condition, store or dispose of radioactive waste.

265. Radioactive waste management in Colombia involves coordinated actions from the Ministry of Mines and Energy, the Group of Nuclear Matters, radioactive waste generators and operators of radioactive waste treatment facilities. Both generators of radioactive waste and operators of radioactive sources require an authorization establishing the conditions under which radioactive waste must be managed. In general, radioactive waste generators have to minimize the generation of such waste by means of an adequate facility's design, operation and closure. Moreover, generators must comply with levels of exempted waste established in the authorization, as well as with the acceptance criteria, prior to sending them for further treatment. Finally, in order to guarantee a cradle to grave protection, radioactive waste generators must have signed contracts with operators of treatment, storage, transport and final disposal facilities.

266. Concerning sealed sources of radioactive waste, Resolution 18005 requires their users to try reusing that source or transferring it to another facility prior to declaring it as radioactive source in disuse. Accordingly, once sealed sources of radioactive waste are declared as in disuse, they have to be sent to adequate facilities for further treatment.

267. Colombia also has a Policy of Radioactive Waste adopted on 20 January 2010. The policy follows the same line and establishes the same requirements of Resolution 18005.

II. Hospital Waste

268. Decree 2676/2000, modified by Decree 4126/2005, regulates the integrated management of hospital waste, including medical and similar waste. Activities of biological and medical waste segregation, storage, collection, transport, treatment and final disposal are covered under Decree 2676/2000. Pursuant to this piece of legislation, those natural or legal persons generating or handling biologically contaminated waste (hospital waste) must implement an integrated management system in order to minimize biohazardous waste generation and mitigate the impact on people's health and the environment.

269. Some of the activities covered by the integrated management system include segregating hospital waste at source, ensuring its proper incineration or landfilling, training employees on hospital waste management and putting in place emergency plans in case of emergencies. Activities concerning waste sterilization, burning or land filing can be outsourced by authorized entities. These entities undertake the hospital waste generator's liability.

270. Furthermore, Resolution 1164/2002 adopts the Manual for Hospital Waste Management, establishing the procedure for the management of medical waste generated in healthcare and similar activities.

III. Non-infectious Waste

271. Although Resolution 1164/2002 establishes the manual for hospital waste management, it does not address those waste originated in hospitals or healthcare establishments that do not exhibit infectious characteristics, such as bags or containers of substances for intravenous use, intra-peritoneal and in haemodialysis, which have not entered in contact with patients' corporal fluids. As a result, the MASD adopts Resolution 482/2009 regulating the management, use and recycling of non-infectious hospital waste (bags or containers of substances for intravenous use, intra-peritoneal and in haemodialysis, which have not entered in contact with patients' corporal fluids). Resolution 482/2009 provides for non-infectious hospital waste classification, packaging and labelling and establishes requirements for waste storage, use or recycling. In order to perform one of the latter activities, natural or legal persons must register with the authority; inform the place of non-infectious waste storage, use or recycling activities; comply with packaging requirements, and fill out the forms provided for identifying non-infectious waste generator, waste quantity, applicable dates, sites and final destination.

IV. Pesticides

A. *Scope*

272. Decree 1443/2004 (Article 2.2.7.1.1.1, Decree 1076/2015) regulates the integrated management of pesticides and pesticide waste as part of the hazardous waste streams provided for in the Basel Convention. Decree 1443/2004 covers any natural or legal person manufacturing, importing, packaging or distributing pesticides; or generating and handling pesticides in disuse (waste pesticides), as well as end-users and consumers. Pesticides are regulated before being placed on the market and during the whole product life cycle.

273. Pursuant to Decree 1443/2004, hazardous waste generated from pesticides includes any pesticides that are no longer in use due to their expiry date, changes in technical specifications or because the government has stated so. Waste pesticides also refer to containers or packaging that have contained pesticides, any surplus content, pesticide by-products and any personal protection equipment or cleaning object that may have been in contact with pesticides, such as working suits or equipment. Article 5 of Decree 1443/2004 (Article 2.2.7.2.1.1, Decree 1076/2015) provides further conditions for a pesticide to be considered waste pesticide.

B. *Obligations*

274. Among the main obligations established in Decree 1443/2004, pesticide manufacturers, importers, distributors and packaging companies are required to implement measures aimed at minimizing hazardous waste generation or facilitating their safe disposal. Moreover, Decree 1443/2004 provides for the implementation of take-back programmes for used packaging and containers of waste pesticides. In addition, Article 15 of Decree 1443/2004 (Article 2.2.7.3.1.3, Decree 1076/2015) requires natural or legal persons handling pesticides to keep a log-book of all pesticides accepted for storage, including information on its origin, quantity, date of entry and name of the depositary, as well as further information regarding final destination and use; and to provide training to all employees responsible for performing activities related to pesticide management.

275. Concerning pesticide transport, Decree 1443/2004 provides that pesticides have to be placed in safe containers displaying a clear label identifying their content, according to the specifications established by Decree 1609/2002 on the transport of hazardous goods by road. Additionally, the storage or transport of pesticides requires an environmental licence prior to starting operations.

C. Liability

276. Decree 1443/2004 establishes that pesticide manufacturers or importers of pesticides are considered waste pesticide generators; thus, they are jointly responsible for the management of pesticides. This liability extends up to the delivery of waste pesticides to an authorized contractor for their final disposal. The waste disposal or treatment contractor assumes the entire responsibility for waste pesticides accepted for further disposal at its facilities. Land filling and open-air burning of pesticides are prohibited by Decree 1443/2004. Pesticide disposal must be carried out in safe conditions at waste management facilities that are duly authorized by the competent authorities.

V. Used Oils

277. According to Law 1252/2008, the use of waste hydrocarbons, including waste lubricant oils for energy generation, is allowed in Colombia as long as they are generated in the national territory and as long as they comply with the conditions established by the competent authorities. In particular, used oils have been regulated through a series of resolutions that have suffered special changes. For example, Resolution 415/1998 regulates and develops some of the principles contained in the Basel Convention by adopting provisions to impede the introduction of toxic waste, such as used oil, and by establishing cases where the combustion of used oils is permitted. Nonetheless, some of the provisions of Resolution 415/1998 have been repealed by Resolution 1446/2005, such as definitions, requirements on the use of used oil (treated and non-treated) and requirements for operators that treat or store used oil.

278. In general, the use of used oil is subject to obtaining a permit for atmospheric emissions and must comply with technical requirements on burners, have knowledge of the final product destination, and carry records on the used oil, including used oil supplier, origin of the used oil, quantities and proportion of the fuel oil used in the mixture and type of fuel that has been mixed with the used oil. The content of Polychlorobifeniles (PCBs) or Polychloroterfeniles (PCTs) and halogens in used oils must be monitored so as to ensure they comply with the maximum concentrations.

VI. RAEE/WEEE Collection and Management

A. Context

279. According to the report from the Registry of Producers and Traders of Electrical and Electronic Appliances (RPCAEE), regulated by Resolution 480 of 2020 from the Ministry of Commerce, Industry, and Tourism, in 2019, 309,715 tons of mass consumption EEE were placed on the Colombian market. Technical analyses by the MASD estimated that around 184,000 tons of waste from EEE imported into the country in previous years were generated in 2019. Of this, 37,008 tons (20.2% of the total generated RAEE and 11.9% of the total EEE placed on the market) were collected through waste collection and management systems for computers and peripherals, batteries and accumulators, bulbs, and other WEEE (RAEE for its initials in Spanish), as per the official report of the ANLA. The Ministry's studies project that by 2026, the generation of WEEE is expected to reach nearly 216,000 tons, representing a 9.4% growth in five years or 1.9% annually in the most conservative scenario.

280. Due to the increasing generation of RAEE and its low rate of environmentally adequate collection and management, the government had deemed it necessary to expand the regulation of collection systems to all mass consumption EEE commercialized in the country and establish long-term national collection and management objectives for RAEE, based on the principle of extended producer responsibility and considering the lifespan of the devices.

B. Objective and Scope

281. Resolution 0851 of 2022 seeks to accomplish three objectives: (i) define the national classification of Electrical and Electronic Appliances (AEE/EEE) and their waste (RAEE/WEEE), (ii) set out the conditions for WEEE collection and management systems implemented by producers, and (iii) establish conditions for the acceptance of RAEE by AEE retailers. The overarching objective is to prevent and control adverse environmental impacts.

282. Resolution 0851 of 2022 covers the comprehensive management of EEE and WEEE across the entire national territory. It applies to producers, retailers, users or consumers of AEE, waste management operators, as well as ANLA and Environmental Authorities. However, the resolution does not extend to AEE that are components of strictly military weapons or ammunition necessary for safeguarding national security.

C. Classification

283. The classification of AEE and their waste is organized into three main categories:

- household appliances, including stoves and ovens, audio and video appliances, major household appliances, personal minor appliances, air conditioning equipment, and domestic and commercial refrigeration, among others;
- electronics and Telecommunications Equipment, including telecommunication antennas, electronic circuits, electronic components, computers and data processing equipment, as well as peripherals, parts, and cards for computers and printers, etc.; and

– machinery and electrical equipment, including cables and conductors, industrial equipment, control and protection equipment, and lighting equipment, among others.

D. RAEE Collection and Management Systems

284. Resolution 0851 of 2022 requires producers of AEE to establish, present, implement and finance systems of collection and environmentally safe management of AEE placed by such producers on the market. The systems can be individual or collective and must comply with the technical requirements for the collection mechanisms, such as fixed points of collection, storage centres, collection campaigns and other requirements.

285. Individual management systems refer to a situation where a producer, acting under its sole responsibility, establishes, presents, implements, and funds their own system for the collection and management of RAEE; whereas in the collective management system, two or more producers, organized as a legal entity, form a collective system with the exclusive purpose of establishing, presenting, implementing, and funding a system. This system must consist solely of AEE producers.

286. The regulation sets out specific conditions for both collection systems and management systems of WEEE.

Collection systems

287. Requirements on WEEE collection systems focus on fixed collection points, storage centres, collection campaigns, and other collection mechanisms.

288. Fixed Collection Points must be strategically located, providing shelter, adequate lighting, and protection against weather conditions. They should be easily accessible and visible to users, implementing measures to prevent theft or unauthorized disassembly of RAEE. Containers used for collection must be compatible with RAEE types, appropriately sized, marked with relevant information, and regularly emptied. Documentation, including records of delivery, installation, and RAEE reception, is crucial for maintaining transparency.

289. Storage Centres are distinct from fixed points and defined as the place where RAEE is temporarily stored or gathered, originating from collection mechanisms within the exclusive framework of the logistical operation of RAEE collection and management systems implemented by producers and approved by the ANLA. Storage centres can be of private, public, or mixed nature, either temporary or permanent. Only separation, classification, weighing, or packaging activities of waste prior to other management activities are allowed in storage centres. These activities must comply with the minimum environmental technical requirements established in Resolution 0851 of 2022. and have specific operational requirements. These centres must operate away from public spaces, ensuring shelter, controlled access, and adherence to environmental regulations. Measures to maintain RAEE integrity, weighing at entry and exit, fire protection equipment, and a storage time limit of six months are mandated, as well as detailed documentation, similar to that of fixed collection points, is required.

290. Collection Campaigns involving organized efforts to collect RAEE must be planned thoroughly. These campaigns include identification of participating actors, specification of accepted waste types, establishment of campaign details (date, duration, hours), communication channels, and campaign locations. Collection campaigns must be communicated to environmental authorities and municipalities at least ten days before commencement.

291. Other collection mechanisms, such as door-to-door collection or postal services, are acknowledged as alternative methods. Irrespective of the mechanism chosen, clear communication to users or consumers regarding operational logistics, geographic coverage, traceability, and associated costs is required.

292. In case a producer intends to terminate a RAEE collection and management system, the representative must inform the ANLA six months in advance.

Special WEEE

293. Since WEEE regulation has existed in Colombia since 2010, the collection and management of certain WEEE, which were already regulated, must comply with specific conditions.

294. For lamps with mercury, measures must be taken to minimize breakage and mercury vapour emissions during collection, transport, and storage. The same applies to monitors, televisions, and other flat-screen technologies, where precautions are necessary to avoid breakage and damage during handling. For waste containing refrigerant gases, steps should be taken to prevent gas release and oil spills during collection, transport, and storage. Specific management considerations for Chlorofluorocarbon (CFC), HCFC, and HFC refrigerants, pursuant to international laws adopted by Colombia, must be complied with.

E. Main Obligations

295. Obligations on collection and management systems are set out according to the type of AEE placed in the market by the producer/importer: AEE of mass consumption, industrial or professional use, and personal use.

296. Mass Consumption Electrical and Electronic Appliances are appliances used in households, commercial establishments, institutions, or other settings. They have a similar market flow to household appliances in terms of nature, quantity, and distribution. Mass consumption producers exceeding annual thresholds fixed in Annex 1 must submit a RAEE collection and management system for approval by

ANLA no later than 30 April of the year following the year in which the thresholds were exceeded.[18] For that purpose, producers must submit all information required for ANLA approval, including producer details, AEE market information, collection mechanisms, identification of RAEE managers, consumer contact information, accepted waste categories, communication strategies, and payment proof for evaluation services.[19] The ANLA has a sixty-day evaluation period to approve or deny presented RAEE collection and management systems once all requirements are fulfilled.[20]

297. To calculate the annual thresholds fixed in Annex 1, the quantity introduced or placed on the market shall be the sum of the annual quantity of imported AEE and domestically manufactured AEE minus the annual quantity of EEE exported, expressed in units or weight. Producers of AEE have the option to deduct the final inventory of the AEE quantity introduced or placed on the market in the immediately preceding year from the evaluation year, provided that the discounted value is fully considered the initial inventory for calculating the AEE quantity introduced or placed on the market in the subsequent year.

298. Industrial or professional use producers must also establish a collection and management system but without ANLA approval. Industrial or Professional Use of Electrical and Electronic Appliances includes appliances that, by exclusion, are not classified as mass consumption appliances. They are specifically designed for industrial or professional purposes.

299. The management of RAEE for personal use, meaning appliances imported or manufactured by the user or consumer for exclusive personal use without the intention of commercialization, requires individuals or entities importing or manufacturing AEE for personal use to ensure proper waste management through ANLA-approved systems.

F. KPIs for the Collection and Management of RAEE

300. Resolution 0851 of 2021 establishes key performance indicators (KPIs) for the evaluation and monitoring of RAEE collection and management systems. There are five KPIs:

- Collection and Management Indicator (IRG for its initials in Spanish): measures the relationship between the weight of RAEE collected and managed compared to the weight collection target for the evaluation year.
- Information and Sensitization to Consumers Indicator (IISC): evaluates the ratio of financial resources invested annually in consumer information and awareness activities to the total financial resources invested in the system's operation.

18. Resolution 0851 of 2021, Art. 16.
19. Resolution 0851 of 2021, Art. 17.
20. Resolution 0851 of 2021, Art. 18.

- Geographic Coverage Indicator (ICG): this KPI seems to measure the same ratio as the IISC KPI. However, this may have been an unintended repetition in the text of the resolution.
- Applied Research and Experimental Development Indicator (IIA): it evaluates the ratio of financial resources invested annually in applied research and experimental development for RAEE utilization to the total financial resources invested in the system's operation.
- Circular Economy Promotion Indicator (IFEC): it measures the ratio of the weight of WEEE collected and prepared for reuse through refurbishment, repair, or remanufacturing to the total weight of RAEE collected and managed by the system.

301. Every KPI has an evaluation criterion in the form of a scoring system. For example, for the KPI on collection and management indicator, a system scoring 100% or more will receive sixty points; otherwise, points will be assigned proportionally. Systems need a minimum of seventy-five points for compliance.[21]

302. Approved systems must submit annual reports through the Online Environmental Procedures Platform (VITAL) detailing the progress in system implementation and compliance with management indicators.[22] Approved systems must update information on the opening, relocation, or closure of collection points within a maximum period of fifteen business days.

G. RAEE Management Certifications

303. Certifications issued by RAEE managers must contain detailed information, including a unique identification, details of the authorized company, recipient information, and environmental authorizations, among other things. Certificates must be issued electronically within a maximum period of ninety days unless justified otherwise.[23]

H. Acceptance of RAEE by Distributors/Retailers

304. Distributors/Retailers of AEE are obliged to comply with Article 2.2.7A.2.2 of Decree 1076 of 2015 starting from 1 January 2024 and are required to coordinate with producers to ensure compliance: AEE distributors must accept the return of RAEE/WEEE from the user or consumer, at no cost to the latter, taking into account the following conditions:

- Distributors must comply with the obligation when RAEE is handed over by the user or consumer at the point of sale. If the RAEE is not delivered at the time of

21. Resolution 0851 of 2021.
22. Resolution 0851 of 2021, Art. 20.
23. Resolution 0851 of 2021, Art. 22.

purchasing the new AEE, the distributor will specify in writing the maximum period the user or consumer has to submit the RAEE at the point of sale, supported by the corresponding purchase invoice of the new AEE. This period cannot be less than thirty calendar days.

- Distributors engaged in remote sales of AEE must have mechanisms in place to inform consumers about their ability to receive equivalent RAEE that has performed the same functions as the purchased device. This information should be communicated to users or consumers at the time of purchase.
- In cases where a user or consumer decides to return an 'orphaned' RAEE or one for which there is no approved RAEE collection and management system by the ANLA, the distributor has the option to accept the RAEE and manage it through licensed handlers of RAEE. If the distributor chooses not to accept it, they must instruct the user or consumer to manage the waste through licensed handlers of RAEE.

I. Derogations

305. Resolution 0851 of 2021 is effective from 1 January 2023 and repeals Resolutions 1297 of 2010 (amended by Resolution 2246 of 2017), 1511, and 1512 of 2010. Approved selective collection and environmental management systems for batteries, bulbs, computers, and peripherals under the aforementioned resolutions must comply with the requirements of Resolution 0851 of 2021. This includes reporting updates, meeting performance indicators in Article 19, and adhering to collection percentages outlined in Annex 3.

VII. Construction and Demolition Waste

306. The management of construction and demolition waste (RCD) is regulated in Resolution 0472 of 2017. Resolution 1257 of 2021 modifies Resolution 0472 of 2017, including definitions, obligations for generators and managers, and adjustments to environmental management measures for RCD disposal sites. The modification aims to enhance RCD recycling, align with circular economy principles, and set specific targets for RCD utilization. The changes also emphasize the need for environmental measures at disposal sites and call for periodic reporting and compliance monitoring. The modifications respond to an evaluation of current infrastructure and technology capabilities, aiming to promote effective RCD utilization and address issues related to waste management.

307. Among the different changes, Resolution 1257 of 2021 emphasizes the promotion of circular economy principles, aligning with the National Circular Economy Strategy. This includes encouraging the reuse of RCD as raw materials within industrial processes through industrial symbiosis. Resolution 1257 attempts to define industrial symbiosis as a collaborative strategy for the exchange of physical flows of materials, energy, or water and the sharing of services among stakeholders, aiming to contribute to the efficient use of resources and the reduction of environmental impacts in industrial systems.[24]

308. RCD generators must comply with recycling goals, requiring them to effectively recycle a percentage of the total weight of RCD generated. The targets are categorized based on the municipality's classification. The goal is to achieve a minimum recycling rate of 30%.[25]

309. Resolution 1257 of 2021 imposes more stringent reporting requirements on large generators, including the submission of detailed reports to the competent environmental authority. This includes documentation of RCD quantities recycled, delivered to receivers, and compliance with recycling targets.

310. Local authorities are mandated to adjust their Solid Waste Management Plans to align with the resolution, promote awareness campaigns, identify areas for the operation of recycling plants and disposal sites, and conduct monitoring and control of RCD management within their jurisdiction.[26]

---

24. Resolution 1257 of 2021, Art. 1.
25. Resolution 1257 of 2021, Art. 9.
26. Resolution 1257 of 2021, Art. 8.

Chapter 5. Soil Pollution

§1. Introduction

311. Soil pollution is mainly evidenced in Colombia in the loss of organic matter, fertility, compacting properties and lixiviation of nutrients. Physical and chemical aspects are polluting factors that have an impact on soil conditions due to natural and anthropogenic causes. Human malpractices in the use of soil, such as the arbitrary use of pesticides, the inefficient use of water for irrigation, urban development, mining activities, waste generation and ecosystems management, have left a considerable footprint in soil pollution. Colombia's current challenges on soil contamination concern erosion, desertification, tree felling, open-air burnings, quarrying and inadequate agricultural practices.

312. Legislation on soil pollution addressing anthropogenic causes is rather scarce in Colombia. Concerning contaminated land, Colombia follows the general approach to environmental pollution and responsibility for environmental damage, contained in the NCRNR, Law 99/1993 and Decree 4741/2005 on hazardous waste; yet, the country lacks a specific regulation on historical soil contamination and contaminated sites. Pursuant to the NCRNR, soil protection includes protection for land use and soil for agricultural purposes. Furthermore, it is worth mentioning that Colombia is a party to the United Nations Convention to Combat Desertification (UNCCD), approved by Law 461/1998.

313. In spite of the need to have a regulation on soil contamination, the government has been preparing proposals, pilot projects and manuals on the subject. These instruments have been initially applied to the hydrocarbon sector and are expected to set the basis for future regulations. Therefore, this section will review the existing legal framework on soil pollution and will explore the main features of the government-proposed instruments.

§2. Existing Legal Framework

314. The NCRNR establishes soil degradation, slumping and erosion, and harmful alterations to the topography as contamination factors. Contamination is defined in the NCRNR as any change in the environment due to substances or energy forms placed in the environment through human activity or nature, in quantities, concentrations or levels likely to interfere with people's health and well-being, endanger plant and/or wildlife, degrade the quality of the environment, or affect resources of the nation or private individuals. The land, soil and subsoil are considered natural renewable sources and, therefore, are protected under Colombian legislation.

315. Article 35 of the NCRNR links soil protection with appropriate waste management by prohibiting the discharge or disposal of waste that may deteriorate soil.

Part VII of the NCRNR regulates land and soil by providing for general duties, powers of governmental authorities, agricultural use of soil, conservation, and soil protection for transport and urban uses. Pursuant to the NCRNR Part VII, soil must be used according to its constitutive characteristics, including physical, ecological and socio-economic factors of each region. In addition, the use of soil must regard technical standards so as to maintain its productive capacity and physical integrity; for example, the standards on conservation and protective measures are the ones provided for in the UNCCD.

316. Concerning powers of authorities on soil protection, they shall coordinate the necessary measures to avoid soil degradation, promote the implementation of pollution prevention measures on land use, regulate irrigation practices, adopt policies on fauna and flora management, gather up information on soil analysis and monitor substances leading to soil contamination.

I. Agricultural Soil

317. The NCRNR establishes a general obligation for natural and legal persons carrying out agricultural activities, livestock rearing, forestry management or infrastructure works, consisting of implementing conservation and recovery techniques to preserve soil conditions. In addition, the NCRNR establishes special measures to be taken when soil conditions demand so; for example, in case of unexploited soil, measures are to be taken when special conditions allow its economic utilization or in case of soil subject to chemical or physical limitations that affect its productive capacity, adjustments and restoration projects should be carried out. Adjustments and restoration projects must be approved and supported by technical studies evidencing their harmlessness to the environment. With regard to other productive activities having an impact on agricultural soil, such as mining construction works, engineering works, excavations or similar activities, they must be preceded by ecological studies and conducted according to soil conservation and protection provisions.

II. Non-agricultural Soil

318. Non-agricultural soil refers to land/soil use for urban or transport purposes. As regards urban soil, the NCRNR provides that urban planning must establish residential, civic, commercial, industrial and recreational sectors, as well as oxygenating and absorbing zones by means of arborization projects. Regarding land use for transport, Articles 192 and 193 require to take into account the trends of the cities on urban expansion in order to control noise emissions produced by airports, and to take the necessary precautions when building highways or railways, so as to impede harmful alteration to the topography. Notably, the environmental protection of land use is more accurately provided for in regulations concerning zoning and land use planning; thus, the corresponding section of this work will address such issues.

III. Contaminated Land

319. As pointed out above, Colombia does not have a specific piece of legislation dealing with contaminated land. However, Decree 4741/2005 on hazardous waste imposes an obligation on those people who have failed to adequately manage hazardous waste and have contaminated sites. The liability of those who have contaminated soil consists of diagnosing, remedying and repairing the damage caused to the environment. That brings liability for soil contamination to the general provisions on tort and applicable administrative and criminal liability.

320. Bearing in mind that Law 1333/2009 on environmental enforcement procedure establishes strict liability for environmental infractions and that it considers environmental damage as an environmental infraction, the responsible person for site contamination is exposed to administrative sanctions under a strict liability system, without prejudice to civil liability for damage caused to third parties. Furthermore, since polluters are jointly and unlimitedly responsible, the extent of historic site contamination goes up to the owner who caused environmental damage. Nonetheless, provided that the court of law may not accurately establish the actual site polluter, it can rule against the current soil tenant/owner and condemn it to full site remediation or damage compensation. Pursuant to the Civil Code, at the request of the condemned individual/company, the Court may establish the degree of responsibility of each owner or tenant involved in soil contamination in order to entitle the condemned individual/company to ask for damage repayment.

§3. Proposed Regulatory Instruments

321. The MASD has been working on legislation for the adequate management of contaminated sites, along with different actors and sectors. Specially, the first efforts have been devoted to implementing technical instruments to prevent site contamination in the oil and gas sector. As a result, the MASD has adopted the technical manual for risk assessment of hydrocarbon derivate distribution sites, a checklist for classification of sensible ecologic receptors and the guidelines for the execution of ecological risk assessments in presumably contaminated sites.

322. Other regulatory strategies have touched basis on Decree 4741/2005 on hazardous waste and the Stockholm Convention on POPs, approved in Colombia by Law 1198/2008, which establishes that the government must eliminate the use of PCB-contaminated equipment by 2025 and make efforts to achieve environmentally sound management of PCB-contaminated waste and equipment by 2028.

323. The IDEAM administers through the Environmental Information System – SIA – the information captured in the PCB Inventory at national level and carries out the processing, analysis, generation of reports and dissemination of the consolidated information at national level. For the collection of PCB Inventory data, a web application has been developed for individual or mass uploading. The environmental authorities must make this application available to the public through their websites.

324. The MASD has been working on a draft regulation on soil protection aimed at granting special protection to human health, groundwater, species and land-investors, from soil contamination. This initiative identifies hydrocarbon activities, petrochemicals, the chemical industry, intensive agriculture and distributors of chemical substances and hydrocarbons as the main activities responsible for historic site contamination. Based on the polluter-pays principle consecrated in Law 99/1993, the NCRNR and Decree 4741/2005 on hazardous waste, the draft regulation would deal with the magnitude of the environmental impact caused by productive activities in contaminated soil; the level of tolerance to the risk posed by the activity; and the risks to be posed when carrying out an activity that is incompatible with land contamination.

325. In order to tackle each one of the aforementioned concerns, the draft regulation would establish a methodology, in accordance with foreign and international experiences on the subject, to determine whether a site is contaminated or not; establish competences among public authorities; and promote the adequate management of contaminated soil in order to lessen the risks to people and the environment. For such purpose, the draft regulation would be focused on two strategies: first, acknowledging and registering existing contaminated sites; and second, implementing an adequate management of potentially contaminated sites. In addition, the proposal would empower the authorities to declare a site as contaminated and then proceed to adopt the necessary corrective measures.

326. Finally, in order to tackle historic contamination, the draft regulation would develop the concept of environmental liabilities (*Pasivos Ambientales*). Environmental liabilities would refer to the obligation to assume the costs of environmental damage caused to soil, water, air or biodiversity, or to the environmental services they provide, that have not been timely and adequately mitigated, compensated, managed or repaired. What is more, the draft regulation would provide for an 'orphan liability' (*pasivo huérfano*), defined as the environmental debt that matches certain criteria, such as lacking a site owner, tenant or possessor, or not having the possibility to identify the polluter; environmental damage caused by illegal groups; or activities where the State has directly assumed recovery activities, among others. The draft regulation on soil contamination is still at an early stage and must undergo all the legal steps before being adopted.

Chapter 6. Noise Pollution

§1. Introduction

327. Acoustic contamination in Colombia is often associated with industrial activities, transport and deficient urban planning. According to technical information,[27] ground and air transit, machinery and engines, construction activities, deafening music from bars, clubs and discotheques, and explosions from specific industries constitute the main sources of acoustic contamination in Colombia. These factors expose individuals to noise pollution, leading to physical and mental disorders, such as deafness, insomnia, irritability or stress. Noise pollution also has an impact on economic and social development, as reflected in real estate value loss, traffic accidents, and low productivity, among others. The city of Bogota is one of the examples where acoustic contamination is patent, as only four of its nineteen communes do not have noise pollution problems.

328. The legislation on noise pollution in Colombia has undergone significant changes from its initial regulation in 1974 to the latest noise standards established in 2006. The NRCNR establishes that noxious noise is a contamination factor, and consequently, conditions and requirements must be established in order to preserve and maintain the health and tranquillity of people by controlling noise from industrial, household, commercial, sportive, transport or related activities. Based on the NRCNR, noise emissions and ambient noise are regulated as part of atmospheric pollution, and therefore, the main requirements are established in Decree 948/1995 (Article 2.2.5.1.5.1 of Decree 1076/2015) and Resolution 627/2006 establishing the national standards on noise emissions and ambient noise.

329. Colombian legislation also regulates workers' exposure to noise. Resolution 1792/1990 establishes the maximum noise levels at workplaces, sets different noise exposure limits according to the exposure period, and prohibits continuous or intermittent noise exposure exceeding 115 decibels (dB). Employers must provide workers with personal protective equipment when exposing them to noise emissions. Yet, these provisions concern a different protection area which exceeds the environmental scope of this work; therefore, noise pollution analysis will be focused on ambient noise and noise emissions.

§2. Noise Emissions

330. Decree 948/1995 lays down the basic provisions on noise pollution control by providing standards on noise emissions and ambient noise. The aim of setting out noise standards is to avoid harmful effects that may affect people's health, ecosystem equilibrium, peace and the tranquil enjoyment of public goods and the environment. Noise standards address the admissible limits of sound pressure in each

27. Movimiento Político Mira, 'Contaminación Ambiental en Colombia I. Problemas Ambientales Globales y Nacionales. Biológica, Química y Física. Fuentes y Efectos', 26 Mar. 2010.

one of the sectors listed in Article 15 of Decree 948/1995 (Article 2.2.5.1.2.13, Decree 1076/2015), like tranquillity and silence sectors, or moderated noise sectors. The standards also establish the allowed noise schedules by taking into account the health concerns of the exposed population.

331. In order to accurately establish noise standards, Colombian legislation establishes different types of sectors and sub-sectors, for which noise emission and ambient noise limits are established as follows:

- Sector A, Tranquillity and Silence: hospitals, libraries, geriatric hospitals, psychiatric hospitals and childcare facilities.
- Sector B, Tranquillity and Moderated Noise: residential zones, hotels, universities, schools and parks in urban areas.
- Sector C, Intermediate Restricted Noise: under this category, noise emissions are established for industrial zones, commercial zones, offices, institutions and related-uses zones.
- Sector D, Suburban Areas or Rural areas: suburban residential areas, rural areas for agriculture and recreational zones.

332. Pursuant to Resolution 627/2006, each one of these sectors and sub-sectors has a maximum permissible level of noise emissions and a maximum permissible level of ambient noise. Resolution 627/2006 adopts the definitions of the International Standard Organization (ISO) 1996, establishes the decibel (dB) as the measurement unit for sound pressure, provides a formula to calculate noise emissions and establishes the maximum limits of noise emissions and ambient noise at daytime and night-time. For example, Sector A has a noise emission limit of 55 dB during daytime and 50 dB at nighttime, whereas the limit in industrial zones in Sector C is 75 dB for both daytime and nighttime. Ambient noise standards closely follow the noise emission standards, although with some variations. For example, ambient noise in Sector A is 55 dB at daytime and 45 dB at nighttime.

333. Finally, Resolution 627/2006 establishes technical instruments to strengthen noise pollution control. These instruments include noise mapping, measurement equipment and noise emission reporting. Particularly, environmental authorities have an obligation to implement noise mapping in cities with more than a hundred inhabitants with the purpose of identifying and taking appropriate measures to prevent noise pollution. What is more, the results from noise mappings are to be used by environmental authorities for the drafting and implementation of decontamination plans in critical areas.

§3. Noise Restrictions

334. Chapter V (Title V, Chapter I, section V) of Decree 948/1995 provides that any continuous, intermittent, transitory or high-impact noise emissions are subject to control and restrictions. This provision is coupled with a general obligation for the noise emitter to implement control systems so that noise emissions do not disturb neighbouring zones. Concerning specific sources of noise pollution, Chapter V imposes noise restrictions and limitations on different noise sources; for example, noise restrictions to zones where noisy activities take place or restrictions to the equipment employed for performing noisy activities. Decree 948/1995 does not establish categories of restricted sources, but it does list activities that are either prohibited or restricted. For the purpose of clarity, it is worth grouping noise restrictions in zones, equipment and activities.

335. As regards restricted zones, Decree 948/1995 prohibits noise emissions above permitted standards in tranquillity and silent sectors. The prohibition covers the construction of industrial or commercial facilities in sectors A or B that may be potentially noisy, such as shops, taverns, bars or restaurants, as well as the operation of industrial machinery in these sectors. In addition, Article 52 (Article 2.2.5.1.5.11, Decree 1076/2015) creates noise buffer zones in order to reduce noise pollution and particularly to minimize noise effects from highways in urban areas or human settlements. Likewise, restrictions on noise emissions apply to special equipment or devices by regulating the use of silencers, alarms and sirens, claxons and horns, and construction equipment. Decree 948/1995 also restricts the manner in which some noisy activities are carried out, including airports, heavy traffic, construction of libraries, clinics and psychiatric clinics; and the use of loudspeakers.

Chapter 7. Radiation and Vibrations

§1. Introduction

336. Radiation is one of the factors amounting to physic contamination in Colombia, manifested in both ionizing and non-ionizing radiation, for as many vibrations are one of the physic agents that workers are exposed to in workplaces and that are likely to cause health problems when surpassing vibration exposure limits. As regards ionizing radiation, defined as the energy in the form of waves or particles that have enough force to remove electrons from atoms,[28] an increasing number of regulations have been adopted on radiological protection, as well as on radioactive waste. Non-ionizing regulation, defined as the radiation that has enough energy to move atoms in a molecule around or cause them to vibrate but not enough to remove electrons, has also gained relevance in terms of legislative proposals due to the rapid demographic concentration in urban areas and the consequent installation of energy generation and transmission lines, antennas, telecommunication equipment and other sources of electromagnetic fields, that expose the public to non-ionizing radiation.[29]

337. From the viewpoint of the Colombian legal framework, the topic of this chapter deserves to be analysed under three subtopics: ionizing radiation, non-ionizing radiation and vibrations. Ionizing and non-ionizing radiation have both a twofold regulatory approach, consisting of regulations concerning occupational health and regulations on radiation sources. Conversely, the existing regulation on vibrations exclusively covers exposure limits of workers to vibrations at workplaces and the appropriate measures that must be implemented in order to avoid health problems.

§2. Ionizing Radiation

I. Sources of Ionizing Radiation

338. Pursuant to Decree 381/2012, the Ministry of Energy and Mines has competence in all matters concerning nuclear and radioactive activities, including regulation, control, licensing and enforcement. One of the competences of the Ministry of Energy and Mines is to draft and adopt standards for the safe management of nuclear and radioactive materials in Colombia and ensure that those standards and correlative international instruments on the subject are complied with. Particularly, the Colombian Geological Service (*Servicio Geológico Colombiano* – SGC), created by means of Decree 4131/2011, is one of the agencies of the Ministry of Energy

28. United States Environmental Protection Agency, 'Ionizing Radiation', https://www.epa.gov/sites/default/files/2015-05/documents/402-k-10-008.pdf, April 2012.
29. Javier I. Torres Osorio and Luz Elena Agudelo, 'Situación actual de la contaminación electromagnética no ionizante en Colombia', https://revistas.utp.edu.co/index.php/revistaciencia/article/view/5495/2801.

and Mines responsible for providing technical information on nuclear matters and for verifying compliance of operators with nuclear regulations. On top of that, Colombia joined the International Atomic Energy Agency (IAEA) by means of Law 16/1960 and committed itself through Resolution 90874/2014 to adopt an appropriate national regulation on radiological protection and nuclear materials.

339. The legal framework on ionizing radiation is therefore composed of one main legal instrument on radiological protection and two regulations on radioactive materials management licensing and the categorization of radioactive sources.

340. Under the auspices of the Group of Nuclear Matters of the Ministry of Energy and Mines, Resolution 181434/2002 was adopted establishing the Regulation on Radiological Protection and Safety. Resolution 181434/2002 establishes the minimum requirements and conditions to be met by legal and natural persons interested in carrying out activities involving exposure to ionizing radiation, as well as the necessary and basic conditions to protect people against radiation and to secure radioactive sources. Resolution 181434/2002 applies to any individual or company carrying out activities related to the use of nuclear energy and practices involving ionizing radiation in the national territory. Consequently, Resolution 181434/2002 addresses three main aspects of radiological protection: practices and sources of radiation; situations of chronic exposure and emergencies; and occupational, medical, and public exposure to ionizing radiation.

341. Among the main obligations for those planning to develop or developing activities entailing ionizing radiation exposure, Resolution 181434/2002 requires developers to notify the authority of the intended practices. The authority grants or rejects the authorization, and assesses the technical conditions under which the activity must be conducted. In addition, the developer has to carry out a radiologic risk assessment during the stage of design, construction, start-up, exploitation and closure of the facility; draft and implement a Safety Protection Programme establishing appropriate measures for the protection of exposed workers, in accordance with the nature and magnitude of the risk; adopt measures to avoid the risk of exposure of the general public to ionizing radiations; have in place emergency plans where measures for incidents or accidents are contemplated; ensure that the equipment is checked and adopt preventive and corrective measures accordingly. Finally, the developer has to keep a record of all the measures adopted as a result of the Safety Protection Programme.

342. Resolution 181304/2004, repealed by Resolution 90874/2014, which at its turn was modified by Resolution 41226/2016, regulates the licence for the management of radioactive materials. This licence must be obtained from the Ministry of Energy and Mines by any natural or legal person handling radioactive materials. The licence application must include information on the internal organization of the applicant's facilities, technical assessments, programmes of radiological protection, and safety procedures to be implemented, among others. The requirements of radiological protection programmes are largely described in Resolution 90874/2014; for example, it must identify responsible persons, the activities for which radioactive material use is required and their purpose, measures on radiological surveillance of exposed workers, training programmes and description of equipment maintenance and calibration. The validity term of the licence depends on the activity for which it is granted, for example, radiotherapy and industrial irradiators: one year; nuclear medicine and mobile measuring equipment: two years; radioactive tracers, non-mobile measurement equipment and research activities: three years.

343. Finally, Resolution 180052/2008 adopts the system of categorization of radioactive sources. The categorization system emerged from the IAEA conferences held in Buenos Aires in 2001 and Vienna in 2003, where the need to fully implement the Code of Conduct on the Safety and Security of Radioactive Sources and review the categorization system of radioactive sources was raised. As a result, the IAEA adopted the categorization of radioactive sources document, Revision of IAEA-TECDOC-1191, providing a numerical relative ranking of radioactive sources and practices, and assigning them 'into one of five categories'.[30] Resolution 180052/2008 transposes the categorization system of radioactive sources in Colombia, paving the ground for issuing further regulations on the technological and physical safety of radiation sources in certain activities, like national infrastructure or national standards on technological safety.

II. Occupational Health

344. Ionizing radiation is also regulated in health and safety legislation, more precisely in occupational health regulations. Although occupational health legal framework exceeds the thematic boundaries of this work, it is worth mentioning where and how ionizing radiation is regulated under this perspective. Resolution 2400/79 on hygiene and safety at the workplace is one of the main regulatory instruments on the subject and provides for exposure limits and protective measures on ionizing radiation. Particularly, Resolution 2400/79 obliges employers to provide workers with radiation dosimeters and personal protective equipment. It restricts the exposure of certain workers to ionizing radiation and establishes exposure limits according to the body parts exposed. More recently and as mentioned above, Resolution 181434/2002 establishing the Regulation on Radiological Protection and Safety requires employers to adopt an internal regulation on radiological protection whereby protective measures are established, namely limiting occasional exposure, ensuring that exposed workers undergo regular medical check-ups, training employees and carrying records on exposure to ionizing radiation.

30. International Atomic Energy Agency, 'Categorization of Radioactive Sources', www.hps.org/documents/IAEATecDoc1344.pdf, July 2003.

§3. NON-IONIZING RADIATION

I. Sources of Non-ionizing Radiation

345. The protection against non-ionizing radiation was earlier developed in Law 9/1979 adopting the Sanitary Code, establishing that any ways of radiating energy, apart from ionizing radiation, were subject to control procedures in order to avoid harmful exposure to such radiation. Law-Decree 1900/1990 provides that telecommunications must foster the political, economic and social development of the country with the aim to upgrade the level and quality of life of the population. The Ministry of Information Technologies and Communications is responsible for the administration, management and control of the electromagnetic spectrum. Concerning non-ionizing radiation, the Ministry has the power to adopt measures to ensure a rational and rightful use of the electromagnetic spectrum.

346. At the international level, Colombia has approved the International Telecommunication Union (ITU) and the treaties adopted thereby in Geneva on 22 December 1992, by means of Law 252/1995. Decree 1900/1990 puts into practice the role of the ITU by establishing that its recommendations have to be regarded in national regulations on telecommunications. One of the recommendations that has shaped the existing legal framework on non-ionizing radiation is the ITU-T K.52 CORR 1 Guidance on compliance with limits for human exposure to electromagnetic fields. As a result of the ITU recommendations and a study carried out by the Universidad Javeriana on human exposure limits to electromagnetic fields produced by telecommunication antennas, Colombia adopted Decree 195/2005 establishing the exposure limits to electromagnetic fields and the procedures for the installation of radio-electric installations.

347. Decree 195/2005 applies to telecommunication activities and services in the frequency range of 9 KHz–300 GHz and establishes exposure limits of the public to radio-electric stations in such frequencies. Any other aspects not provided for in Decree 195/2005 are to be covered by the international recommendation ITU-T K.52 CORR 1 Guidance on compliance of limits for human exposure to electromagnetic fields. Decree 195/2005 excludes non-intentional emission of non-ionizing radiation, radio frequency receiving antennas and radio-electric terminal equipment or end-consumer devices from its scope.

348. Any entities rendering services or carrying out telecommunication activities must ensure that the emission levels of their installations comply with the limits established in Decree 195/2005. Exposure limits are set out in accordance with the operation frequency for occupational exposure and exposure of the public. In addition, Decree 195/2005 includes exposure limits and emission restrictions in case of multiple emission sources (simultaneous exposure). Furthermore, in order to meet emission limits, operators must carry out measurements and report them according to the parameters established in Article 2.2.2.5.2.1 of Decree 1078/2015.

II. Occupational Health

349. Exposure to non-ionizing radiation is also regulated in health and safety legislation, namely, Resolution 2400/79. This piece of legislation provides for exposure to ultraviolet radiation and infrared radiation. For the former, employers must take preventive measures to avoid risks relating to insulation, like water provision or creams to protect employees from the sun; if such radiation comes from welding activities, then, protective equipment must be provided, as well as training on the risks that such activity poses. For the latter, employers must install absorbent screens, water curtains or any other devices to reduce infrared radiation risks.

§4. Vibrations

350. As mentioned at the beginning of this chapter, the regulation on vibrations in Colombia is part of the system of laws of health and safety at workplaces. No environmental regulations on outdoor vibrations have been adopted. Indeed, due to the problems caused by vibrations to workers' health, neurological- and bones-related problems, Resolution 2400/79 limits the exposure of workers to vibrations. Employers, thus, are required to adopt appropriate measures to control vibrations and minimize further symptoms, such as improving the design of the tools and machinery, complying with the speed limits of industrial equipment, training exposed workers on the correct use of the machinery, reducing vibration-exposure hours and enhancing staff selection for tasks involving vibrations.

Chapter 8. Noxious Substances

§1. Introduction

351. Article 32 of Decree-Law 2811 of 1974 requires the establishment of requirements and conditions for the importation, manufacturing, transportation, storage, commercialization, handling, use, or disposal of toxic or hazardous substances to prevent environmental deterioration or harm to human health and other living beings.

352. The CONPES 3868 document from 2016, titled 'Policy for the Management of Risk Associated with the Use of Chemical Substances,' aims to cohesively integrate risk management processes with the life cycle stages of industrial chemical substances. It recommends defining technical and regulatory elements for managing risks associated with the use of industrial chemical substances.

353. By means of Decree 1496 of 2018, Colombia adopted the Globally Harmonized System of Classification and Labelling of Chemicals (GHS) to standardize and harmonize the classification and hazard communication of chemical products.

354. In 2019, Law 1950 of 2019 was enacted to approve the 'Agreement on the Terms of the Accession of the Republic of Colombia to the Convention of the Organization for Economic Cooperation and Development (OECD)' signed in Paris on 30 May 2018. To comply with Law 1950 of 2019, necessary actions must be taken to implement the action plan accepted by the OECD regarding industrial chemical substances and adopt the instruments for their management. This aligns with Colombia's commitment to fulfil OECD requirements and international standards in the regulation of industrial chemicals.

§2. Industrial Chemical Substances

I. Management of Chemical Substances

355. Decree 1630 of 2021 modifies Decree 1076 of 2015, by adding a chapter on comprehensive management of chemicals for industrial use, including risk management, with a specific focus on risk management. The regulation aligns with the United Nations Globally Harmonized System of Classification and Labelling of Chemicals (GHS), following the guidelines set forth in Decree 1496 of 2018.

356. To achieve this purpose, Decree 1630 of 2021 sets out specific tools to achieve its objective of managing chemicals for industrial use, with a particular focus on risk management. These mechanisms include:

- National Inventory of Chemical Substances for Industrial Use: A comprehensive list of chemical substances used in industry, serving as a foundational tool for effective management.

- Instrument for Prioritization of Chemical Substances: This instrument operates within the National Inventory, employing defined criteria to prioritize chemical substances. This helps in identifying and addressing high-priority substances efficiently.
- Risk Assessment for Health or Environment: The regulation incorporates a process for assessing the risks posed by chemical substances concerning their identified use. This assessment is crucial for developing targeted risk management strategies.
- Programs for Risk Reduction and Management: To actively address and mitigate risks, Decree 1630 of 2021 introduces programs specifically designed to reduce and manage risks to both the environment and human health. These programs aim to ensure a proactive approach to potential hazards associated with industrial chemical use.

357. Chemical substance manufacturers or importers shall be responsible for the information included in the framework of compliance with the management instruments set out in the decree.

A. Scope

358. Decree 1630 of 2021 applies to both natural and legal persons involved in various activities related to the management of substances specified in the regulation, including chemical production, import, use, marketing, distribution, and transport.

359. Certain chemical substances are excluded from the scope of Decree 1630 of 2021. Exclusions include substances with specific regulations, those with unknown or variable composition, articles, impurities, substances of natural origin without chemical processing, and those resulting from exposure to environmental factors or during the end use of other products. The list of substances outside the scope of Decree 1630 of 2021 further includes substances not manufactured, imported, or marketed as such, along with hydrates, polymers, substances in transit, non-isolated intermediates, and samples with no commercial value.

B. Relevant Definitions

360. Decree 1630 of 2021 includes crucial definitions to facilitate its proper interpretation, including:

- Chemical substance: A chemical element and its compounds in their natural state or obtained by any production process, including additives necessary to preserve the stability of the product and impurities resulting from the process used, excluding solvents which can be separated without affecting the stability of the substance or changing its composition.

- New chemical substance: A substance imported or manufactured in the country after the deadline established in paragraph 6 of Article 2.2.7B.1.2.2, meaning six (6) months after the entry into force of Decree 1630 of 2021 and which is not found in the National Inventory of Chemical Substances for Industrial Use.
- Integrated management of chemical substances for industrial use, including their risk management: This refers to the safe use of chemical substances throughout their life cycle, which allows preventing, reducing, mitigating or eliminating risks to health or the environment.
- Industrial use: Refers to any transformation, formulation, consumption, storage, preservation, treatment, packaging, transferring, mixing, production of an article or any other use of a chemical substance or mixture in industry.
- User of chemical substances for industrial use: Any natural or legal person established in the country, who uses a substance, whether mono-constituent, multi-constituent or in the form of a mixture, in the course of its industrial activities.
- Mono-constituent Chemical: Describes a chemical substance in which a constituent is present at a minimum concentration of 80% (w/w) and contains up to 20% (w/w) of impurities. Naming is based on the main constituent.
- Multi-Constituent Chemical Substance: Defined by quantitative composition, where more than one constituent is present at > 10% (w/w) and < 80% (w/w). It results from a chemical reaction in the manufacturing process.
- Mixture: It is a solution obtained from intentionally joining two or more substances without a chemical reaction.

C. Main Obligations

361. In terms of key requirements, they can be classified for each actor in the value chain of chemical substances, including manufacturers and importers, distributors, carriers and users.

i) Manufacturers and Importers

Information

362. Natural and legal persons who import or manufacture chemical substances for industrial use, whether mono-constituent, multi-constituent and those incorporated in mixtures whose volumes exceed 100 kilograms per year, will be obliged to provide the following information through the computer application, to feed the database of information on chemical substances produced or imported in the national territory:

- Identification data of the manufacturer or importer of the chemical substance.
- Quantity of annual production or import of the chemical.
- Identification of the chemical, including CAS number (where applicable).
- Classification of hazards in accordance with the United Nations Globally Harmonized System of Classification and Labelling of Chemicals, in accordance with the provisions of Decree 1496 of 2018.
- Identified Uses of the substance.

363. When the manufacturer or importer ceases the importation or manufacturing activity of the chemical substance for industrial use, they must notify it, following the guidelines outlined in the computer application instructions.

Environmental and Health Risk Assessments

364. Importers or manufacturers of new industrial chemicals meeting priority or environmentally and health-relevant criteria (Article 2.2.7B.1.2.3), must conduct environmental or health risk assessments for these substances. This assessment aims to understand the risks associated with the identified use within the national territory.

365. In case the importer or manufacturer identifies a new use for an inventoried substance categorized as a priority or of interest to health or the environment (Article 2.2.7B.1.2.3), a subsequent risk assessment for the environment or health must be carried out.

Risk Reduction and Implementation Program

366. For chemical substances meeting priority or health/environmental interest criteria, based on the instrument in Article 2.2.7B.1.2.3 and technical analyses derived from the information in Article 2.2.7B.1.2.1, importers or manufacturers must establish and implement a risk reduction and management programme. This programme should guide the understanding and control of risks linked to the identified use of the substance.

Additional Obligations

367. Manufacturers and importers must:

- Ensure comprehensive management of the risk associated with the industrial use of chemical substances in the manufacturing and import stages.
- Identify, classify, label and prepare the Safety Data Sheet (SDS) of chemical substances for industrial use, in accordance with the Globally Harmonized System of Classification and Labelling of Chemical Products (GHS), in accordance with the provisions of Decree 1496 of 2018 or the regulations that modify or replace it.
- Make available on a permanent basis to users of chemical substances for industrial use, information on risk assessments and programs for the reduction and management of risk to health or the environment.
- Provide the information required by the competent authorities regarding the instruments for the management of chemical substances for industrial use and to carry out the actions requested by them as a result of the inspection, surveillance and control process.
- Support and participate in research processes on the management of the risk associated with chemical substances for industrial use.

- Comply with the provisions of section 8 of Chapter 7 of title 1 of book 2 of Decree 1079 of 2015, Single Decree of the Administrative Transport Sector, on the transport of chemical substances for industrial use.

ii) Distributors

368. As part of their obligations, distributors must:

- Ensure comprehensive management of the risk associated with the industrial use of chemical substances in the marketing or distribution stages.
- Verify that chemical substances are labelled according to the Globally Harmonized System of Classification and Labelling of Chemical Products (GHS) and that they have their respective Safety Data Sheet (SDS), in accordance with the provisions of Decree 1496 of 2018. Marketers or distributors will in turn be responsible for providing the respective Safety Data Sheet to their customers.
- In the case of repackaging, they must label the chemical substances for industrial use in accordance with the Globally Harmonized System of Classification and Labelling of Chemical Products (GHS), in accordance with the provisions of Decree 1496 of 2018 or the regulations that modify or replace it, based on the information provided by the importer or manufacturer in the Safety Data Sheet (SDS).
- Carry out the corresponding actions according to the programs for the reduction and management of the risk to the environment or to health defined by the importer or manufacturer.
- Follow the safe handling instructions provided by the manufacturer or importer of the industrial chemicals.
- Comply with the provisions of section 8 of Chapter 7 of title 1 of book 2 of Decree 1079 of 2015, Single Decree of the Administrative Transport Sector, on the transport of chemical substances for industrial use.

iii) Carriers

369. The transporter of chemical substances for industrial use must comply with the provisions of section 8 of Chapter 7 of title 1 of book 2 of Decree 1079 of 2015 when transporting chemical substances for industrial use.

iv) Users

370. Users must also comply with obligations on the safe management of chemical substances, which include:

- Verifying that chemical substances are labelled in accordance with the Globally Harmonized System of Classification and Labelling of Chemical Products (GHS) and that they have their respective Safety Data Sheet (SDS), in accordance with the provisions of Decree 1496 of 2018.

- Informing the manufacturer or importer of the new uses for which the substance is intended and which are not listed in the inventory referred to in Article 2.2.7B.1.2.2 of this decree. In the event that the new use is accepted by the importer or manufacturer, provide the information required for the formulation of the evaluation and the risk reduction and management programme, except for that which is legally protected.
- Requesting from the importer or manufacturer of chemical substances for industrial use that require programs for the reduction and management of risk to the environment or health, the additional information that it deems pertinent to implement the actions that correspond to them in said programme.
- Carrying out the actions that correspond to them in the programs for the reduction and management of the risk to the environment or health defined by the importer or manufacturer, adapted to their particular conditions of use.
- Informing the competent authorities when it is evident that the manufacturer or importer does not have permanently available to users of chemical substances for industrial use, programs to reduce and manage the risk to the environment or to health, or in the case of finding inconsistencies in the available information.

D. Compliance Deadlines

371. Manufacturers and importers handling chemical substances for industrial use, with volumes exceeding 100 kilograms per year, must provide the required information in the National Inventory of Chemical Substances for Industrial Use within a compliance deadline of up to three years from the establishment of the computer application and its processing instructions.

372. For annual quantities below 100 kilograms or produced before the three-year period mentioned above, manufacturers and importers have the option to voluntarily input the required information into the computer application for the National Inventory.

373. For new chemical substances for industrial use exceeding 100 kilograms per year, importers or manufacturers must complete the necessary information within a maximum period of six months.

374. The information gathered through the aforementioned mechanisms, will help the Ministries of Environment and Sustainable Development, Health and Social Protection and Labour, to define the criteria and conditions that make it possible to identify the substances that are considered a priority or of interest to health or the environment, which will be required to provide additional detailed or specific information to allow decision-making for their comprehensive management.

E. Monitoring of Environment and Health Effects

375. There are two mechanisms for monitoring the effects of chemical substances, intended to support competent authorities in monitoring, controlling and adopting the necessary measures with regard to activities regulated under Decree 1630 of 2021.

376. The first one is for capturing environmental information on emissions and transfers of pollutants generated from the use of the substances. This mechanism will be established by the MASD, within the framework of the Environmental Information System of Colombia (SIAC) (Article 2.2.7B.1.4.1).

377. Second, the creation of a Toxicological Management System to determine the components, processes, procedures and those responsible for providing information on the identification of hazards, exposure and health effects of chemical substances for industrial use (Article 2.2.7B.1.42). This system will be administered by the Ministry of Health and Social Protection and will develop the necessary aspects related to the definition, organization, and operation of the Toxicological Management System, and other components essential for its implementation, with the support of the Ministry of Labour.

F. Data Collection and Exchange of Confidential Information

378. Decree 1630 of 2021 require that all data employed in the management instruments outlined in Article 2.2.7B.1.2.1 must originate from reliable sources meeting the criteria specified in points 2 and 3 of Article 5 of Decree 1496 of 2018 or those recommended by the Ministries of Health and Social Protection and Environment and Sustainable Development (Article 2.2.7B.1.6.1).

379. If reliable data is unavailable, and non-clinical safety studies for industrial chemicals are required, these studies should be conducted by a testing entity adhering to the Principles of Good Laboratory Practice (GLP) as set forth by the OECD. Acceptance of such data is contingent on the use of OECD test methods or their equivalents, with testing entities subject to inspection by the National Accreditation Body (ONAC) in Colombia. For testing entities outside the national territory, inspection must be conducted by their national monitoring authority of the OECD GLP principles, and their monitoring programme should be part of the Mutual Data Acceptance Agreement (Article 2.2.7B.1.6.2).

380. Regarding the exchange of confidential information on industrial chemicals, the national government is authorized to engage in such exchanges in compliance with relevant international laws and standards. Furthermore, the suggestions put forth in the OECD's Recommendation LEGAL/0204 shall guide this process.

G. Institutional Framework

381. An inter-ministerial technical working group, comprising representatives from the Ministries of Health and Social Protection, Labour, Trade, Industry and Tourism, and Environment and Sustainable Development, will be established to oversee the outcomes of the instruments outlined in the decree for managing chemical substances for industrial use. The group will assess the effectiveness of these instruments in the comprehensive management of such substances and convene at least two times a year.

382. The MASD will take charge of the operational coordination of the Inter-Ministerial Technical Group on Chemical Substances for Industrial Use. (Article 2.2.7B.1.5.1)

II. GHS – Classification and Labelling

383. Decree 1630 of 2021 adopts the Globally Harmonized System of Classification and Labelling of Chemicals and establishes other chemical safety provisions.

A. Context and Objective

384. In the process of Colombia's accession to the Organization for Economic Cooperation and Development (OECD), recommendations have been made to the country regarding the incorporation of instruments for the management of industrial chemicals and the prevention of major accidents.

385. In recognition of the importance of adopting a system of classification of chemical substances that allows for the availability of tools for the identification and communication of their hazards, the Globally Harmonized System of Classification and Labelling of Chemicals (GHS), which was approved by the Economic and Social Council of the UN in 2002, has been recognized as the official tool to classify chemical products, including the hazard indications, symbols and warning words, as well as for the creation of Safety Data Sheets.

386. Prior to that, Articles 101 to 104 of Title III 'Occupational Health' within Law 09 of 1979, provided some guidance on chemical safety. These articles were crafted to safeguard the health of workers within their occupational environments, emphasizing the prevention of harm arising from the production, handling, and storage of chemical substances. Notably, these measures included the implementation of labelling systems for the classification and communication of hazards.

387. Further on, Law 55 of 1993 ratified Convention 170 and Recommendation 177 on Safety in the Use of Chemicals at Work. These international standards were adopted during the 77th Amendment meeting of the General Conference of the International Labour Organization (ILO) in Geneva in 1990. This development imposed an obligation on authorities to establish specific systems and criteria for classifying chemicals based on their physical and health risks. The aim was to ensure a comprehensive framework for managing chemical substances in the workplace.

388. Finally, with the adoption of Decree 1496 of 2018, Colombia formally adopts the United Nations Globally Harmonized System of Classification and Labelling of Chemicals – GHS (or SGA, for its initials in Spanish), 6th revised edition (2015), with application in the national territory, for the classification and communication of hazards of chemicals.

B. Scope

389. Decree 1496 of 2018 applies throughout the national territory to all natural and legal persons, public or private, in all economic activities in which the extraction, production, import, storage, transport, distribution, marketing and different uses of chemical products that have at least one of the hazard characteristics in accordance with the criteria of the GHS are carried out.

390. Pharmaceuticals, food additives, cosmetics, and pesticide residues in food are exempt from the application of the GHS, as well as hazardous waste.

Applicability of existing legislation

391. While chemicals used in workplaces, as well as direct-to-consumer chemicals must be classified and labelled according to GHS, except for (i) household hygiene products and absorbents, covered by Decision 706 of 2008 of the Andean Community of Nations and (ii) pesticides for domestic use and public health, which are governed by Decree 1843 of 19910 (Article 11), other activities related with chemicals classification and labelling are governed by existing legislation.

392. For example, (i) the classification and labelling of chemical pesticides for agricultural use must follow the provisions of the Andean Technical Manual for the Registration and Control of Chemical Pesticides for Agricultural Use regulated by Resolution 630 of 2002 of the General Secretariat of the Andean Community; and (ii) the transport of chemical products by road remains regulated by section 8 of Chapter 7 of Title 1 of Part 2 of Decree 1079 of 2015 and the applicable provisions of the GHS.

C. Hazard Classification and Communication

393. The hazard classification of chemicals will be based on the guidelines of the GHS. The data used to classify chemical hazards should be generated through tests carried out in accordance with the methods and techniques referenced in the GHS or be in reliable sources of information, according to the requirements further developed in Decree 1496 of 2018.

394. Labels and Safety Data Sheets (SDS) may be complemented by other communication mechanisms, as long as the information is consistent between the mechanisms used. The label of chemicals shall contain the elements defined in the system, and products must be labelled even if they are intended for workplace use only.

395. When the transfer of chemical products is carried out, the destination container shall be labelled according to the packaging of the original product. The transfer of chemical products in containers that have food labels or shapes that represent or indicate food is prohibited. The use of hazardous chemical containers to store food is prohibited.

396. The manufacturer and/or importer must prepare the SDS in accordance with the GHS and guarantee the competent authority access to the technical and scientific support used for its preparation.

397. The Ministries of Labour, Health and Social Protection, Agriculture and Rural Development and Transport may define specific guidelines for the preparation of labels and SDS.

398. Manufacturers and importers will need to incorporate significant new information about the hazards of a chemical by updating the relevant label and SDS. New and significant information is information that changes the hazard classification of the chemical and requires a change in the label or SDS. Every five years, manufacturers and importers must review the information indicated thereof.

399. If emergency response agencies deem it necessary to access confidential information about a chemical in an urgent or emergency situation, the manufacturer, importer, and/or distributor must promptly provide all specific information required for emergency treatment, and the competent authority shall comply with the duty of confidentiality (Article 10).

D. Obligations

400. Key requirements arising from Decree 1496 of 2018 have a direct impact on manufacturers and importers, distributors and employers.

401. Manufacturers and importers of chemicals are responsible for classifying hazards and generating the respective labels and SDS in accordance with the GHS (Article 15).

402. Distributors and other end-users handling chemicals should require manufacturers and importers to supply chemicals classified and labelled in accordance with the GHS, and in turn, be responsible for providing the respective SDS to their customers.

403. Employers must ensure that in the workplace when chemical substances are handled, the identification of chemicals, exposure assessment, operational controls and training of workers are complied with as established in articles 10 to 16 of ILO Convention 170 approved by Law 55 of 1993 and in Chapter 6 of Title 4 of Part 2 of Book 2 of the Decree 1072 of 2015 (Article 17).

E. Role of Public Authorities

404. The implementation of GHS requires an active and coordinated role of the ministries of Labour, Health and Social Protection, Transport, Agriculture and Occupational Risk Administrators.

405. The Ministry of Labour must define the actions to be developed by employers for the application of the GHS to chemical products in the workplace and the actions aimed at protecting the safety and health of workers from the use and handling of such products, in coordination with the Ministry of Health and Social Protection. This involves carrying out dissemination and socialization campaigns on the application of the GHS aimed at employers; and establishing, the sources of information that will be recommended for the classification of hazards of chemicals used in the workplace.

406. The Ministry of Health and Social Protection must, with the support of the Ministry of Trade, Industry and Tourism, set out actions aimed at the application of the GHS in the field of chemicals aimed at consumers, while the Ministry of Transport shall carry out actions aimed at disseminating the provisions of Decree 1496 of 2018 to the various participants of the chain of transport of dangerous goods. The Ministry of Agriculture carries out the same exercise, in the broader context of updating the Andean Technical Manual for the Registration and Control of Chemical Pesticides for Agricultural Use, aligning with Decision 804 of 2015 from the Andean Community of Nations.

407. Occupational Risk Managers have a key role in helping employers implement the GHS. They are responsible for (i) carrying out education and prevention programs, campaigns and actions aimed at ensuring that its affiliated companies are aware of and comply with the requirements of the GHS, (ii) providing advice and technical assistance to employers in the application of the system, and (iii) and carrying out promotion and prevention actions in the workplace.

F. Enforcement

408. These public authorities must each, within the scope of their competences, exercise the functions of inspection, surveillance and control of compliance with the provisions of health, occupational safety and health, commerce, transport and agriculture, contained in Decree 1496 of 2018, in accordance with the rules applicable to each sector.

§3. Ozone Depleting Substances

409. Colombia adopted the Vienna Convention on the Protection of the Ozone Layer by means of Law 30/1990 and the Montreal Protocol on ODS by means of Law 29/1992. Under these instruments, the import or export of ODS is subject to restrictions and special requirements. The ODS are listed in different annexes of the Montreal Protocol and contain the deadlines for the elimination of such substances. ODS are used in the Colombian industry for different applications, such as refrigerants, aerosol propellants, foam-blowing agents, solvent degreasers, and fire protection equipment.

410. Pursuant to Law 29/1992, the import of products containing recycled CFCs should not be allowed and, once the corresponding deadline for zero level of consumption has been met, the production or emission of substances or equipment listed in Law 29/1992 should be forbidden. In particular, the manufacture and import of equipment or substances or products containing substances of Annex A, groups I and II; and Annex B, groups I, II and III, are forbidden by Resolution 1652/2007 and Resolution 2507/2018. Resolution 301/2008 bans the use of CFCs in pharmaceutical, hygienic and cleaning products. Concerning ODS export measures, Decree 423/2005 (Article 2.2.5.2.1.1, Decree 1076/2015) establishes a list of substances that are subject to control by the MASD. Control activities on ODS export are carried out by taking into account the schedule established in Law 29/1992 and the national consumption levels of ODS.

411. Resolution 304/2001, modified by Resolution 734/2004, regulates the registry for the import of ODS administered by the Ozone Technical Unit (*Unidad Técnica de Ozono* – UTO) of the MASD. Any natural or legal persons interested in importing ODS must be duly registered, and have a plan of gradual reduction of ODS imports and a statement on the use of imported ODS. Resolution 304/2001 also provides for ODS packaging and labelling requirements, for substances in pure state or in mixtures. For example, ODS in pure state must be presented in hermetic packages displaying information in Spanish on its trade and technical name, country of origin, producer's name, etc.

I. Ban on Equipment and Products Containing Controlled Substances

412. Resolution 0634 of 2022 prohibits the fabrication or importation of equipment and products containing or requiring controlled substances of annexes A, B, C, E and F of the Montreal Protocol.

413. This regulation is enacted for two primary reasons. First, in line with the National Plan for the Elimination of HCFC (Hydrochlorofluorocarbons) Consumption, it aims to strengthen the domestic regulatory framework to prohibit the manufacturing and importation of equipment and products containing, or requiring for their production, HCFC. Second, aligning with the Kigali Amendment to the Montreal Protocol and Colombia's climate actions under the Nationally Determined Contribution to the UNFCCC, including the NAMA Project for the domestic refrigeration sector, the resolution is issued to prohibit the manufacturing and importation of products and equipment when they contain or require substances listed in Annexes A, B, C, E, and F of the Montreal Protocol. Additionally, Colombia has committed to banning all uses of pure HCFC-141b and HCFC-141b contained in premixed polyols, starting 31 December 2020, contingent on the execution of seven projects for the polyurethane foam production sector.

414. The purpose of Resolution 0634 of 2022 is therefore to prohibit the manufacturing and importation of equipment and products containing and/or requiring for their operation or functioning substances controlled in Annexes A, B, C, E, and F of the Montreal Protocol. The resolution extends this prohibition to four groups of products: (i) refrigeration and air conditioning equipment and systems; (ii) polyurethane foams, polystyrene, formulated polyols and products made from these foams; (iii) fire extinguishing equipment and products; and (iv) other products containing substances controlled by the Montreal Protocol, especially aerosols and solvent products.

415. For each of the product categories mentioned above, Resolution 0634 of 2022 specifies an explicit prohibition on manufacturing, an explicit prohibition on importation of products identified with the tariff codes of each item, and some exceptions depending on the product. For instance, the importation of fire extinguishers containing and/or requiring for their operation or functioning substances from Annex A Group II of the Montreal Protocol is allowed exclusively for the civil, commercial, and private aviation sector, provided they meet certain criteria, including the requirement that fire extinguishers with a Halon load not exceeding 4 kg must be for exclusive use in extinguishing fires in passenger cabins, cargo, kitchens, aircraft cockpits, and use Halon 1211 as an extinguishing agent.

416. The Importation of products detailed in this resolution, unless explicitly prohibited, requires approval through the Single Foreign Trade Window (VUCE). For that purpose, they are required to present to the ANLA the certification issued by the foreign manufacturer, confirming that the equipment and/or product intended for importation neither contains nor has required, for its production or functioning, any of the substances controlled as specified for each case in the equipment and/or product to be imported. This submission is necessary to secure environmental approval from ANLA. Furthermore, they have the option to include under a single certificate the equipment and/or product families associated with batches or related groups, provided that the comprehensive identification of the equipment and/or products slated for importation under the same certificate is feasible.

417. Resolution 0634 of 2022 repeals Resolutions 1652 of 2007, 0171 of 2013, and 2507 of 2018.

§4. Restricted Chemicals

418. In 2007, Colombia ratified the Rotterdam Convention on the Prior Informed Consent Procedure for Certain Hazardous Chemicals and Pesticides in International Trade (Rotterdam Convention), by means of Law 1159/2007. The Rotterdam Convention, signed in 1998, establishes the PIC as a regulatory instrument to restrict the import and export of the chemicals listed in Annex III, including industrial use chemicals and pesticide formulations, among others. The Rotterdam Convention elaborates on the principle of shared responsibility for chemical handling and requires countries to exchange information on chemicals for future imports. The Rotterdam Convention provides all parties with decision-guide documents to assess the convenience of accepting, banning or restricting the import of chemicals listed in Annex III.

419. Colombia is a party to the United Convention Against Illicit Traffic in Narcotic Drugs and Psychotropic Substances of 1998, which seeks to tackle illicit narcotic drug trafficking at the international level. One of the measures established therein is to implement controls over the substances used in the manufacture of narcotic drugs and psychotropic substances, including precursors, chemicals and solvents. Decree 2530/2009 regulates the requisite of pre-notification for this kind of substance, consisting of giving notice to the Ministry of Trade, Industry and Tourism of the materials, goods or substances that are intended to be exported, and that are listed as controlled substances. Decree 2530/2009 lists thirty-one substances that are subject to pre-notification of the competent authority, including Acetone, Ethyl Ether, Sulphuric Acid, Hydrochloric Acid, and Toluene.

§5. Persistent Organic Pollutants

420. Colombia adopts the Stockholm Convention on POPs by means of Law 1196/2008. POPs are POPs that possess toxic properties, resist degradation, bioaccumulate and are transported through air, water and migratory species, across international boundaries and deposited far from their place of release, where they accumulate in terrestrial and aquatic ecosystems.[31] The Stockholm Convention

31. Stockholm Convention on Persistent Organic Pollutants, http://chm.pops.int/Convention/tabid/54/language/en-US/Default.aspx, 22 May 2001.

seeks therefore to eliminate or restrict the production and use of POPs. Colombia has started preparing the implementation plan for the Stockholm Convention and has drafted proposals on soil pollution prevention relating to POPs.

§6. Transport of Hazardous Materials

421. Decree 1609/2002 is the key regulatory instrument on the transport by road of hazardous goods, covering activities like hazardous goods segregation, loading, unloading, packaging, storage and delivery. Decree 1609/2002 establishes requirements for vehicles, the authorizations to be obtained for transporting hazardous goods by road and the responsibilities of all the actors involved in the activity, including the cargo sender, receiver, transport company, vehicle driver and the owner or holder of the vehicle. Remarkably, Decree 1609/2002 follows the United Nations Recommendations on the Transport of Dangerous Goods and includes the nine categories of hazardous goods. These categories are developed through Colombian Technical Standards (Norma *Técnica Colombiana* – NTCs) that, pursuant to Decree 1609/2002, are mandatory: explosives (NTC 3966), flammable gasses (NTC 2880), flammable liquids (NTC 2801), flammable solids (NTC 3967), organic peroxides (NTC 3968), toxic and infectious substances (NTC 3969), radioactive materials (NTC 3970), corrosive substances (NTC 3971) and other hazardous substances (NTC 3972).

422. The transport of specific materials is regulated by special regulations. For example, Resolution 181682/2005 establishes the Regulation for the Safe Transport of Radioactive Materials. Likewise, the transport of dangerous materials or substances by means other than road is regulated in specific pieces of legislation. For example, the transport of hazardous goods by air is regulated in Resolution 3208/2003 by the Colombian Civil Aeronautic.

Part II. Nature Conservation and Management

Chapter 1. Monuments and Landscapes

§1. Monuments

423. The notion of monuments in Colombia goes back to 1959 with Law 163/1959 establishing measures for the defence and conservation of monuments, and historic and artistic heritage. Law 163/1959, regulated by Decree 264/1963 and mostly repealed by Law 1185/2008, declares the historic and artistic heritage of the monuments, pre-Hispanic tombs and other objects from nature or human activity that hold a special interest for the study of history, art, civilization and antique cultures. Pursuant to the obligations of the 7th International American Convention of 1933, Colombia adopts as unmovable monuments the ones intimately related to the national independence campaign and the initial part of the republican period, as well as nature manifestations with great scientific interest in the study of flora and geology. As a result, the old towns of the cities of Tunja, Cartagena, Mompox, Popayan, Guaduas, Pasto and Santa Marta, especially the country house of San Pedro Alejandrino are declared national monuments. Departmental governors and mayors are responsible for the enforcement of the provisions of Law 163/1959, and thus, they have to verify that works in their jurisdiction are carried out in accordance with the regulation on national monuments.

424. At the international level, Colombia adopted the Convention Concerning the Protection of the World Heritage Convention (WHC) of 24 May 1983. Up-to-date, Colombia has nine sites registered in the World Heritage List, divided into cultural, natural and mixed properties: (i) cultural sites: the Coffee Cultural Landscape (2011); Historic Centre of Santa Cruz de Mompox (1995); the National Archaeological Park of Tierradentro (1995); the Port, Fortresses and Group of Monuments of Cartagena (1984); the Qhapaq Ñan, Andean Road System (2014) and the San Agustin Archaeological Park (1995); (ii) natural sites: Los Katios National Park (1994), and the Malpelo Fauna and Flora Sanctuary (2006); and mixed sites: Chiribiquete National Park – 'The Maloca of the Jaguar' (2018). Colombia has submitted six additional sites to register in the Tentative List of the WHC, including

Buritaca 200 – Ciudad Perdida – Sierra Nevada de Santa Marta, the Pre-Hispanic Hydraulic System of San Jorge River, and the Sea flower Marine Protected Area.[32]

425. The adoption of the 1991 Constitution and the General Law of Culture (Law 397/1997) marks a significant step towards the protection of cultural heritage, defining Colombia as a multi-ethnic and multicultural nation. One of the advances of Law 397/1997 is the replacement of the term 'monuments' for 'goods of cultural interest'. The new notion covers not only magnificent and monumental goods but also representations of cultural heritage as an understanding of Colombian social dynamics. Law 397/1997 obliges the State to protect, conserve, rehabilitate and spread the Colombian cultural heritage, by coordinating tasks among public and private entities. Accordingly, the Ministry of Culture and, in particular, the Directorate of Heritage of the Ministry of Culture are responsible for the management of cultural heritage in Colombia. Law 388/1997 on Land Planning also plays an important role in monument conservation, as it seeks to harmonize the regulation on land planning with cultural heritage protection.

426. The Colombian Inter-sector Commission of World Heritage, created by Decree 2406/2005, is the national entity in charge of assessing and rendering expert opinions on the new proposals for the register of goods in the World Heritage List. The Commission articulates the relationship between the United Nations Educational, Scientific and Cultural Organization (UNESCO), Colombia and local entities for the adequate management of goods of natural or cultural interest. The Commission is integrated by the ministers of culture, public affairs and environment, the director of the Colombian Institute of Anthropology and History, and the director of the national geology service. The executive secretary of the UNESCO National Cooperation Commission and the President of the International Council of Monuments and Historic-Artistic Sites may attend the Commission meetings as permanent invitees. In addition to the cultural and natural goods, Colombia has declared other goods and sites as part of its cultural heritage. These goods include historic urban collections, such as the historic centres of Ambalema, Barichara, Concepcion and Santafe de Antioquia; and archaeological zones and excavation sites.

427. The protection of monuments and the procedure for their declaration are mainly governed by Law 397/1997.[33] Law 397/1997 provides that national cultural heritage is integrated by all material goods, immaterial manifestations, cultural products and representations expressing Colombian nationality, as well as the movable and unmovable goods with historic, artistic, scientific, aesthetic or symbolic significance. Within this framework, the policy on the national cultural heritage aims at the safeguard, protection, recovery, conservation, sustainability and divulgation of cultural heritage, so it stands as a testimony of the national cultural identity for the present and future generations. For the purpose of achieving the ends of

32. UNESCO. State Parties, Colombia, http://whc.unesco.org/en/statesparties/CO, 2021.
33. Modified by Law 797/2003, Decree 2106 of 2019 and Law 2070/2020. Further regulated by Decree 358/2000, Decree 833/2002 and Decree 2941/2009.

the cultural heritage policy, territorial entities, such as departments, municipalities and districts must harmonize their local development plans with the National Plan of Development and the ten-year plan of culture and must appropriate the economic resources for cultural heritage protection within their jurisdiction.

428. The protection of a monument requires its declaration as a material good of cultural interest. The declaration of goods of cultural interest is made through an Administrative Act issued by the national authority, or by territorial, indigenous or Afro-descendent authorities, depending on their powers. Once the Administrative Act is in force, the good of national interest enjoys the special regime of protection or safeguard established in the law. Any goods that prior to the entry into force of Law 397/1997 have been declared as monuments, areas of historic, archaeological or architectonic conservation, or any other denomination, are considered goods of cultural interest and therefore receive special protection.

429. The declaration of goods of cultural interest consists of two phases: the project listing and the final declaration. The project listing is a procedure whereby the competent authority lists a good in the Indicative List of Candidates for Goods of Cultural Interest. The same authority establishes whether the project requires a Special Plan of Management and Protection. Once this phase has been completed, the National Council of Cultural Heritage, or the respective Departmental or District Council, depending on the location of the good (national, departmental or district/municipal), renders its technical opinion on the declaratory of the project as good of cultural interest, and the convenience of the management and protection plan. If the opinion of the respective council is favourable, the authority that listed the project declares it good for cultural interest and approves the Special Plan of Management and Protection. In case the petition on the project declaratory is requested by individuals or companies, the petitioner has to draft and present the management and protection plan itself for the later approval of the authority.

430. The Special Plan of Management and Protection is an instrument that establishes the necessary actions to guarantee the protection and sustainability of goods. In case of unmovable goods, the plan must detail the affected zone, buffer zones, the permitted intervention level, management conditions and a disclosure plan, which should help the community to integrate with the conservation aspect of the project. The public Registrar Office of Public Instruments registers the affection of the unmovable good in its corresponding record, stating that such good is subject to a special plan of management and protection. The elements of the management and protection plan are to be defined by the Ministry of Culture.

§2. Landscapes

431. The NCRNR sets out general provisions on landscape protection. According to the NCRNR, the community has the right to enjoy urban and rural landscapes that contribute to their physical and spiritual welfare. In this context, the national government must determine the places or zones where construction works are forbidden; prohibit tree felling, growing or alteration of the landscape configuration deserving special protection; establish height limits or style guidance to preserve aesthetic and historic uniformity; and adopt all the measures to protect landscapes. Concerning the private sector, natural or legal persons carrying out urbanization projects or construction works are prompted to keep harmony with the landscape structure.

432. Decree 1715/1978 regulates landscape protection as established in the NCRNR. The former national INDERENA was empowered to establish those landscapes deserving special protection, by taking into account the criteria set in the NCRNR. However, as the INDERENA was terminated and its competences were assumed by the MASD, the establishment of protected landscapes is currently made by the MASD. This level of protection must be compatible with the legislation on protected areas; thus, the establishment of protected landscapes shall fit in the categories established within the SINAP, or the national system of natural parks.

433. One of the measures on landscape protection provided for in Decree 1715/1978 consists of protecting the adjacent zones to roads so that national road users enjoy the surrounding landscape. The width of these zones is to be determined by the Ministry of Transport with the technical advice of the environmental authority. The environmental authority helps establish prohibitions, restrictions and provisions on the sticking of billboards, and the alteration or deformation of landscape natural elements such as rocks, stones, rocky outcrops, meadows or trees for advertisement purposes, even if artistic reasons are argued. Remarkably, landscape harmful or unsightly alteration is considered by the NCRNR as an environmentally detrimental factor; thus, offenders of such provisions are subject to sanctions like paying fines or removing billboards. The sanctions established in Decree 1715/1978 must be understood in accordance with Law 1333/2009 establishing the environmental enforcement procedure.

434. The Colombian Institute for Archeology and National History advises environmental authorities and other actors so that, in the process of granting environmental licences or the approval of environmental management plans, the Preventive Archeology Program (Title V, Decree 138 of 2019) is complied with and thus avoid that, in the development of works, projects or activities, valuable information from the human past is affected.

Chapter 2. Parks and Reserves

§1. Introduction

435. Nature conservation and management is organized under the national *SINAP*. Although the configuration and regulation of the SINAP only came in 2010 with Decree 2372/2021, Colombia has had a system of parks and reserves since 1974, known as the System of National Nature Parks (*Sistema de Parques Nacionales Naturales – SPNN*), which constitute the backbone of protected natural areas. The SPNN was recognized in 2010 and made part of one of the categories within the SINAP.

436. Since the 1991 Political Constitution, the importance of conserving the country's biological diversity has been established. Earlier on, the Natural Resources Code recognized the environment as a common heritage and established responsibilities for its preservation and management. In 1994 with the signing of the Convention on Biological Diversity (CBD) and the formulation, in the following year, of the National Policy on Biological Diversity, Colombia acquired the commitment to form and consolidate a national SINAP. Subsequently, in 1998, the National Environmental Council approved the strategy for a National SINAP, the objective of which is to ensure the conservation of biological and cultural diversity and the sustainable production of environmental goods and services indispensable for the economic, social and environmental development of the nation. In parallel, Law 388 of 1997 recognized that land use planning must take into account the protected areas declared by the Regional Autonomous Corporations, the areas that make up the SPNN and the National Forest Reserves.

§2. System of National Nature Parks

437. The SPNN is provided for in Chapter V of the NCRNR and further regulated in Decree 622/1977 (Article 2.2.2.1.7.1, Decree 1076/2015) as a system of areas with an exceptional national value due to their natural, cultural and historical characteristics, as well as the benefits they render to inhabitants. The SPNN seeks to preserve the outstanding worth of flora, fauna, landscapes, and historical, cultural or archaeological relics; keep samples of biotic communities, genetic resources, biogeographical units, physiographic regions and threatened species in their natural state; and protect species from natural, cultural and historical phenomenon, in order to enrich the preservation of the common heritage of the mankind.

The types of activities that are permitted, and on some occasions restricted in the SPNN, include conservation, recovery and control, investigation, and cultural, educational and recreational activities.

438. Conservation activities seek to keep the inner state of renewable natural resources and panoramic views and foster the ecosystem's biological equilibrium. Recovery and control activities refer to assessments or investigations aimed at restoring an ecosystem and/or accumulating the elements that determine the basic conditions of such an ecosystem. Investigation activities concern works leading to ecosystems' knowledge, including cultural and archaeological aspects, in order to use that knowledge in the management and use of historical and natural resources in Colombia. Complementarily, education activities seek to teach and spread knowledge in resource conservation, management and use, with the purpose of raising awareness of Colombian natural wealth and the need to conserve it, whereas cultural activities are focused on promoting knowledge of the cultural richness of a certain region. Finally, recreational activities refer to the provision of a leisure space for National Nature Park visitors.

439. Decree 622/1977 regulates further the NCRNR and sets specific goals for the SPNN (Article 2.2.2.1.10.1, Decree 1076/2015). These include: technical regulation on area management and use; reservation of special areas; conservation of natural genetic banks; investigation of the natural renewable sources in the country, within and out of protected areas; maintenance of biological diversity and ecological balance by protecting natural areas; provision of recreational services to visitors, according to the objectives of the SPNN; enhancement of inhabitants welfare by preserving outstanding values of the national heritage; and the promotion of the use of SPNN resources for educational purposes, so as to raise awareness on the importance of nature conservation.

I. Areas Within the SPNN

440. The areas comprised within the SPNN include national parks, unique nature areas, sanctuaries of flora and fauna, and road-parks. National Parks refer to areas whose ecosystems have not been substantially altered by human exploitation or occupation, and which allow for self-ecological regulation, and the fauna, flora, geomorphological complexes or historic manifestations have a scientific, cultural, educational or recreational value. All the six kinds of activities foreseen in the NCRNR (conservation, investigation, education, recreation, cultural, and recovery and control) are permitted in national parks.

441. Colombia has fifty-nine national parks representing 65% of the national ecosystems, equivalent to 17 million hectares of biodiversity. Ecotourism is allowed in the national parks of Sierra Nevada de Santa Marta, Sumapaz, Tayrona, Tuparro, Utria, Malpelo and Los Nevados, and Purace, among others. The main threats to the SPNN are illicit crops and high levels of deforestation.[34]

442. Colombia has two nature reserves: Nukak, with a total area of 855,000 hectares (ha), located in the Department of Guaviare, and Puinawai, with a total area of 1,092,500 ha, located in the Department of Guainia. According to the NCRNR, nature reserves consist of areas with primitive conditions of flora, fauna and earth,

34. Diario La República. 'Entre los 59 parques nacionales naturales del país, 49 tienen algún tipo de amenaza', available at, https://www.larepublica.co/economia/de-los-59-parques-nacionales-naturales-del-pais-49-tienen-amenazas-en-sus-ecosistemas-3223677, 28 Aug. 2021.

for which only activities of conservation, investigation and education are allowed. Likewise, unique nature areas are defined as areas that due to their special conditions of flora and earth are deemed as rare natural scenarios. The activities allowed in such areas include conservation, investigation and education. Colombia has only one unique nature area, created in 1988 with a total area of 640.62 ha in the Department of Norte de Santander, named Estoraques.

443. Sanctuaries of flora and fauna are defined in the NCRNR as the areas for the conservation of species or communities of vegetables and wild animals, with the purpose of preserving their genetic value. Pursuant to the NCRNR, the activities that are permitted in the sanctuaries of flora or fauna include conservation, recovery and control, investigation and education. According to the information system of the SPNN, Colombia has twelve sanctuaries of flora and fauna, including the Cienaga Grande de Santa Marta, El Corchal, Galeras, Guanenta Alto Rio Fonce, Iguaque, Los Colorados, Isla de la Corota, Los Flamencos, Malpelo, Otún Quimbaya and Orito Ingi Ande, among others. The last category of SPNN areas concerns road-parks (vía-parque). Road-parks are defined as a land strip along the road that has particular beautiful panoramic characteristics or cultural and natural values, which must be preserved for education and leisure purposes. Conservation, education, cultural and recreational activities are allowed in road-park areas. The SPNN has registered one road-park area named Isla de Salamanca, with an extension of 56,200 ha, bordering the Colombian Atlantic coastline in the Department of Magdalena.

II. Reservation and Delimitation

444. Pursuant to Decree 2915/1994 and Decree 622/1977, the national competent authority for the management and administration of the SPNN is the Special Administrative Unit of the System of National Nature Parks (UAESPNN). The UAESPNN is in charge of accomplishing the purposes of the nature parks system, by exercising administrative powers on the regulation, investigation, biodiversity protection, use and information of the areas comprised under the SPNN. Notably, Law 99/1993 provides that the establishment, delimitation and exclusion of the SPNN areas correspond to the MASD, as well as the licences and concessions required to perform activities in these areas. The UAESPNN serves as the technical body of consultation of the MASD when establishing, demarcating or excluding an area from the SPNN.

445. The SPNN administration involves establishing and removing areas from the system; regulating its management; ensuring the conservation, restoration and promotion of wildlife; enforcing compliance with applicable provisions; drafting and implementing management plans for each one of the SPNN areas; and fixing fees for SPNN visitors. The UAESPNN must coordinate the management of the SPNN areas with local and regional authorities, especially concerning area zoning. Indeed, the Council of State has ruled that coordination among public authorities must be guided by the effective protection of the environment by both territorial and environmental authorities in the area of their jurisdiction and that the concerned authorities must monitor compliance with environmental laws.[35]

446. The UAESPNN must also establish and demarcate buffer zones for each one of the area categories of the SPNN. Buffer zones refer to those areas that are intended to lessen the effects caused by human activities in neighbouring areas, and aim at avoiding ecologic alterations or disturbance in SPNN areas' wildlife. The management programmes to be established in buffer zones must be coordinated with territorial entities, such as municipalities, departments or districts.

447. When establishing areas of the SPNN, the competent authority must verify whether there are indigenous reserves settled in such areas. If the declaration of an SPNN area involves the inclusion of an indigenous reserve, the competent authority must have prior technical advice from the consulting bodies, in order to establish an advantageous regime for indigenous communities. The applicable regime must seek to ensure the indigenous community's permanence in the area and the use of renewable natural resources, by observing the compatible technologies with the management plan of the said area.

III. Expropriation and Incentives

448. The National Constitution establishes that any form of property can be expropriated for reasons of social and public interest. Decree 622/1977 and Law 99/1993 establish that the SPNN areas and the establishment of future areas under such a system are considered reasons of public interest. The MASD may expropriate the properties and any improvements made over those properties for the development of the SPNN areas. The negotiation process, voluntary or direct, is regulated by non-environmental regulations; however, if the expropriation concerns the establishment of SPNN areas, the Geographic Institute Agustin Codazzi will establish the price of the property under negotiation. The Colombian State must not allocate territories from the SPNN to new possessors.

449. Law 1536 of 2012, named 'Gloria Valencia de Castaño' law, promotes nature conservation by establishing fiscal incentives to taxpayers that give donations for the conservation of the National Natural Parks and natural forests. Donors have the right to deduct 30% of the value of the donation from their tax revenue. Donors may specify to which natural park the donations go, although they do not grant rights to these areas or to carry out activities therein.

35. Council of State, Sentence of 24 Sep. 2009. First Section. Magistrate Rafael E. Ostau de Lafont Pianeta.

A. Acquisition of Real Estate and Purchase of Improvements Within the SPNN Areas

450. Decree 1785 of 2021 sets out the conditions for the automatic correction of defects in titles and ownership traditions (*saneamiento* automático) for State entities acquiring properties within the areas of the National Natural Parks System (SPNN), with the aim to foster preservation and conservation strategies and ensuring legal certainty. This process follows the aims of Law 1955 of 2019, which issues the National Development Plan 2018–2022 'Pact for Equity' seeking to correct legal defects arising after the acquisition process. In addition, Decree 1785 of 2021 allows the State to buy the material elements installed by the occupants of the land within the SPNN, such as constructions, crops, or modifications, under certain conditions of vulnerability and legality.

Correction of defects

451. The process of automatic correction of defects arises in the context of an acquisition process, where State entities must conduct a legal study of the property, accompanied by an ecological and convenience study by Colombia's National Natural Parks. The legal study should include information and records from all state entities with competence in identifying rural real estate and resolving land tenure conflicts. If legal or administrative processes with regard to the target area exist, the automatic correction of title defects cannot proceed.

452. In the event of no agreement for voluntary acquisition, and when the property is crucial for conservation goals, the acquiring entity may initiate expropriation proceedings according to constitutional and legal provisions.

453. The intention of automatic correction of defects must be registered by the Public Instruments Registry Office and recorded in the property's real estate folio. The registration request must be accompanied by a topographic survey and property appraisal is ordered with the registration request. Those with registered real rights affecting property ownership may oppose the automatic correction of defects until a substantive decision is issued.[36]

454. Once the topographic survey, property appraisal, and opposition resolutions are complete, a motivated administrative act declaring the public utility basis for automatic correction is issued. The cadastral authority must update its databases within two months of the automatic correction decision, establishing or updating the property's cadastral identity.[37]

Purchase of Improvements

455. Purchase of improvements is a legal process where the possession of a property, along with any improvements made on it, is transferred from the seller to the

36. Decree 1785 of 2021, Art. 2.2.1.1.19.2.3.
37. Decree 1785 of 2021, Art. 2.2.1.1.19.2.6.

buyer. The primary purpose is to recognize and facilitate the transfer of possession and any improvements (such as renovations, modifications, or additions) made by the occupant to the State entity. The purchase process requires a motivated administrative act based on a study, confirming that the properties were characterized within SPNN areas post-declaration (of protected area) and before 30 November 2016.[38]

456. In order to be eligible for the process, improvement holders must meet the following eligibility conditions: (i) they must not be landowners; (ii) they must experience conditions of vulnerability or dependence on land and natural resources for subsistence; (iii) the improvements to the property must not be linked to illicit crops, processing, marketing, or illegal mineral extraction. Parques Nacionales Naturales de Colombia is responsible for conducting a characterization study to evaluate eligibility and appropriateness.

457. The procedure to purchase the improvements initiates when the public entity sends a motivated purchase offer to the improvement holder, including improvement value, purchase offer, and payment instructions. The improvement holder must accept or reject the offer within fifteen business days, providing necessary payment information. The improvement purchase is formalized through a public deed.[39]

458. In addition to general conditions, the improvement holder commits to not returning to the sold property and agrees to payment and property delivery conditions.[40]

IV. Area Management and Uses

459. Each one of the areas integrating the SPNN must have a management plan where the developments, facilities, use, and administration of the area are established. The activities to be carried out within the areas of the SPNN must not admit foreign governments or stakeholders, nor can they have rights over these areas. SPNN areas may include the following zones: intangible, primitive, natural recovery, cultural-historic, general recreation, high-density and buffer zones. High-density zones are not established for nature reserves. The execution of works, projects or any other activities that may cause a significant damage to the environment or natural resources in the SPNN areas requires an environmental licence.

V. Users and Obligations

460. Activities authorized under the SPNN must not significantly alter the natural environment. The use of the SPNN areas is conditioned to obtaining an

38. Decree 1785 of 2021, Art. 2.2.1.1.19.3.1.
39. Decree 1785 of 2021, Art. 2.2.1.1.19.3.3.
40. Decree 1785 of 2021, Art. 2.2.1.1.19.3.4.

authorization, which follows the conditions established in the management plan of each area. In addition, the permanence of users in the SPNN areas is subject to the time allocated in the authorization. Users' obligations in the SPNN areas include obtaining the authorization according to the objectives of their visit, complying with the conditions of the area, exhibiting the authorization to the authorities and denouncing any infraction against the area. In case SPNN users intend to carry out investigations, they will have to provide the authority with a detailed report on their activities and findings, send copies of their publications, and provide at least one unit of the species, subspecies, objects or samplings used in the investigation.

461. Finally, Decree 622/1977 prohibits conducts that may affect the organization of the SPNN and those that may alter the natural environment in such areas. Regarding the former group, Article 31 includes abandoning vehicles, objects or equipment, selling non-authorized products, carrying firearms or any other element used for hunting, fishing, tree felling, etc. Concerning conducts that may alter the environment in the SPNN areas, Article 30 prohibits modifying, removing or altering signs, boards or any other banners; generating noises that disturb other visitors or the environment; discharging, introducing, using or abandoning toxic substances; using chemical products that have harmful effects; developing agricultural, industrial, mining, oil or hospitality (hotels) activities.

§3. National System of Protected Areas

I. Background

462. The term protected area was introduced in Colombian legislation with the ratification of the CBD by means of Law 165/1994. According to Article 2 of the CBD, a protected area is defined as *a geographically defined area, which is designated or regulated and managed to achieve specific conservation objectives.*[41] Prior to the entry into force of the CBD and apart from the categories of the SPNN, regulations like Law 99/1993 and the NCRNR made reference to protected areas but without defining or regulating those areas. Furthermore, protected areas have been mentioned in national development plans from 1994 to 2010, and have been addressed in national policies, including the policy on biodiversity, the strategies for creating a SINAP, the policy on social participation for conservation, forest management policy, national territory zoning guidance, and wildlife protection, among others. At regional and municipal levels, some departments and municipalities have created systems of protected areas, such as the Autonomous Corporation of Risaralda in 1999 or the Capital District of Bogota in 2000. The notion of protected areas, thus, has long developed the Colombian experience in nature management and conservation.

41. Convention on Biological Diversity, 'Protected Area on Provisions in CBD', www.cbd.int/protected-old/background.shtml, 25 May 2007.

463. The ratification of the CBD in 1994 and the subsequent decisions adopted by the CBD's Conference of the Parties have propelled the creation, regulation and implementation of a SINAP in Colombia. In 2010, Decree 2372/2010 was adopted regulating the SINAP. Decree 2372/2010 provides for SINAP definitions, conservation objectives, compounds, authorities, management, principles, administration and main agents; among others. The participation of the Institute Alexander Von Humbolt in the design and legal framework of the SINAP has also been crucial for the achievement of this project.[42]

464. In addition, a National Policy for Comprehensive Management of Biodiversity and Ecosystem Services (PNGIBSE) has been adopted encompassing the SINAP. The policy seeks to promote comprehensive management for biodiversity conservation and ecosystem services so that the socio/ecological systems improve at local, regional and national levels. According to the PNGIBSE, the productive sector is encouraged to foster conservation and achieve sustainability of economic activities, such as agriculture, livestock and industrial extraction. Economic incentives for environmental investment must be geared towards biodiversity protection.

II. Regulation

A. *System Definition*

465. SINAP is defined as the nationwide set of protected areas governed by public, private and communitarian entities at national, regional and local levels, and involving public and private agents. As a system to achieve Colombia's conservation objectives, the SINAP involves competent authorities at national, regional and local levels; regional and thematic subsystems of protected areas, as well as the areas comprised within the SNPNN; management categories that follow international guidance on the matter; and land zoning plans at different levels, such as departments and municipalities. The SINAP is guided by principles that ensure its correct implementation and operation, like considering protected areas as the central element for biodiversity conservation; subjecting protected areas to management actions for conservation purposes; allowing the SINAP flexibility so as to adapt to biodiversity intrinsic and external changes, without disregarding its conservation purposes; coordinating existing environmental principles with the SINAP implementation; making the national government, CARs, Sustainable Development Corporations and other actors jointly accountable for SINAP areas management; and fostering legal instruments for the conservation of areas in privately owned lands.

466. The SINAP shall be coordinated by the UAESPNN. The UAESPNN must propose to the MASD policies, plans, programmes, regulations and procedures

42. Eugenia Ponce de León Chaux. 'Estudio jurídico sobre categorías regionales de áreas protegidas'. Presented to Alexander Von Humbolt Institute, October 2003.

related to the SINAP. In addition, it coordinates with environmental authorities, territorial entities, ethnic representatives, non-governmental organizations and private parties the strategies for the consolidation, development and running of the SINAP, as well as the homologation, categorization and establishment of areas under the existing regional or thematic subsystems of protected areas.

B. SINAP Objective

467. The SINAP seeks to address conservation *in situ* objectives established in the CBD, by creating a national SINAP, management categories and general procedures. In line with the aims of the Constitution, the areas are designated to ensure the continuity of natural evolution and ecological processes to maintain biological diversity; guarantee the offer of environmental services and goods for human well-being; and guarantee the permanence of the natural environment and its compounds, as the basis for keeping national cultural diversity and nature's worth. Additionally, governmental authorities are to be provided with specific criteria to determine whether a protected area amounts or not to the conservation objectives of Colombia. The conservation objective must be evidenced by the competent authority in the Administrative Act that creates, reserves, delimits, declares or designates a protected area.

C. Categories

468. The SINAP categories reflect the existing groups of protected areas in Colombia and include a few new ones, as established in Article 10 of Decree 2372/2010. In addition, it includes those areas created by private entities. Each area is subcategorized under one of the two subsystems: regional or thematic. The SINAP categories include: the existing SPNN, Protective Forest Reserves, Natural Regional Parks, Districts of Integrated Management, Districts of Soil Conservation, Recreational Areas, and Areas established by the civil society.

469. While the SPNN remains regulated by Decree 622/1977, the Protective Forest Reserves and Districts of Integrated Management may be established at a national scale by the MASD, which will set out the parameters for delimitation, establishment, demarcation or exclusion. The Districts of Integrated Management with strategic ecosystems and landscapes at a national scale follow the provisions of Decree 216/2003 on their declaration, reserve and administration. Districts of Soil Conservation, Recreational Areas and Natural Regional Parks shall exclusively be established at the regional level by the corresponding CARs. Natural reserves from the civil society remain regulated by Decree 1996/1999 and allow coexistence with public protected areas under specific conditions, meaning that private areas have to be compatible with the zoning and management plans of the public area. Areas proposed to be designated as natural reserves of the civil society have to register with the UAESPNN.

D. Existing Protected Areas

470. The areas legally established before the entry into force of the new regulation remain protected as conservation *in situ* strategies. As regards internationally protected areas, such as Ramsar sites or the common heritage of mankind, Decree 2372/2010 does not include them within the SINAP, for they are considered complementary strategies of biodiversity conservation. In order for the existing protected areas to become part of the SINAP, they have to undergo a homologation process whereby the new area denomination, use, management and other conditions match the categories of the SINAP. The competent environmental authorities can change the categories of the protected areas under their jurisdiction and have to ensure that protected areas categories do not overlap. Additionally, the competent environmental authorities are able to grant ecological protection to *paramos* and *subparamos* zones, water sources and aquifers, by designating them as SINAP areas.

471. 'Páramos', which can be translated as 'highland' or 'moorland' in English, represent a distinctive type of high-altitude ecosystem located in the northern Andes, at altitudes ranging from 3,400 to 5,000 meters above sea level, primarily in certain regions of South America, with over 60% situated in Colombia.[43] Possessing unique environmental conditions, they contribute significant ecosystem benefits to their respective areas. Their altitude and climate enable them to retain water, maintaining a balance between inputs and losses within the ecosystem. During dry periods, water flows to lower areas, supplying nearby populations and ensuring the provision of drinking water, irrigation, and hydroelectricity. Species in páramos have adapted to extreme conditions, including daily temperature fluctuations, high radiation, desiccating winds, and soil freezing.

472. The conservation of páramos is crucial due to their significant ecological importance and vital role in water management and biodiversity. They receive specialized protection through sector-specific regulations, such as those governing agricultural and mining activities.[44]

E. Designation and Exclusion of SINAP Areas

473. The designation of protected areas is based on technical, social and environmental assessments that seek to ensure that biophysical, socio-economic and cultural criteria are met. The designation of protected areas at national and regional levels requires the favourable technical opinion of the Colombian Academy of Exact Physic and Natural Sciences or the entities ascribed to the MASD. The

43. Ecología Verde. Páramo: características flora y fauna, https://www.ecologiaverde.com/paramo-caracteristicas-flora-y-fauna-2546.html.
44. Resolution 1294 of 7 Dec. 2021, which establishes the guidelines for the development of low-impact and environmentally sustainable agricultural activities in páramos, and Resolution 1488 of 20 Dec. 2021, which establishes the environmental guidelines for the regulation of the substitution program that involves the closure, dismantling, restoration and reshaping of the areas intervened by mining activities and the reconversion program or job relocation within the Páramo ecosystems.

authorities involved in the process of protected areas declaration, recategorization or homologation have to request information from the competent entities in order to analyse aspects like land possession, ethnic groups, mining rights, infrastructure projects in those areas, and hydrocarbon exploration and exploitation activities. Provided that the designation of protected areas may involve ethnic groups living in such areas, these groups have to be provided with mechanisms to get involved in the decision-making process.

474. The exclusion of areas from the SINAP is conditioned to the requirements established in Decree 2372/2010. Withdrawal of an area shall only be allowed when public utility or social interest reasons support the development of activities that may contravene the management and uses of a protected area. In this case, the developer will have to request the exclusion of the area from the SINAP to the authority that created it. Likewise, the authority will have to take into account criteria like the area's ecological importance, number of species, environmental benefits, and cultural significance, in order to determine whether the exclusion request is conceded or denied. The Administrative Act excluding an area from the SINAP shall include a motivation part describing the criteria that the authority has taken into account for rendering its decision.

F. Protected Areas Zoning and Authorized Activities

475. The authorized activities to be carried out in each area category correspond to their management and conservation purposes. Decree 2372/2010 establishes zones of preservation, restoration, sustainable use and public use, as well as different types of allowed uses, such as sustainable, preservation, restoration, knowledge and leisure uses. The activities or uses to be carried out in SINAP areas are subject to authorization from the competent authority, and in some cases, to a fee payment fixed in the protected area management plan.

G. SINAP Coordination

476. In order to ensure coherence and full coordination with territorial entities, Decree 2372/2010 conditions zoning plans and land use regulations to the designation and demarcation of SINAP areas. Municipalities, districts and departments must establish their zoning plans in accordance with the SINAP parameters and the CARs have to assist municipalities, districts and departments in the implementation of appropriate zoning plans. Additionally, zoning plans of SINAP neighbouring areas must establish buffer zones so that human activities do not interfere with the conservation purposes of the SINAP. Finally, with the purpose of harmonizing national and regional protected areas, the regulation creates the following regional subsystems: Caribbean, Pacific, Orinoco, Amazon, Northeast Andes and Northwest Andes regions.

Chapter 3. Wildlife Protection

477. According to the Clearing House Mechanism for Colombia, created in the CBD as a means to achieve the CBD goals, Colombia is the fourth most biologically diverse country in the world: the second country in plants, first in amphibians and birds, third in reptiles, and fifth in mammals. The country has a total number of 3,357 species of fish, amphibians, reptiles, birds and mammals, and nearly 41,000 plant species. These numbers correspond approximately to 14% of the world's species. Biodiversity levels in Colombia depend on the region; for example, the Andean region is the most diverse in wildlife species, while the Amazon region is the most diverse in fish species. In terms of endemic species, Colombia reports 32 species of mammals, 400 amphibians, 66 birds, and the third part of plant species are considered endemic. As regards threatened species, by 2002 Colombia reported 213 high plants, 41 mammals, 78 breeding birds, 14 reptiles and 8 fish species. Finally, the estimation of invasive species in the country is 117, with 20 fish, 2 amphibians, 7 invertebrates, 9 birds, 9 mammals and 70 plants.

478. In Colombia, wildlife protection has been developed in the NCRNR, Law 17/1981 approving the Convention on International Trade in Endangered Species of Wild Fauna and Flora (CITES), Decree 1608/1978 and Law 611/2000. Notably, Law 99/1993 establishes the protection and sustainable use of biodiversity as an environmental principle. Law 99/1993 allocates competences among national and regional authorities for wildlife protection and empowers the MASD to adopt measures for the protection of wild fauna and flora species, adopt measures for the defence of threatened species, and issue the certifications referred to in the CITES.

§1. Flora

479. The NCRNR defines wild flora as the vegetable species or individuals in the national territory that have not been cultivated or improved by human beings. The adoption of wild flora protective measures is aimed at regulating the management, use, transport and market of public and/or private wild flora species, and their by-products; promoting and restoring wild flora; and controlling wild flora species or individuals by means of ecologic practices. The administration and management of wild flora involve conservation and preservation of its natural renovation, the direct use of wild flora by the State, when ecological, social or economic reasons demand so, and the creation of zones for the development of wild flora species.

480. Law 299/1996 regulates Colombian flora and declares it of national priority. Particularly, Law 299/1996 (Article 2.2.1.1.16.1, Decree 1076/2015) regulates the commissioning and operation of botanic gardens and the way they must contribute to flora promotion and conservation. Botanic gardens must advise the national government on how to achieve compliance with the CITES, regarding the trade of threatened plants; additionally, botanic gardens must administrate confiscated species of flora. In order to control the illegal trade of threatened flora species, Law 299/1996 provides that customs, sanitation, environmental, police and airport authorities must control the import and export of biological material.

481. Decree 690 of 2021 regulates the sustainable management of wild flora and non-timber forest products, such as fruits, leaves, bark, seeds, resins, roots and other parts of potential commercial value from wild flora. In alignment with the national goal of zero deforestation by 2030, the decree provides communities in natural forests with an alternative economic opportunity that enables them to subsist without resorting to deforestation. Interested parties may access non-timber resources through permits, concessions, and authorizations, subject to the completion of the National Single Format and a technical study for commercial utilization.

482. The decree classifies sustainable management into two types: domestic, for meeting vital needs without commercialization, and persistent, for renewable use. Different permit modalities are established based on expected monthly income, categorized as small, medium, and large. Moreover, the regulation addresses the sustainable use conditions for indigenous and Black communities, respecting the provisions of existing laws. This ensures their right to participate in the utilization, administration, conservation, and commercialization of these valuable resources.

483. Decree 690 of 2021 also regulates the mobilization and commercialization of wild flora and non-timber forest products, emphasizing the need for a national online Unique Safe Conduct for mobilization and compliance with specific resolutions.

§2. Fauna

484. Wild fauna is defined in Law 611/2000 (Article 2.2.1.2.7.1., Decree 1076/2015) as living organisms of land and aquatic animal species that have not been domesticated, genetically modified or bred, or those that have returned to their wild state. The main pieces of legislation regulating wild fauna protection are established in the NCRNR, Decree 1608/1978 (Article 2.2.1.2.1.1, Decree 1076/2015) regulating wild fauna related activities and Law 611/2000 on sustainable use of wild and aquatic fauna. The legal protection of wild fauna is basically structured under three main action lines: rational use, conservation and promotion, and export and import activities. Wildlife export and import are dealt with in the CITES section.

485. Fauna rational use is enhanced through the regulation of hunting, animal resettlement, and zoological gardens, museums and collections. Pursuant to the NCRNR, hunting is classified as hunting for subsistence, and commercial, sportive, scientific, control or promotion purposes. Decree 1608/1978 (Article 2.2.1.2.4.3, Decree 1076/2015) regulates hunting rights, hunting facilities and the obligations for obtaining hunting permits, including the establishment of hunting areas and seasons; the allowed quantity, sizes and species; and the hunting quota allocation.

Natural or legal persons holding hunting permits, as well as those entities authorized to operate wildlife breeding facilities, museums, collections, zoological gardens or circuses, are required to obtain a licence for wild fauna mobilization.

486. Wild fauna promotion and conservation are implemented through fauna territories, reserved areas, and areas for sportive hunting. The NCRNR and Decree 1608/1978 create fauna territories with the purposes of species conservation, investigation, management for later exhibition, restoration and preservation. Reserved areas of hunting refer to areas that are demarcated and reserved for the promotion and conservation of specific wildlife species. Concerning areas for sportive hunting, Decree 1608/1978 requires an inventory of wildlife species in the area, a special permit, compliance with national laws, and observation of hunting bans. Notably, Colombian legislation provides for another instrument of wild fauna promotion and conservation: wildlife breeding centres (*zoocriaderos*).

487. Wildlife breeding centres are regulated in Law 611/2000 as public or private facilities intended for the maintenance, promotion, breeding or use of fauna for scientific, commercial, industrial, resettlement or subsistence purposes. Wildlife breeding centres require an environmental licence, which is subject to the approval of the EIA for the facility's experimental and commercial phase. The EIA provides information on the adaptability of the species, information on the proposed area, species population, and biólogical and ecological information on the species, among others. The mobilization of wild fauna species requires a licence, as described above.

488. In order to achieve wildlife protection goals, environmental authorities are provided with specific powers. Environmental authorities must classify wild animals and establish the appropriate species for hunting activities; establish the species requiring special management; establish hunting areas, and species' size and quantity; establish fauna's products subject to economic uses; establish hunting bans or restrictions; regulate hunting activities; grant, deny, suspend or revoke permits; and impose sanctions for non-compliance.

§3. CITES

489. The CITES was signed in 1973 and entered into force in Colombia in 1978, by means of Law 1/ 1978. According to the International Union for Conservation of Nature (IUCN), the main aim of the CITES is to ensure that international trade in specimens of wild animals and plants does not threaten their survival. The CITES has established a permitting system for the export, transit and import of specimens listed in the appendices of the convention. The CITES appendixes cover approximately thirty-three thousand species of wild fauna and flora, grouped in three lists that reflect how species are threatened by international trade, and the desire of CITES parties to protect other species. The Conference of the Parties of the CITES has provided a mechanism to include plants and animals in appendixes I and II.

490. As part of its international obligations with the CBD and CITES, Colombia has established and implemented a categorization system to identify fauna and flora specimens considered threatened species in the country. The Research Institute of Biological Resources 'Alexander Von Humbolt' carried out a study pointing out the main causes of biodiversity loss in Colombia, including habitat transformation and fragmentation, introduction and exclusion of species, overexploitation of biological resources, pollution factors and climate change. In spite of the results obtained from this study, the MASD has appointed a Categorization Committee in cooperation with other technical bodies to start a species categorization process based on the red lists of the IUCN. The Categorization Committee adopts a series of red books of threatened species in Colombia, which have been inserted in Resolution 584/2002, establishing the list of threatened wildlife species. Resolution 584/2002, modified by Resolution 572/2005, establishes that research, sustainable use and any other management activities aimed at threatened species conservation are subject to prior authorization by environmental authorities.

§4. Wildlife Movement Within the National Territory

491. The movement of biodiversity species in Colombian territory is subject to the obtaining of a species mobilization authorization, known as '*salvoconducto*'. According to Resolution 1909/2017, mobilization authorization must be requested by any natural or legal person transporting biodiversity species, excluding household fauna and flora, fishing resources, or biological samples covered by investigation permits. The characteristics and information that the mobilization authorization must contain are detailed in Resolution 1909/2017, such as type of biological resource, transport means, types of resource uses, dimensions, and carrier identification. The species mobilization authorization is valid for eight days within which the transport must take place.

Chapter 4. Agricultural Resources

492. The NCRNR devotes a whole title to agricultural soil, providing for general principles, powers of the authorities, and the use and conservation of soil. Notwithstanding, the relationship between agriculture and the environment has not been clearly dealt with in policy instruments and has resulted in divergent approaches leading to environmental problems in the agricultural sector. The creation of the Ministry of Environment and the national system of environmental information in 1993 marked a change with respect to environmental protection and conservation in different sectors of the economy. New environmental institutions undertook the environmental powers of the different public sector authorities, which haltered a sector-based focus on the enhancement of agricultural soil regulation.

493. In Colombia, agricultural policy has been focused on sector development by promoting the modernization and competitiveness of productive activities, and the development and improvement of the rural population. The so-called Green Revolution policy adopts specific models of agricultural development towards the realization of the said purposes, gaining acceptance within the sector and creating resistance to new models. Yet, compounds such as environmental protection, conservation or sustainability remain out of the sector priorities. On top of that, agricultural soil conservation is pressured by factors like illegal mining, illegal crops, poverty, violence and land allocation, which require urgent attention at the policy level.

494. The combination of the aforementioned factors has led to unsustainable agricultural practices. The lack of internalization of agricultural environmental externalities is evidenced in the inappropriate use of land and water; the indiscriminate use of fertilizers, agrochemicals and pesticides; and a lagging agricultural technology. Regarding land and water use, malpractices are observed in the use of outdated work tools that pulverize soil surface and make soil more compact; land surface with agricultural aptitude is used for other activities, including cattle feeding in pasture fields; inefficient irrigation systems that fall short of coverage; contamination of water bodies, and a lack of available drinking water. As to the use of fertilizers and pesticides, sector policies aiming at developing agriculture, such as the Green Revolution, have indirectly contributed to the indiscriminate use of chemical products resulting in high levels of water and soil contamination.[45]

495. The main provisions on agricultural soil conservation are developed in the NCRNR. Pursuant to the NCRNR, soil must be used according to their conditions and constitutive factors, so that its physical integrity and productive capacity are protected. The potential use of soil must be established by taking into account physical, ecological and socio-economic criteria, which will also render the basis for soil classification. Indeed, the main aim of soil utilization is to avoid soil loss or degradation, in order to achieve restoration and ensure conservation. The NCRNR

45. Agricultura Sensitiva, 'La problemática Ambiental del Sector Agropecuario en Colombia', www.angelfire.com/ia2/ingenieriaagricola/sectoragropecuario.htm, 14 Sep. 2007.

establishes a general obligation to truly achieve soil conservation by requiring natural or legal persons carrying out agricultural, livestock breeding, forestry or infrastructure activities, which affect or may affect soil, to undertake conservation and recovery practices.

496. The NCRNR also grants public authorities specific powers to meet soil conservation targets. Governmental authorities must enforce legislation to prevent and control erosion, degradation, desertification and land sliding. Likewise, authorities must promote the adoption of measures on land use towards the conservation of soil and aquifers, as well as the implementation of cultivation methods, and fauna and flora management. Public authorities are empowered to intervene and take corrective measures in areas of private tenure, in case of erosion, degradation, landslide risk or desertification. Finally, the NCRNR puts special interest in the conservation of soil in islands, savannas and beaches; hence, the competent authorities must overlook and promote the sound management of these zones.

497. Agricultural soil is subject to special management and restoration activities once they fall into one of the circumstances foreseen in the NCRNR. The NCRNR circumstances include soil non-exploitation, so the soil is subject to management practices in order to reactivate its productive capacity; inappropriate soil application leading to environmental unsteadiness; soil subject to physical or chemical limitations affecting soil productivity; and soil affected by inadequate exploitation. Other measures on agricultural soil conservation concern ensuring forest coverage in soil located at sloped terrains; the presentation of ecological studies detailing soil protection and conservation measures, for mining, construction and engineering projects; and the obligation to obtain an authorization for activities involving the removal of natural vegetation from the slopes of communication ways or canals.

498. Law 1776 of 2016 creates the zones of rural, economic and social development Interest (Zidres), as special territories, suitable for agriculture, livestock, fishing or forestry development, and far from urban centres, with low population density and limited infrastructure. The Zidres have been created to develop comprehensive rural plans, strengthen environmental sustainability and promote the economic and social development of their inhabitants. To be part of the Zidres, it is necessary to present a productive project to the Ministry of Agriculture. The project must be administratively, financially, legally and environmentally viable; it must guarantee the purchase of production at market prices; it must be compatible with the country's food security policies; and it must be in line with the territorial planning of the region where it will be implemented.

§1. Low-Impact Agricultural Activities in Paramo Ecosystems

499. The Ministry of Agriculture and Rural Development, through Resolutions 464 of 2017 and 261 of 2018, established strategic guidelines for public policy regarding peasant, family, and community agriculture. The objective is to guide state action and influence private or social institutions in strengthening the social, economic, and political capacities of these agricultural sectors. Additionally, Resolution 261 of 2018 defined the national agricultural frontier and adopted a methodology for identifying such frontier, while charging the Unit of Agricultural Rural Planning (Upra) with the task of continually updating this identification. The legislative context, particularly in Law 1930 of 2018, emphasizes the need for progressive actions by environmental authorities to control agricultural frontier expansion. Foremost, the past regulations have fostered the continuation of low-impact agricultural activities in delimited páramo zones, provided they adhere to environmental standards and good practices.

500. Resolution 1294 of 2021 provides a framework for the development of low-impact and environmentally sustainable agricultural activities in páramos, aligning with the provisions of Law 1930 of 2018. It applies to both current and prospective individuals and entities engaged in such activities within delimited páramos, as well as those transitioning to low-impact practices while adhering to environmental standards and páramo preservation.

501. Environmental and social guidelines for low-impact agricultural activities are grounded in principles of reciprocity, cooperation, solidarity, and recognition of local knowledge. They describe the roles and responsibilities of relevant ministries, environmental authorities, and territorial entities for the monitoring and evaluation of the regulation. It prohibits detrimental practices such as deforestation, mining, burning, and the use of agrochemicals, and stresses on the adoption of good practices to minimize impacts on páramo ecosystems, including preserving natural coverage, protecting water sources, managing soil fertility, and utilizing substances derived from living organisms.

Chapter 5. Forests

§1. Introduction

502. Forests embody an important compound of Colombia's wealth representing 59.9 million hectares of natural forest covering 52% of the territory.[46] The special geographical conditions of the country, including flat coastal lowlands, Andean Mountains, plateaus and lowland plains, amounted to Colombia's tropical climate with temperatures ranging from 5°C to 35°C yield different types of forests: lowland tropical rainforest in the northern part of the Amazon, humid lowland rainforests between the mountains and the Pacific Ocean, mountain and sub-mountain forests in the Andean mountain range, and dry tropical forests in the Caribbean area. These forests are home to biodiversity species, indigenous communities and African descendant communities; and provide crucial environmental services by ensuring the provision and quality of water, protecting soil against erosion and counterbalancing GHG emissions. Additionally, forests serve the round timber industry, two-thirds of the internal pulp production, small-scale paper supplies and fuel for rural farmers.

503. Forests face severe challenges in terms of conservation, exploitation and restoration, bearing in mind that Colombia has one of the largest deforestation rates worldwide. According to the MASD, the unsustainable exploitation of forest resources, the widening of agriculture borders, wood consumption for energy purposes, forest fires, open-pit mining, deficient implementation of infrastructure projects, bad practices with flora and fauna, introduction of invasive species and the growing of illicit crops are the main factors threatening Colombian forests. Notably, the expansion of agricultural frontiers and colonization account for 73% of deforestation causes, whereas timber production for 12%, wood consumption for 11%, and forest fires and illicit crops for 2%. Due to the internal circumstances of Colombia, the effects of illicit crop growing in forestry loss deserve a special analysis.

504. The armed conflict in Colombia involving guerrillas and paramilitary groups against the State and civil society, fuelled by the trade of prohibited drugs, has had a direct impact on deforestation, land colonization and aerial spraying of herbicides. Thousands of forest hectares are cleared in order to grow illicit crops such as poppy, marihuana and cocaine. Studies show that 'two hectares of forest are depleted for the production of one hectare cocaine, and for every hectare of poppy, 2.5 hectares are depleted'. Farmers in agricultural areas switch from legal crops to illicit ones, due to the economic benefits they receive from drug lords and belligerent groups, all of which cause deforestation, ecosystem and biodiversity loss. In

46. MASD, 'Importancia de los bosques, Colombia tercer país de la región en cobertura boscosa', https://archivo.minambiente.gov.co/index.php/redd/importancia-de-los-bosques#:~:text=Por%20Qu%C3%A9%20los%20Bosques%20de%20Colombia%20Son%20Tan%20Importantes&text=Los%20bosques%20y%20las%20selvas,erosi%C3%B3n%2C%20evitando%20derrumbes%20y%20deslizamientos.

response to this problem, the national government, in cooperation with international agencies, has started programmes to counter illicit crop growth.

505. Furthermore, armed conflict occurring in forested areas has brought along the displacement of the rural population and environmental authorities. This phenomenon has triggered forest abandonment leading to a lack of appropriate management, inefficient enforcement of laws, ecosystem loss and proliferation of illicit crops. What is more, the eradication policy of aerial herbicide spraying has significantly contributed to ecosystem loss and deforestation. In spite of this reality, the government and lawmakers have been drafting policies and laws aimed at guaranteeing forest conservation and fostering economic activities in the forest sector.

§2. Policy

506. The first policy and planning instruments on forests date back to 1959 with Law 2 regulating the conservation of forestry resources. In 1974, the first plan for pulp, paper and cartons, as well as the first national reforestation plan were launched. Later on, Law 37/1989 set out the basis for structuring the National Plan of Forest Development (NPFD) in order to keep the social and economic benefits of forests and to tackle forest-related problems. In 1996, the MASD and the National Department of Planning (NDP) adopted the Forests Policy establishing strategies for land zoning, forest ecosystems restoration and reforestation for commercial and industrial purposes, which resulted in Decree 1791/1996 establishing forest uses (Article 2.2.1.1.2.1, Decree 1076/2015). After gathering up the objectives and principles of former forest policy and planning instruments, including strategies on protected areas, threatened species and biodiversity conservation, the NPFD was approved in December 2000.

507. The NPFD is meant to be a roadmap to consolidate the forest sector by 2025, as a strategic market in the national economy, with high participation in agricultural production and employment generation, and based on the sustainable use and management of natural and plantation forests. The NPFD is guided by nine principles, including the protection of forest social and economic benefits, investigation and knowledge, international cooperation, forest production, productive forest chains, sustainable use and management, and environmental sources. The main objective of the NPFD is to include the forest sector in the national development programme by enhancing its comparative advantages, promoting competitiveness in timber and non-timber products in national and international markets, and ensuring the sustainable use of natural and plantation forests.

508. The NPFD sets out three main programmes to accomplish the goals set therein: programme for forest planning, conservation and restoration; programme for the development of forest commodity chains; and programme for institutional development. The three programmes are intended to work harmonically under an eco-systemic approach, which consists of acknowledging the ecological processes of forests and their productive capacity and making them compatible with the expectations of society on goods and services production. This approach must take note of the knowledge of forest management that native communities have. Notably, the NPFD programme on forest planning, conservation and restoration, articulated with the eco-systemic approach, represents the gross impact of the policy on nature conservation; therefore, this section is devoted to analysing the five strategies and subprogrammes conceived under the said NPFD programme.

509. The subprogramme of forest zoning and planning aims at defining new processes and approaches for the planning of forest ecosystems, with the purpose of taking note of the regional and local needs for forest goods production and environmental services. This subprogramme seeks to tackle transformation, fragmentation and loss of forested areas, for they have led to increased biodiversity loss, soil degradation and reduction of forest environmental services. The action lines under this subprogramme include the redefinition of local zoning plans, a national inventory of forested areas, the redefinition of forest borders and the redefinition of forest ownership, where indigenous and African descendent communities shall be included.

510. The second subprogramme aims for the conservation *in situ* of ecosystems and biodiversity. Under this programme, the environmental authorities guarantee the ends of protective forested areas and micro river basins. In order to achieve so, the MASD, the UAESPNN and the CARs must include forest ecosystems into the existing categories of protected areas, such as the SPNN or the SINAP, putting special interest in rainforests, mangrove swamps and dry forests, and guaranteeing the participation of the main actors.

511. The third subprogramme is the conservation *ex situ* subprogramme, which seeks to protect forest germplasm, preserve the genetic basis and diversity, generation of knowledge and economic benefits to society. Environmental authorities must identify endangered species, define protocols for their management, identify the sources of forest germplasm in endangered or threatened species, and look for commercial activities through activities of genetic enhancement. Likewise, a national system of conservation, production and distribution of forest germplasm must be launched to strengthen the Andean Network of Forest Seeds and to enhance knowledge of botanic gardens.

512. The fourth subprogramme on restoration and rehabilitation of forest ecosystems promotes the establishment and management of vegetable cover in order to restore forests, gain a larger offer on environmental services and improve the population's quality of life. This subprogramme involves the gathering and analysis of information that allows determining the priorities on forest restoration, soil rehabilitation and establishment of forests. Restoration and rehabilitation activities are carried out by taking into account the peculiar attributes of the ecosystems, and ensuring that forests comply with their very purpose, meaning, protection and conservation of soil, reduction of landslides and floods, regulation of the hydrological cycle, conservation of wildlife, supply of timber goods, improvement of the productivity and sustainability of agriculture and cattle farming, among others.

513. The NPFD programme on forest planning, conservation and restoration includes a final subprogramme on protection against wildfires. The subprogramme on the protection of wildfires seeks to diminish the occurrence and negative effects of this phenomenon. The areas with high wildfire risks have priority under this strategy, and the national government must strengthen coordination among institutions, such as the National System on Disaster Prevention and Management and its regional committees, CARs, the MASD and the UAESPNN. In addition, public authorities have to consolidate a national network for the prevention and control of wildfires, including fire monitoring and fire detection programmes by means of observation towers, tools and assets for ground squads, satellites and local communities.[47]

§3. Main Regulation

514. The main regulation on forest conservation can be grouped into three chronological stages: natural forest management and conservation; forest resources planning; and environmental management and promotion of the forest sector. Natural forest management and conservation has its first records in Law 2/1959, creating seven forest reserves located in the Amazon region, the snow-capped Cocuy, the mountainous region of Motilones, the Sierra Nevada de Santa Marta, along the Magdalena River, in the centric zone and in the Pacific region. The forest reserves created by Law 2/1959 aim at developing the national economy, protecting soil and wildlife by establishing forest reserves in 65 million hectares (ha), subjecting those forest reserves to special management plans and restricting land allocation to interested parties in reserved areas. Additionally, Law 2/1959 empowers the national government to create areas known as National Nature Parks, which currently accounts for the creation of 275,000 ha of protective forested areas, 453 ha of productive forested areas and 17,000 ha of forested areas managed by the civil society.

515. However, even with these protective measures, certain circumstances may warrant the subtraction of specific areas. In Colombia, the MASD may permanently remove a portion from the Amazon Forest Reserve in line with the restitution principles outlined in Law 1448 of 2011, which establishes measures for the attention, assistance, and integral reparation of victims of the internal armed conflict. This is exemplified by Decision 061 of 2022 of the MASD, there the Ministry, with the collaboration of the UAE for the Management of Restitution of Dispossessed Lands, has decided to start the procedure to ensure the effective execution of this land restoration effort for the benefit of victims.

47. Ministerio del Medio Ambiente, 'Plan Nacional de Desarrollo Forestal', https://archivo.minambiente.gov.co/images/BosquesBiodiversidadyServiciosEcosistemicos/pdf/Plan-Nacional-de-Desarrollo-Forestal/553_plan_nal_des_forestal.pdf.

516. The second stage of forest resource planning has its main source in the NCRNR. The NCRNR draws up a comprehensive legal framework for the protection of forests by regulating forest uses, logging and the industry of timber and non-timber products, and providing for basic criteria for environmental protection. The NCRNR establishes three kinds of forest areas: productive areas, meaning those areas protected and preserved in order to obtain forest products for sale or consumption; protective areas, concerning forests that must be conserved and protected, as well as their natural resources; and productive-protective areas, which are protected and preserved for both purposes: commercial and nature conservation. In order to ensure the protection of these forest areas, the NCRNR only allows forestry activities in these areas, conditions infrastructure projects to permitting systems, prohibits land allocation, and restricts the development of activities that are not compatible with forest purposes. The protection is reinforced in the NCRNR by restricting the use of forest resources and subjecting this usage to meeting special conditions, such as the implementation of forestry techniques, clean-up of the forest area and payment of fees intended for reforestation programmes.

517. In 1987, Law 37 was adopted, setting out the basis for structuring an NPFD and creating the National Forest Service (NFS). The NFS is conceived as a coordination system among territorial and administrative authorities that articulates the actions of these entities towards achieving compliance with the objectives of the NPFD. Law 37/1989 foresees the creation of a forest police responsible for the enforcement of provisions on wildlife, use and forest protection. In addition, Law 37/1989 vests the NFS with powers on nature conservation matters, such as carrying out a national inventory of forests; overseeing and controlling forestation, reforestation and forest use; and the administration, management and conservation of forests.

518. The third stage of environmental management and promotion of the forest sector is marked by the Earth Summit in Rio de Janeiro in 1992, and the subsequent adoption of Law 99/1993, creating the national environmental system in Colombia. Law 99/1993 assigned the Ministry of Environment the task of coordinating the drafting of the NPFD, as well as the organization, implementation and harmonization of the NFS established in Law 37/1989. As a result of the adoption of Law 99/1993 and the competences provided therein, Decree 1791 was adopted in 1996, regulating the use of forests in Colombia.

519. Decree 1791/1996 (Article 2.2.1.1.2.1, Decree 1076/2015) regulates the activities of the public administration and the private sector with respect to the use, management, economic exploitation and conservation of forest and wild flora, in order to achieve sustainable development. Decree 1791/1996 establishes a permitting system for the three types of forest uses provided in the regulation, namely single, persistent and domestic use, as well as for the studies on future forests and wild fauna works.

520. In order to foster forest conservation and ensure its life cycle, Colombian legislation provides for incentives on reforestation activities. Law 139/1994 (Article

2.2.9.9.1.1, Decree 1076/2015) creates the Certificate of Forest Incentive (*Certificado de Incentivo Forestal* – CIF), as a monetary benefit for those entities, including the public and private sector, carrying out reforestation activities. The monetary benefit consists of paying the costs for the growing of forest plantations for protective-productive purposes. The monetary benefit covers 50% of the aforementioned costs when planting introduced species, and 75% for native species.

521. In 2006, Law 1021 'Forest Law' was adopted as part of the 2000 forest policy establishing a twenty-five-year plan for the forest sector. Law 1021/2006 was intended to channelize the targets and objectives of the 2000 forest policy and to correct the lacunas and flaws of Decree 1791/1996, as well as to continue developing the postulates on sustainable use of forests and promotion of the forest sector. However, the Colombian Constitutional Court found that during the law-making process of Law 1021/2006, native communities were not consulted. Based on those facts, the Court ruled the unconstitutionality of Law 1021/2006, excluding it from the legal framework and disabling its application in Colombia.[48] As a consequence, forest activities and the provisions on forest conservation remain regulated by Decree 1791/1996.

48. Constitutional Court, Sentence No. C-30 of 23 Jan. 2008, Magistrate Rodrigo Escobar Gil.

Chapter 6. Fish Resources

522. Fishing and fish farming activities contribute to a large extent to food supply and employment generation in the national economy. The Colombian territory, characterized by tropical weather with a variety of climates, a considerable number of river basins, and coastal access to both the Pacific and Atlantic oceans, enables the country to have one of the largest fish species and hydrological species biodiversity in the world. In addition, the amount of freshwater and saltwater areas allows the development of aquaculture (fish farming) activities throughout the country. Colombia cultivates marine prawns, tilapia, tambaqui (known in Colombia as cachama) and trout. The Fish and Agriculture Organization of the United Nations (FAO) reports aquaculture as a rapid and sustained activity in Colombia that may have a positive economic impact in the long term.[49]

523. The NCRNR lays down general provisions to ensure the conservation, promotion and rational use of hydro-biological resources and the aquatic environment. The main aim of the NCRNRN regulation is to protect the permanent availability of biological resources and the aquatic environment and guarantee their rational management pursuant to social, economic and ecological techniques. The NCRNR establishes the State ownership over fish resources, thus conditioning their exploitation to a fee payment. Furthermore, Law 13/1990 on the General Fishing Statute sets out the legal framework for fish resources, providing for competent authorities, regulatory measures, permitting system and fishing and aquaculture activities.

§1. Institutional Framework

524. The Ministry of Agriculture and Rural Development is the national entity responsible for setting out, executing and following up on fisheries and aquaculture policy in Colombia, along with the MASD to ensure the sustainable use of these resources. The policymaking process involves the adoption of regulatory and non-regulatory measures that respond to interdisciplinary research on biological, fisheries, technological, social, economic and environmental factors. In addition, the policymaking process integrates governmental agencies with associations of regional fisheries and rural communities so that the measures agreed thereby are the result of a participative process. The National Authority of Aquaculture and Fishing (AUNAP), created by Decree 4181/2011, replaces the Institute of Rural Development (*Instituto Colombiano de Desarrollo Rural*) and takes charge of the administration, investigation, promotion, zoning, project implementation and surveillance of fishing and aquaculture activities at the national level. Most importantly, it grants the required authorizations, permits, licences and concessions, and administers the general register of fisheries and aquaculture.

49. FAO, 'Visión General del Sector Agrícola Nacional. Colombia', www.fao.org/fishery/countrysector/naso_colombia/es#tcNA009C, 1 Feb. 2005.

§2. Regulatory Measures

525. The main piece of legislation on fishing and aquaculture is Law 13/1990 on the General Fishing Statute. Law 13/1990 aims to establish a framework for the integrated management and rational exploitation of fish resources in order to ensure their sustainable use. Law 13/1990 regulates the fisheries sub-sector composition and operation; fishing activities, such as research, extraction, fish processing, marketing, and aquaculture; the permitting system and the applicable fees; close seasons and reserves; infractions and sanctions; the general register of fisheries and aquaculture; fisherman; coordination among public institutions; and incentives to fishing activities. Decree 2256/1991 regulates Law 13/1990 by setting out quotas to the main marine resources; establishing control systems for fishing fleet with respect to the number, size, type and ownership of vessels; regulating close seasons for fishing in marine and continental water; establishing exclusive areas for small fisherman and capture methods to be used at this level; providing for minimum species sizes for capture; regulating a permitting system of concessions, authorizations and permits; providing for inspections and visits; and establishing methods for law enforcement.

Decree 2256 creates the Executive Committee for Fisheries (CEP). The CEP brings together representatives of the Ministry of Agriculture and Rural Development, the MASD and the AUNAP to decide on the definition of species authorized for cultivation or the setting of catch volume quotas, among others.

§3. Permitting

526. Fishing and aquaculture activities are subject to different kinds of permits depending on the activity scale. Decree 2256/1991 establishes the following types of permits: concessions, artisanal fishing, commercial and industrial fishing, exploratory commercial fishing, ornamental fishing, investigative fishing, sportive fishing, fish processing, fish marketing permits, aquaculture permit and an integrated permit for fishing. Environmental aspects are dealt with in each one of those permits, as well as in water concessions and plans for environmental management, which are directly enforced by the CARs, or by requiring the developer to follow the applicable environmental guidelines. Environmental guidelines aim at harmonizing the activity performance with environmental standards, so the fishing activity is compatible with sustainability criteria; for example, in the case of shrimp fishing activities, the developer has to comply with the existing environmental guidelines. Furthermore, when fish farming activities involve the introduction of parental specimens for the reproduction of exotic species that may affect ecosystems and wildlife, an environmental licence is required as provided for in Decree 2041/2014.

§4. Fishing Activities

527. In Colombia, fisheries are regulated by national conservation provisions and international agreements, which are implemented through the former Colombian

Institute of Rural Development (INCODER) resolutions. The main regulatory measures impacting this industry include the establishment of annual closed seasons on marine and continental fish resources, such as piranha, arapaima, shallow and deep-water prawns; regulation on fishing methods and techniques; the obligation to use turtle excluder devices and the prohibition to use marine turtles incidentally captured; the adoption of the International Program on Conservation and Protection of Dolphins of the Inter-American Tropical Tuna Commission; restrictions on ship's capacity for tuna fishing; establishment of maximum dolphins mortality rate; restrictions on the use of trawls in the first nautical mile; and zoning plans on the Pacific and Atlantic coastline for small-scale fishing areas; among other measures.

528. Notably, the fishing quota allocation to those people holding a valid permit for maritime fishing is made in accordance with the global quotas established for each ocean. For continental water, the quota is established according to the hydrological resources availability of Colombia. The Food and Agriculture Organization of the United Nations presents figures for fish resources for the Pacific and Atlantic Oceans. For example, Colombia has established the fishing quota in the Pacific Ocean for shallow and deep-water prawns, oceanic fish, medium and small pelagic fish and demersal fish; and for lobsters and shellfish in the Atlantic Ocean.

§5. Aquaculture

529. Aquaculture is legally defined as the cultivation of hydro-biological species by means of appropriate techniques in natural or artificial environments and under special control. In Colombia, aquaculture activities are subject to the obtaining of an aquaculture permit (Permiso de Cultivo). The permit is granted once the developer has provided information on the project's technical aspects and infrastructure, implemented a plan of environmental management, proposed a sound system of water management and established the aquatic organism to be farmed. Apart from permit requirements, the regulation on aquaculture focuses on the introduction of exotic species in the country, the use of fresh or saltwater, the implementation of clean and sustainable production systems, aquaculture for investigative purposes, water recovery, technical assistance, technology transfer and training. Some of the main regulatory measures impacting national aquaculture concern the regulation on red tilapia farming in artificial or natural environments of 1995; the establishment of permits and restrictions to freshwater and saltwater movements with exotic species, also of 1995; and the mandatory presentation of a sanitary certification for the import of shrimps, lobster, brine shrimp and polychaetes, in order to avoid transboundary disease transmission.

Chapter 7. Subsoil and Minerals

530. In the mining sector, coal has been the most important mineral, turning Colombia into the first coal producer in Latin America and the eleventh coal exporter worldwide.[50] Regarding oil and gas activities, the exploitation of these resources has guaranteed energy self-supply and has contributed to the national and regional economic growth through tax and royalty payments.

531. According to Constitution Articles 332, 360 and 361, the State is the owner of the subsoil and the non-renewable resources, without prejudice of pre-existing or acquired rights. The exploitation of non-renewable resources involves the payment of a royalty, in addition to other payments the State may impose. Departments and municipalities where exploitation activities take place, as well as the places where such resources are transported or delivered to, are entitled to participate in those royalties and compensations.

§1. Hydrocarbon Sector

532. The extraction of hydrocarbons is regulated in the Petroleum Code. The Code ratifies the State ownership over subsoil resources, especially on hydrocarbons, and regulates surface exploration, contracts of exploration and exploitation, procedure for area proposals and objections, notices of perforation and titles review, royalties, taxes on hydrocarbon resources of private property, transport, refineries and distribution, tax benefits and repayment, sanctions and contract revocation.

533. The hydrocarbon sector in Colombia is exposed to a series of ethnic, cultural, social and environmental problems. The main factors amounting to these problems include the dependency on fossil fuels, the fiscal benefits of the oil and gas industry, the energy demand from importer countries, and the rapid expansion of hydrocarbon exploitation. The ANH has pointed out the main environmental problems of the hydrocarbon sector: lack of planning strategies with respect to ecosystems; lack of guidelines on extraction activities in areas of high ecological, social and cultural susceptibility; the absence of reliable, updated and available environmental information; the current model of EIA does not accurately evaluate long-term impacts in certain areas; and the different environmental performance levels of each hydrocarbon operator. In spite of this problem, the ANH has proposed a socio-environmental policy aimed at achieving the sustainable exploitation of the resource, respect for the cultural values of the communities and contribution to social development.

534. The socio-environmental policy on hydrocarbons is guided by the principles of transparency, sustainability, participation, responsibility, legitimacy and

50. Asociación Colombiana de Petróleo, 'Sector Minero y Petrolero en Colombia', www.acp.com.co/assets/documents/asuntos%20economicos/exploracion%20y%20produccion/2010/doctecnico_prorroga_aranceles_2010.pdf, December 2010.

equity. The main objective is to conduct and structure hydrocarbon resource exploitation by fostering the participation and transparency of all interested parties. The specific objectives of the socio-environmental policy include the harmonization of sector plans with social, cultural and environmental national policies; incorporation of social and environmental criteria in the management of land occupation; strengthening of public participation mechanisms; promotion of transparent administration of oil revenues towards the contribution of social development, environmental protection and economic growth; implementation of Corporate Social Responsibility guidelines; research and innovation in environmental, social and cultural issues related to the oil and gas industry; consolidation of a contractual framework of the ANH; facilitation of the relationship between the oil industry and the environmental authorities.

535. Added to the aforementioned measures, Resolution 22/2013 establishes the requirements that oil tankers must comply with while navigating territorial waters. Ships transporting hydrocarbons in waters under the jurisdiction of the Colombian DIMAR must be provided with double hulls so as to prevent leaks or damages in the outer hull. The DIMAR will verify compliance with this requirement.

§2. Mining Sector

536. Mining production in Colombia is mainly focused on coal and precious metals. According to official reports, 2.5% of the total area of the country is engaged in mining activities. Although construction materials do not occupy a large surface of the mining areas, they represent almost 47% of the national mineral production. Additionally, the mining sector represents 27% of the national exports with a trend to grow in the near future. As a result of these circumstances, Colombia has developed legislation and has designed interesting investment vehicles towards the strengthening of the mining sector.

537. The institutional framework on mining activities in Colombia is led by the Ministry of Mines and Energy and its Directorate of Mines, which delegates the main powers on the mining sector to two entities: delegated departmental governments and the Colombian Geological Service (SGC). The SGC is in charge of the hiring, enforcement, royalty payment, promotion, cadastre and register of mining activities in Colombia. The basic procedure for carrying out mining activities includes the acknowledgement of receipt of all the necessary documentation; an assessment and further approval of the proposal; the signature, securitization and register of mining titles; enforcement; and payment collection and distribution.

538. The main piece of legislation on mining activities is the Mining Code adopted by Law 689/2001. The Mining Code regulates several matters, including the definition of the mining activity as a social and public activity, the allocation of equal rights and duties to foreign and national investors, the establishment of the mining contract phases and the regulation of the instruments that Mining Concession holders are provided with for ensuring their technical, economic and commercial autonomy in the development of their contracts. The developer of mining activities must have a signed contract, be registered with the Mining Register and undertake an environmental-mining insurance.

539. Regarding environmental protection, mining activities can be seen in two ways: those activities considered illegal and those executed under a mining concession and the corresponding environmental licence. Regarding the first group, the Constitutional Court has acknowledged that polluting activities produced by illegal mining can have direct impacts on people's health and, additionally, other indirect impacts on human well-being, such as the reduction of forest products that affect the food and medicinal balance, and can produce changes in the traditional practices, uses and customs of ethnic communities associated with biodiversity.[51] For the second group, authorized mining activities, they are requested to comply with environmental compromises during the whole concession term, from the initial contractual phase to the termination and abandonment phases. The inscription in the National Mining Register triggers the obligation to follow and comply with the environmental guide on mining for the technical exploration phase. Once the exploration phase has successfully concluded, the environmental performance of the project must regard the terms established in the environmental licence. Notably, the legislator wanted to simplify the procedures for obtaining an environmental licence in the mining sector, and created the global environmental licence, as regulated in Decree 2041/2014. The global environmental licence allows all developers to obtain all the necessary permits involving environmental aspects, as detailed in the EIA, in one single procedure. The environmental licence for mining activities is exclusively granted by the MASD.

I. Mining Activities in Paramo Ecosystems

540. Part of the responsibilities of the MASD include establishing rules and criteria for environmental land use and adjacent seas to ensure sustainable utilization of renewable natural resources and the environment. This involves regulating general conditions for environmental sanitation and the use, management, exploitation, conservation, restoration, and recovery of natural resources. Particularly, the MASD determines minimum environmental standards and general regulations applicable to, among others, mining activities.[52]

541. Law 685 of 2001 defines mining reconversion projects as those in which it is not possible to take advantage of the mining resource and, therefore, are redirected towards the labour reconversion of miners and the environmental and social readjustment of the areas of influence of the exploitations.[53] The Government's

51. Constitutional Court, Sentence T-622, 2016, Magistrate Jorge Iván Palacio.
52. Law 99 of 1993, Art. 5.
53. Law 685 of 2001, Art. 248, para. 2.

action in these projects is aimed at training miners on new economic activities, or complementary to mining activity, its financing and social management.

542. Given that the development of mining exploration and exploitation activities is not permitted in paramo ecosystems,[54] the Ministry of Mines and Energy, in coordination with environmental authorities and following guidelines from the MASD, must establish procedures for mining substitution projects that take place in paramo ecosystems, including the closure, dismantling, restoration, and reshaping of areas affected by mining activities. In addition, the Ministry of Mines and Energy is also responsible for designing, financing, and implementing programs for the conversion or relocation of traditional small-scale miners with mining titles and environmental authorizations.

543. To regulate mining substitution projects and labour conversion programs, the MASD issued Resolution 1468 of 2021 setting out environmental guidelines for the substitution programme involving the closure, dismantling, restoration, and reshaping of areas affected by mining activities, as well as the programme for conversion or relocation of labour within the páramo ecosystems. The guidelines shall inform the design, training, and implementation of both the substitution programme and the programme for the conversion or relocation of traditional small-scale miners as addressed in Articles 5 and 10 of Law 1930 of 2018.

544. Resolution 1468 of 2021 is structured under three chapters, setting out general guidelines, regulating substitution programs and regulating reconversion or relocation programs. General guidelines apply to both the substitution programme and the reconversion or relocation programme, and include principles such as articulation of resources, differential approach, public participation, guarantee of time and means, education and sensitization, monitoring and research and technical assistance. Regarding substitution programs involving the closure, dismantling, restoration and reshaping of areas intervened by mining activities within the delimited páramo ecosystems, Resolution 1468 of 2021 sets out criteria for the mine closure, risk and climate change analysis, stability and permanence of slopes and works, chemical stability of water and soils, maintenance and monitoring programme, the introduction of cleaner technologies and the restoration of ecosystems. Finally, Chapter 3 outlines the guidelines for the design, training and implementation of the reconversion or relocation programme of small traditional miners within the delimited páramo ecosystems, such as the promotion of associativity for productive inclusion, planning and participatory management, and promotion of viable and sustainable production systems.

54. Law 1930 of 2018, Art. 5.

Chapter 8. Genetic Resources

545. The regulation of genetic resources is grounded in the nation's Political Constitution, specifically in Article 81, which confers authority upon the State to oversee the entry, exit, and utilization of genetic resources in alignment with the country's national interest. The objectives of biodiversity conservation and equitable participation in benefits, endorsed by Law 165 of 1994, which approved the CBD, are explicitly detailed in this constitutional context.

546. These objectives include the conservation of biodiversity, aimed at protecting and preserving the variety of life on Earth; sustainable use of its components, in a way that maintains such components' long-term viability and benefits for the present and future generations; access to genetic resources, including those of plants, animals and microorganisms, for research, development and commercial purposes; transfer of appropriate technologies, with the aim to promote sustainable use and development; and fair and equitable participation in benefits.

547. The legal framework extends further with Decision 391 of 1996 from the Andean Community of Nations, establishing a Common Regime on Access to Genetic Resources. This decision complements the national constitutional provisions by regulating access to genetic resources and their derived products among member countries, ensuring confidentiality and protection against unfair commercial use.

548. Individuals, whether nationals or foreigners, natural or legal entities, intending to access genetic resources owned by the Colombian nation, along with their derived products or associated intangible components of native species, including viruses, and similar entities, must seek permission. This permission is formalized through a contract for access to genetic resources, as stipulated in the guidelines established by Resolution 1348 of 2014. For those uncertain about whether their activities constitute access to genetic resources and their derivatives, a concept request can be submitted to the MASD.

549. The requirement for a contract arises when undertaking activities involving native species, whether in the wild, domesticated, cultivated, or escaped from domestication, both within and outside the national territory. Activities triggering the need for a contract include the separation of functional and non-functional units of DNA and/or RNA in all their natural forms, the isolation of one or more molecules produced by the metabolism of an organism, and any endeavour seeking a patent for products or procedures derived from genetic resources or their products, as set forth in Andean Decision 486 of 2000.

550. According to Article 24 of Law 1437 of 2011, information safeguarded as a trade secret may be deemed confidential. Consequently, entities engaged in the application or execution of contracts for access to genetic resources have the option to request protection for such confidential information. As illustrated by Decision 313 of 2022 from the MASD, confidentiality is extended to all data and pertinent details concerning the specific objectives, materials, methods, methodology, use, technology, and outcomes of activities undertaken by Casaluker S.A., a food company. This confidentiality pertains specifically to their study of microbial communities associated with the cultivation and harvesting of cacao in Colombia.

Part III. Zoning and Land Use Planning

§1. Introduction

551. Colombia is a central republican State, territorially decentralized in thirty-two departments containing municipalities and districts, which represent the basic administrative unit of land, management and planning. Colombia develops the concept of territorial planning (*Ordenamiento Territorial)* that gathers the notions of zoning, land use planning, land management and land planning. Although zoning and land use planning receive a separate treatment in other jurisdictions, they will hereinafter be jointly referred to as 'territorial planning'. Territorial planning is defined as the spatial distribution of territory, geographical conditions, human settlements, political-administrative units and land use management, in a given country. The main aim of territorial planning is to harmonize territory, population and government by ensuring environmental sustainability, population development and administrative efficiency.

552. Environmental considerations have played a key role in territorial planning. The incorporation of environmental factors in zoning and land planning has been the result of a deep change in philosophical, political and social conceptions, which has taken almost four decades to become a reality, and still faces serious challenges. The consideration of the environment in territorial planning has been prompted by historic crises demanding effective solutions, such as urban migration, armed conflict in rural areas and uncontrolled city expansion. The adoption of environmentally sound criteria in territorial planning is regarded not only as an environmental protection and nature conservation imperative but also as a meaningful step in the redefinition of national development and social well-being.

553. Environmental considerations in modern territorial planning would not have been possible in Colombia without rethinking the right of property, and providing such right with social and ecological duties. The former Constitution of 1886 understood property as an absolute right, which enabled the owner to use, abuse and profit from its property without limitations. The introduction of socialist ideas in 1936 marked a change in the conception of the right to property in Colombia, yielding important notions such as not allowing the abusive usage of property and establishing the inherent social purpose of property, later enacted as constitutional amendments to the 1886 Constitution. At present, the 1991 Constitution consecrates the right of property, not as an absolute right, but as a right that implies social and ecologic duties, and hence, is to be exercised by taking into account factors that contribute to public well-being. These factors are evidenced in protected public interests like urban regulations, natural protected areas, cultural heritage and land-added value.

554. In this context, the aim of this part is to point out how environmental considerations shape territorial planning in Colombia. First, the main regulatory instruments will be chronologically analysed in order to understand the origins of land use planning and where Colombia's regulations stand on territorial planning. Second, the zoning powers of national and local authorities will be highlighted in order to establish the importance of environmental criteria in the harmonization of national and local regulations. Third, the legal framework on zoning and land use planning, including the urban permitting system, will be considered to illustrate how concrete environmental provisions work in conjunction with land planning and planning instruments. Finally, the main environmental challenges to the existing legislation will be highlighted.

§2. Main Territorial Planning Legislation

555. Legislation on territorial planning experienced a significant change with the adoption of the 1991 National Constitution. Before the 1991 Constitution, land planning was regulated by Law 9/1989 establishing the urban reform, and complemented by the general provisions of the NCRNR on land use. The enactment of the 1991 Constitution as well as the creation of the national environmental system in 1993 with Law 99/1993 triggered a thorough review process of the existing regulation on urban planning, which culminated in the adoption of Law 388/1997 on territorial planning, modified by Law 614/2000 and Law 2079/2021. The main legislation on territorial planning is thus contained in the NCRNR, Law 9/1989, the 1991 Constitution, Law 99/1993 and Law 388/1997.

556. The NCRNR regulates territorial planning by laying down general provisions on non-agricultural use of land. Articles 187–192 establish the manner under which planning for urban, housing and industrial land use, as well as airports, roads and railways, must be carried out. Specially, the NCRNR provides that urban planning must establish residential, civic, commercial, industrial and recreational sectors, as well as buffer and oxygen zones. Moreover, the NCRNR sets out the basic environmental considerations that urban planning must take into account, such as regulating construction and housing development programmes according to protection and restoration needs of environmental quality, giving priority to the zones with more problems. Bearing in mind that these considerations remain applicable, they will be further highlighted in the section on environmental law and territorial planning.

557. Before 1991, Law 9/1989 emerged as a regulatory solution to urbanization problems in Colombia, after a number of legislative initiatives were discarded along with their goal of tackling urban disorder and uncontrolled city expansion. With the 'right to a city' principle, Law 9/1989 regulated planning on municipal development, public space, real state acquisition by voluntary sale and by expropriation, protection to dwellers in urban renovation projects, social housing, urban licences and sanctions, banks of plots and adjustment of terrains, property confiscation on urban properties, and financial instruments to finance urbanization projects. Law 9/1989 required municipal land use plans to include zones of environmental interest and save areas for environmental protection. Law 9/1989 also provided for a group action in order to defend the essential elements of public space and the environment, established the setting of reserved zones for environmental and water resource protection as legal justifications for expropriation processes and created urban renovation projects as a means to avoid physical and environmental deterioration of urban centres. Law 388/1997 gathers these provisions and harmonizes them with the current regulation on territorial planning.

558. The 1991 Constitution introduces noteworthy transformations in the Colombian legal framework, with a marked impact on institutional, economic, social, political and environmental fields, and hence, on urban planning. The 1991 Constitution sets out the basis for the decentralization process and entrusts territorial entities (departments and municipalities) with the responsibility of developing their territories. Particularly, municipalities are expressly given the power to plan and administrate urban land and take care of the physical development of the cities. These powers were later ratified by Law 152/1994 on the Organic Law on Development Plans, stating that municipalities have to implement a Development Plan including the programmes and projects of the government and a Territorial Zoning Plan (*Plan de Ordenamiento Territorial – POT*). Notably, the enactment of the new Constitution led to an assessment of the constitutionality of legislation adopted prior to 1991, all of which evidenced the need to review Law 9/1989 on urban planning.

559. Law 99/1993 establishing the national environmental system introduces the concept of land environmental zoning and allocates responsibilities at national, regional and local levels on territorial planning. Article 7 of Law 99/1993 defines land environmental zoning as the power of the State to regulate and guide the design and planning process of the use of land and natural renewable resources, in order to ensure their sound exploitation and sustainable development. Concerning competences on territorial planning, Law 99/1993 appoints the MASD as the responsible authority at the national level for establishing environmental criteria for land use; preparing plans, projects and programmes on land environmental zoning; and issuing and updating the zoning regulation on the adequate use of land and river basins in the national territory. At the regional level, CARs are required to participate in land planning and zoning projects of their jurisdiction to ensure that environmental factors are taken into account in the decision-making process. Finally, Article 65 expressly empowers municipalities, districts and the Capital District of Bogota to establish, within the limits set out in laws, regulations or superior norms, the regulation on territorial planning and land use for the municipality or district.

§3. Government Powers on Zoning and Land Use Planning

560. Law 388/1997 distributes public powers on zoning and land use planning in four political-administrative levels: the national level, departments, metropolitan areas, and municipalities and districts. Essentially, the national governmental authority is responsible for the general policy on territorial planning in those matters involving national interests, such as national parks and protected areas, large infrastructure projects, areas for security and defence, etc. Departments are in charge of establishing parameters and guidelines for the zoning of the whole departmental territory or specific portions, with the purpose of creating opportunities for space use and occupation in accordance with environmental conditions, development objectives and biophysical limitations; defining policies on human settlements and urban centres pursuant to national policies; and integrating space distribution projects in sector, municipal and indigenous zoning plans. Metropolitan areas, which are not territorial entities pursuant to the 1991 Constitution but administrative entities composed of municipalities sharing economic, social or physical elements, are responsible for drafting integrated plans and establishing mandatory standards for municipalities in relation to shared metropolitan aspects. Municipalities and districts represent the main political-administrative unit of the Colombian decentralization system, provided that they are the closest governmental entities to citizens and can directly address citizens' concerns on land planning aspects. Municipalities and districts are responsible for drafting and adopting POTs for their territories, in accordance with Law 388/1997 and the Organic Law on Development Plans, Law 152/1994. In so doing, municipalities and districts have to regulate land use in urban, expansion and rural areas, enhance land use in available plots and coordinate sector plans, by harmonizing land use planning with national policies and departmental and metropolitan plans.

561. Article 7 of Law 388/1997 establishing the government powers on zoning and land use planning was challenged before the Constitutional Court. According to the arguments presented by the plaintiff in the lawsuit, the powers attributed to the departments on *defining the parameters and guidelines for the zoning of the whole territory or specific portions* violated the rights of indigenous people to participate in the zoning and land use planning decision-making process. The arguments supporting the lawsuit explained how the Constitution provides for a multicultural and multi-ethnic State where equal conditions must be granted to all its citizens. In addition, the powers of indigenous communities and territorial entities (departments, municipalities and districts) must be established by means of an organic law and not by an ordinary law, given that the organic law has a superior hierarchy and its legislative procedure involves more stages. Any attempt to establish zoning and land use plans in territories where indigenous communities dwell contravenes the constitutional provisions as indigenous communities are deprived of exercising their sovereign rights. The power of departments to establish parameters and guidelines for the zoning of a territory where indigenous communities may be settled contravenes the Constitution and therefore such power must be void.

562. The Constitutional Court conceded the argument of the plaintiff but grounded its ruling on a different basis. The Court held that a law for distributing and allocating land use in a certain territory has the highest relevance for citizens and their fundamental rights since such a decision-making process involves the development of the physical space of a certain territory, and therefore land use establishes the relationship between the population and its cultural and natural environment. In the view of the Court, a matter of such importance deserves to be regulated by a special law requiring a comprehensive legislative enactment procedure.

563. According to the Court, the distribution of powers is a subject that according to the Court's analysis of the 1991 Constitution must be regulated by an organic law and not by an ordinary one; thus, it has to undergo the legislative procedure of an organic law. Law 388/1997 went through the legislative procedure of an ordinary law and was adopted as such. The Court finds that the government power attribution of Article 7 of Law 388/1997 should have been done by a law of a superior hierarchy, such as the organic law; therefore, the regulation of zoning and land use competences via ordinary law is not compatible with the 1991 Constitution. Consequently, the Constitutional Court ruled the unconstitutionality of Article 7, voided its further application and removed it from the legal framework.

564. The aftermath of the Court's ruling has left two visible levels in zoning and land use planning in Colombia: the national level, and the municipalities and districts. Departments and metropolitan areas have been removed from the whole process.[55]

§4. Environmental Protection in Zoning and Land Use Planning

I. National Code of Renewable Natural Resources

565. The NCRNR is a key regulatory instrument in the configuration of zoning and land use planning from an environmental point of view. The NCRNR attempts to ensure a minimum environmental protection by laying down basic rules on urban planning. Urban planning conditions the housing construction and development projects to the existing needs on environmental quality protection and restoration, by giving special importance to certain factors, such as problematic zones; adequate localization of public services so the project operation does not harm the environment; the establishment of recreation places and their organization, so the environment remains healthy and friendly to the community; and appropriate regulation on the dimensions of plots and dwellings, and the number of people that can inhabit in urban zones.

566. Regarding polluting industries, the NCRNR establishes that special zones must be created for the settlement of industries that may cause environmental damage. The purpose of special zone creation is to avoid causing nuisance or harm to

55. Constitutional Court, Sentence No. 795 of 29 Nov. 2000, Magistrate Eduardo Cifuentes Muñoz.

neighbouring inhabitants and their activities. For the establishment of industrial zones, urban planners must take into account geographical aspects, wind direction, uncontrolled emissions and other characteristics of the environmental-media. Regarding the settlement of industries in rural areas, planners must take into account additional elements, including a prior research on the area to establish likely emissions, discharges or damages to human settlements, soil, water, air, fauna or flora. Industries located in other-purpose areas, such as residential or silent areas, have to move to the zone established for industrial purposes and adopt all the necessary measures to avoid causing nuisance to the neighbours.

II. Law 388 of 1997

567. Law 388/1997 incorporates environmental protection from its very objective, as it aims to articulate urban planning and land use with the ecological heritage of the municipality or district. Municipal land or territorial planning refers to an agreed set of political, administrative and physical planning measures that seek to guide the development of a territory and regulate the use, transformation and occupation of the municipal space. This process must be carried out within the limits of the Constitution and in accordance with the strategies that the municipality may establish on socio-economic development, the environment and historic and cultural traditions. Municipal territorial zoning must also serve as a means of integration among economic planning, social planning, land use considerations and reasonable regulatory intervention, towards the sustained development and use of the specific area (municipality or district). Notably, the definition of strategies on land use, occupation and management in municipal territorial planning must be done so as to fulfil economic, social, urban and environmental objectives.

A. *Urban Action (Acción Urbanística)*

568. Urban action is the actual tool that municipalities and districts are provided with to exercise powers on territorial planning. Urban action includes the power to establish: zoning in urban, rural and urban expansion land; the sitting and characteristics of infrastructure projects for transport, public services, solid and hazardous waste treatment and disposal facilities, and services of public interest, such as airports, schools and hospitals; zoning and sitting of production centres, residential areas and other activities, and the definition of specific land uses, land use intensity, mandatory transfers, occupation percentages, types and uses of buildings, and other urban provisions; free spaces for parks and public green areas; areas entailing risks for human settlements that have no aptitude for urban projects; social housing construction projects; and the expropriation of real state declared properties of social interest or public utility. Urban action includes the power to establish and locate critical areas of recovery and control for disaster prevention, as well as areas for landscape conservation and recovery; and the identification and characterization of ecosystems with environmental importance for the municipality/district. These actions are to be carried out in coordination with the environmental authority for their environmentally sound management and protection.

B. Conditions in POTs

569. Law 388/1997 creates 'conditions' (determinants) of POTs as a way to ensure that local plans obey pre-established legal parameters. Law 388/1997 states that POT conditions have a higher hierarchical legal standing than municipal or district zoning plans, and therefore the conditions established in Law 388/1997 must be fulfilled and included in municipal and district POTs. The four zoning plans' conditions established in Law 388/1997 include those related to environmental conservation and protection; policies, guidelines and regulations on the conservation, preservation and use of the cultural heritage of the nation; the establishment and sitting of basic infrastructures for national and regional roads, harbours, airports, drinking water and sanitation services, and energy supply; and the components included in POTs of metropolitan areas.

570. The first zoning plan condition is the one involving environmental conservation and protection, natural resources, disaster and natural risk prevention. This condition covers four aspects that every territorial plan must refer to and comply with. First, local plans must follow the guidelines, provisions and regulations adopted by the entities of the national environmental system on aspects related to zoning and land use planning: especially, the provisions of Law 99/1993 and the NCRNR regarding zoning environmental aspects. Second, POTs must regard and respect: regulations on the environment and renewable natural resources use, conservation, preservation and management in marine and coastal zones; regulations adopted by the CARs or the corresponding environmental authority on the establishment and reservation of Districts of Integrated Management, Districts of Soil Conservation, Forest Areas, Regional Nature Parks; provisions on the management of river basins; and regulations for the conservation of areas of eco-systemic importance. Third, local plans must be drafted under the limits of the national system of nature parks and national forest reserve regulations. Finally, the fourth aspect covered under the condition of environmental conservation and protection consists of the policies, guidelines and regulations on the prevention of natural risks, the establishment and setting up of high-risk areas for human settlements, as well as management strategies for zones exposed to threats and natural risks. In this context, municipalities and districts must ensure that the environmental condition of zoning plans is fully inserted in their local zoning plans (*Planes de Ordenamiento Territorial – POT*); otherwise, the POT is deemed unlawful.

571. Furthermore, Law 388/1997 establishes an additional layer of protection for environmental and natural resources. According to Article 11, the POTs must have a general, urban and rural component. The general component is composed of the objectives, strategies and contents for the long term. The urban component is integrated by policies, actions, programmes and provisions to channelize and administrate urban physical development. The rural component concerns the policies, actions, programmes and standards that guarantee the appropriate interaction between rural settlements with the municipality, as well as the adequate use of land. Notably, the three components of the POT deal on some scale with environmental issues.

572. The Final Peace Agreement between the National Government and the FARC-EP of 2016 defined in point 1.1.10 the formulation of an Environmental Zoning Plan with the '*purpose of delimiting the agricultural frontier, protecting areas of special environmental interest and generating for the population that borders or occupies them, balanced alternatives between the environment and well-being and good living under the principles of Participation of Rural Communities and Sustainable Development*'.[56] To this end, point 1.1.10 established that the Environmental Zoning Plan delimits the agricultural frontier and allows updating and, if necessary, expanding the inventory, and characterizing the use of areas that must have special environmental management, such as: forest reserve areas, areas of high biodiversity, fragile and strategic ecosystems, watersheds, moors and wetlands and other water sources and resources, with a view to protecting biodiversity and the population's progressive right to water, promoting its rational use.

573. In compliance with this mandate, the MASD issued Resolution 1608 of 2021 adopting the Environmental Zoning Plan derived from the Final Peace Agreement, within the framework established by Decree Law 902 of 2017, Decree 893 of 2017, the Implementation Framework Plan – PMI (CONPES 3932 of 2018), the National Development Plan – PND 2018 -2022 and the 'Peace with Legality' Policy.

574. The Environmental Zoning Plan responds to three purposes: (i) the closure or stabilization of the agricultural frontier; (ii) the effective protection of Areas of Special Environmental Interest – AEIA; and (iii) the orientation of balanced alternatives between conservation and good living for the communities that live in and/or that border AEIA.

575. The Environmental Zoning Plan is formulated for the 16 subregions and 170 municipalities prioritized by the Development Programs with a Territorial Focus – PDET for the implementation of the National Sectoral Plans – PNS (CONPES 3932 of 2018) and the Action Plans for Regional Transformation – PATR for Comprehensive Rural Reform (Decree 893 of 2017). It contains an Indicative Environmental Zoning of the territory and establishes a Strategic Framework and an Action Plan to harmonize and guide the programs, plans and actions for the sustainable development of the subregions and municipalities of PDET. The environmental management of the PDET subregions must close the agricultural frontier, and stabilize its expansion over forest reserve areas, protected areas and strategic ecosystems, both Amazonian, Pacific, Andean and Caribbean.

56. Government of Colombia, 2016.

Part IV. Liability Questions

§1. Introduction

576. The adoption of the 1991 Constitution has raised awareness about environmental rights protection and the legal response to their violation. The three branches of power have contributed to the notion of environmental liability. Particularly, the executive power has used regulatory and enforcement instruments to act on environmental infractions and their consequences. In turn, the courts have rendered binding opinions on how the application of a certain type of liability encompasses specific conducts affecting the environment. Lawmakers have worked on legislative mechanisms to answer the questions emerging from environmental damages and the breach of environmental provisions.

577. Colombia has adopted the 'polluter-pays' principle to ensure the polluter internalizes the costs of the environmental damage it has caused or the risks it has posed to the environment. The establishment of environmental liability regimes based on the polluter-pays principle promotes the prevention of environmental damages and the internalization of environmental costs. In this context, three systems of environmental liability can be distinguished in Colombia: administrative, civil and criminal.

578. This part discusses substantive rules on liability for environmental matters. First, administrative liability will be analysed as it has developed significantly in recent years and has helped build the notion of environmental liability in Colombia. Second, special attention will be given to criminal liability for environmental damage, given the high impact it has had on individuals as well as companies. Finally, this part will deal with civil liability, also known as private law liability or tort law. This work does not intend to study in depth each system and the numerous issues they cover, but to illustrate the purpose of each system, how they tackle environmental damage and how, if at all, they accomplish the goals of the Colombian State on environmental matters.

§2. Administrative Liability

579. Administrative liability on environmental matters can be seen from two different perspectives: citizens breaching environmental provisions or causing environmental damage and environmental damage caused by the actions or omissions of the government. The first part of this chapter, hence, will be devoted to analysing the relationship between citizens and the government whenever an environmental provision has been infringed or an environmental damage caused. The second part will then illustrate how the government may be held liable for the direct or indirect cause of environmental damages. It is important to note that, while the former liability regime has been thoroughly and recently developed through regulatory instruments, the latter one has emerged from case law and jurisprudence of the Council of the State and the Constitutional Court.

I. Administrative Liability of Citizens for Environmental Damage

580. In general, administrative liability refers to the power of the State to sanction offenders of environmental laws and perpetrators of environmental damages. Administrative liability is triggered when an environmental law, standard or regulation is breached, and the authority sanctions the offender for its wrongful action or omission. The sanction involves the duty to repair the wrongdoing, carry out the applicable prevention and mitigation measures, and meet the corresponding costs. Administrative liability elaborates on the polluter-pays principle evidenced in the cost internalization that this liability system seeks to achieve through the imposition of sanctions and preventive measures on offenders. Administrative sanctions on environmental matters are mainly regulated in Law 1333/2009 and the specific pieces of legislation concerning infringements of specific matters, like the illegal introduction of hazardous waste in the territory.

581. In order to have a full picture of the manner in which administrative liability responds to pollution issues and prevents environmental degradation, this section will now analyse the regulatory evolution of administrative liability. The analysis includes the definition of the different elements constituting this liability system, administrative sanctions, the powers of environmental authorities, parallel administrative enforcement measures and the legal challenges set up by the application of administrative liability.

A. *Regulatory Structure*

582. The 1991 Constitution granted the public authorities enforcement powers to achieve the ends of the Colombian State and the full protection of constitutional rights. Regarding the environment, Article 80 established the duty of the State to plan the use and management of natural resources, as well as to prevent and control pollution factors. For such purpose, authorities were provided with the powers to impose sanctions and demand the reparation of environmental damages from offenders. These powers are exercised through disciplinary measures, which are intended to punish the conduct of officers and citizens for the breach of their duties, obligations and prohibitions. Likewise, the powers of governmental authorities are developed through corrective measures, which seek to sanction the infractions of citizens with respect to violations of regulations, orders, obligations or limitations established by Law. The punitive instruments that authorities are provided with are limited by the principles established in Law 99/1993 and by constitutional rights, especially by the right to due process.

583. Administrative sanctions for environmental liability are contained in Law 1333/2009. In addition, Law 23/1973 provides general criteria on administrative liability for the State and the citizens. According to Article 16, the State is responsible for the damages to mankind or to privately owned natural resources caused by State acts generating contamination or deterioration of the environment. Likewise, citizens are accountable for contamination or deterioration of the environment and for the damage or inadequate use of natural resources. In both cases, the elements of administrative liability must be demonstrated: wrongful conduct, damage and the causal link between them. These elements will be analysed in the following section.

B. Elements of Administrative Liability System

1. Environmental Infraction

584. According to Law 1333/2009, environmental infractions consist of breaching any environmental duty established in the law, regulation or permit, and causing damage to the environment. Some examples of environmental infractions include causing harm to the environment, natural resources or landscape, or putting such elements at risk; breaching the conditions of an environmental permit, concession or authorization; constructing or operating projects without authorization; and obtaining wild or exotic species, and products or by-products of fauna or flora without a permit. The administrative liability system draws from civil law to establish the elements that configure liability for damages.

585. For example, in Decision 246 of 2022, the MASD undertook an environmental sanctioning procedure, prompted by a resolution from the Regional Autonomous Corporation of Valle del Cauca (CVC). The resolution imposed a preventive measure of activity suspension due to identified environmental violations in a specific area. The violations included carrying out earthwork of approximately 1,600 m^2 in the village of El Remolino, Calima el Darién Municipality, Valle del Cauca, without the required environmental permits, and making interventions that altered the land use in a Pacific Forest Reserve without the proper subtraction procedure. These infractions were discovered during an inspection visit on 23 January 2022, leading to the suspension of activities and the initiation of the environmental sanctioning procedure. The findings, including the presence of machinery and excavated areas without permits, served as crucial evidence for the regulatory actions taken.

586. Under the Colombian Civil Code, damages must be certain and personal in order to be fully indemnified. These two characteristics of civil damage appear not to be compatible with the nature and specificities of environmental damage. First, the scientific uncertainty on the causes and effects of contamination hinders the proof of environmental damage as they vary in intensity and immediateness.

Although it is possible to establish the origins and consequences of polluting acts, their magnitude and short-term or long-term impact remain uncertain. Unlike civil damages, environmental damage assessment involves considering the human being in its relationship with all the elements of the ecosystem, providing the environment itself with rights that may be claimed regardless of the consequences that polluting acts may have on human beings or their properties.

587. Second, the personal notion of civil damages seems not to fit with the collective and diffuse character of environmental damages. While civil law looks at the personal interest of the presumed right holders, environmental damage involves several unknown victims, as well as many polluters. The notion of environmental damage enables the community as a whole to claim the protection of collective rights and to ask for damage compensation, under the administrative liability system. The latter implies the abandonment of the traditional notion of damage in civil law, towards a more comprehensive notion that takes into account the relationship between man and his surroundings.

588. Article 42 of Law 99/1993 defines environmental damage as 'the one affecting the normal running of ecosystems or the renewability of their resources and compounds'. According to the doctrine, the definition contained in Article 42 reflects a broad and pure understanding of environmental damage, as the concept applies not only to the particular repercussions it may have on individual rights but also to the actual deterioration it causes to environmental services. In this context, the compensation for environmental damages must involve the whole affected community and its relationship with the environment.

2. Causation

589. One of the challenges facing the law is to establish if environmental damage can be fully attributed to a specific polluter. The link between the conduct and the harmful effect, referred to as causation, exhibits some problems of proof and accuracy due to the nature of environmental damages, as contamination episodes are caused not only by one polluter but also by the collective action of different agents operating in the area of contamination. In Colombia, the Superior Tribunal of Judicial District has acknowledged this difficulty when ruled over a case of contamination due to the inadequate establishment of a landfill, by illustrating that environmental damages suffered by the community were due to not only the landfill but also unpaved streets, and the existence of brick and asphalt manufacture facilities in the vicinity, among other factors.[57] Additionally, environmental damages are often not easily attributed to one or another agent, due to the distance from the source of contamination to the place where damages occur, and the time they may take to evidence themselves.

57. Superior Tribunal of Judicial District, Sentence of 15 Sep. 2004, Civil Section, Magistrate Pedro Pablo Torres Beltrán.

590. Law 1333/09 establishes strict liability for environmental infractions, which can be reflected in the burden of proof and the available defence mechanisms; yet, it does not provide for joint liability in contamination cases with multiple polluters. Furthermore, the Constitutional Court has denied pleadings based on the failure of plaintiffs to demonstrate who is actually responsible for the contamination, and at the same time, the Court has opened the possibility of challenging operators for environmental damage, even though they have been granted different licences and authorizations. In spite of these circumstances, judges and academics have tried to ease the rigid link between damage and conduct, by elaborating on different causation theories and by construing operators' joint environmental liability on a different basis. Regardless of the causation theory that the judge or governmental authority decides to adopt, in Colombia, the causal link must be duly demonstrated so that the authority can establish that the operation or execution of a certain activity, project or work caused environmental damage, and therefore can impose the sanction.

3. Conduct

591. Under administrative liability, the fault of the alleged offender is presumed. The offender has the burden of proof and demonstrates he has not committed the infraction. Regardless of whether the offender acted diligently or safely, as long as there is an environmental infraction derived from the conduct, operation or omission of the offender, the offender will be held liable. The Constitutional Court has backed the constitutionality of Article 1 of Law 1333/2009 establishing strict liability for environmental infractions.

592. Certainly, the balance between the constitutional right to due process and a strict liability system has brought along doubts about the constitutionality of Article 1 Law 1333/09. According to the charges against Article 1, the exercise of punishing powers must be done by observing all the guarantees of due process so that the presumed offender can defend himself against the enforcement powers of the State, and the public and private burdens remain fairly balanced.[58] In Colombia, due process principles include the express establishment of government punishing powers in the law, the observance of the presumption of innocence principle, the express establishment of unlawful conduct and the corresponding sanction in the law, non-retroactivity and proportionality of the sanction. The establishment of a strict liability system for environmental matters, reflected in the presumption of environmental offenders' fault and the burden of proof, appears not to be compatible with the rights and principles of the Constitution.

593. The Constitutional Court has settled the matter and reaffirmed the constitutionality of Article 1 Law 1333/2009. According to the Court, the sanctioning powers of the authorities seek to guarantee the operation of the public administration, achieve the ends of the State and prosecute the breach of duties, orders and

58. Constitutional Court, Sentence No. T-1263 of 29 Nov. 2001, Magistrate Jaime Córdoba Triviño.

obligations. The preventive nature of administrative sanctions and the aims that guide this liability system differ from the ones supporting criminal liability, and hence, the constitutional right to due process must be applied under different parameters. This does not mean that environmental liability admits the violation of the due process, for Law 1333/2009 establishes a clear, expedited and protective procedure that enables defendants to destroy the presumption of fault. According to the Court, the importance of environmental values in the Constitution reflected in fundamental rights, collective rights and constitutional duties is such that the procedural mechanisms to protect these values must allow their efficient and effective protection. Presuming the fault of an alleged offender does not prevent him from exercising all the available defence mechanisms and bringing the necessary evidence; rather, it switches the burden of proof and frees the State from demonstrating the offender's fault. The State must still demonstrate the occurrence of an environmental infraction or damage.[59]

C. *Preventive Measures and Sanctions*

594. According to Law 1333/2009, preventive measures seek to prevent, impede or avoid any fact, conduct or activity harming the environment, natural resources, landscape or human health. Preventive measures include: written warnings; preventive confiscation of resources, products, equipment, etc., used to infringe environmental law; confiscation of fauna and flora products or specimens; and, temporary cancellation of the project or activity when it might generate damage to the environment, natural resources, landscape or human health. The procedure to impose preventive measures is set forth in Title III of Law No. 1333/2009. Furthermore, environmental sanctions seek to prevent, correct or compensate for environmental infractions, by ensuring the effectiveness of constitutional principles, international treaties, law and regulations. Depending on the seriousness of the infraction, the following sanctions can be imposed on the offender: daily fines up to 5,000 monthly minimum wages; temporary or permanent closure of the facility; cancellation of the environmental licence; demolition of the whole project; confiscation of the resources, products, equipment, etc., used to infringe the environmental law; restitution of fauna and flora specimens; and community work.

II. Administrative Liability of the State for Environmental Damage

A. *State Liability*

595. The Constitution of 1991 consecrated the basis on which the Colombian State may be held liable for damages. Article 90 makes the State responsible for the actions or omissions of its public authorities when these conducts result in damages. Three elements must be demonstrated in order to make the State responsible

59. Constitutional Court, Sentence No. C-595 of 27 Jul. 2010, Magistrate Jorge Iván Palacio.

for the occurrence of damages and their corresponding compensation: an unlawful damage; that such damage has been caused by the action or omission of the public authority; and that such damage is imputed to the State. Bearing in mind that State liability derives directly from the Constitution, the elements of such liability have been largely developed in the jurisprudence of the Constitutional Court and the Council of State.

596. The first element of State liability is unlawful damage. Adopting the Spanish theory of unlawful damage, the constitutionalists of 1991 understood unlawful damage as that sort of damage that lacks a valid legal justification and breaks the public burdens that citizens have to bear when living in society. Therefore, the State cannot be held liable for any type of damage, but for unlawful damages. The question of when the citizen is to bear damage caused by the State has been analysed by the Colombian doctrine, explaining that damages are justified, and thus lawful, under two circumstances: when there is a cause that obliges the citizen to suffer damages, such as legitimate defence, victim's consent or when the affected values are not legitimately protected interests; and, when such damage does not distort the balance of the common burdens that imply living in society.[60]

597. Second, the occurrence of unlawful damages must be linked with the actions or omissions of the State. This element seeks to establish whether the action or omission of the public authority has triggered damages. At this point, the Council of State has ruled that in order to establish the causal link, it must be assessed whether the public authority has the legal obligation to act or proceed in a certain manner. If the public authority had failed to act when it had the obligation to do so, the judge will analyse the third element of State liability: the capacity to be imputable to the State.

598. Accountability is the element of liability that attributes causation of the damage to the State and therefore makes the latter responsible for its compensation. The high court's jurisprudence has largely discussed the factors under which an unlawful damage may be attributed to the State, including service failure, exceptional risk, distortion of public burdens and special damage. If any of these latter factors is demonstrated, the State will be held liable, and therefore, will have to pay damages.

B. State Liability for Environmental Matters

599. State liability for environmental matters can be studied under three circumstances: the State causing damage to the environment; the State allowing contamination from third parties; and the State causing transboundary environmental damage. This analysis departs from a description of regulatory instruments to

60. Palacio, Bermúdez Muñoz, *Responsabilidad de los jueces y del estado* (Bogotá: Librería del Profesional, 1998), 109 and 110.

review State liability on environmental matters.[61] The study of any of the three circumstances mentioned above requires a systematic interpretation of the underpinning principles of State liability and its three elements, as established in Article 90 of the 1991 Constitution. With respect to international environmental liability, this work will focus on the main issues impacting Colombia's international obligations on environmental protection, and the cases the State faces for transboundary pollution.

1. Damage Caused by the State

600. As already discussed in the previous section of this part, Law 23/1973 establishes the polluter's liability regardless if the polluter is the State or the citizens. The causation of environmental damage by the State triggers environmental liability and the consequent duty to fully repair it. In this case, the State is a victim of environmental damage as the first owner of national natural resources, but it is also responsible for guaranteeing the right of citizens to enjoy a pollution-free and healthy environment. The restoration of natural resources and the environment indeed concerns the whole population and the appropriate conditions to make life possible in the national territory. For that reason, the State must proceed to repair, when possible, or pay for damages it has caused to the environment.

2. Damage Caused by Third Parties

601. The second circumstance triggering State liability for environmental matters occurs when the State allows environmental pollution from third parties. In this case, the application of Law 23/1973 does not fit the purpose of internalizing pollution costs or making the actual polluter responsible for environmental damage since the State cannot be liable for every damage caused by third parties. In the absence of a regulatory instrument establishing State liability for allowing contamination, the source of this liability is to be found in Article 90 of the Constitution. As explained above, State liability requires three main elements to be demonstrated: unlawful damage, the relationship between the conduct of the State and the damage, and a legal provision attributing such liability to the State. According to case law, the State is responsible for allowing third parties' pollution in two circumstances: service failure and exceptional risk.

602. The State is responsible when a failure in service is demonstrated, meaning that the State service was not provided, was provided in an inappropriate way or was provided too late. Service failure takes place when the State deliberately knows about harmful actions leading to damages and does not take measures to counter such harmful actions. Under this approach, the State could be held liable when it knowingly allows the operation of polluting activities. For example, when the State

61. Juan Carlos Henao, 'Responsabilidad del Estado Colombiano por Daño Ambiental', www.mamacoca.org/FSMT_sept_2003/es/doc/henao_responsabilidad_ambiental_es.htm, September 2003.

knows the existence of water courses posing flood or contamination risks to neighbouring dwellers and does not take any action to counter likely water pollution, or when the State does not take any precautions knowing guerrilla's plans to attack the population, the State is liable for those damages. The failure in service operates when the State has the chance to know the causation of damage in advance and does not use its enforcement and judicial powers to avoid such damage.

603. Exceptional risk is the second concept that makes the State accountable for allowing pollution. The exceptional risk theory comes from a case where a terrorist attack is committed against the military and it results in the death of an occasional pedestrian. Under this theory, the State is responsible for the commission of terrorist attacks against publicly exposed people or national institutions resulting in damages to third parties, like the occasional pedestrian, provided that an exceptional risk has been created to citizens and thus, the balance of public burdens that citizens shall bear has been broken. The use of this theory in environmental damages opens the possibility of condemning the State for the creation of exceptional risks of contamination, such as the execution of public works or nuisance.

3. Transboundary Pollution

604. The State may be internationally responsible for causing environmental damages itself, or for allowing the use of its territory to cause damage. Certainly, the two scenarios described above involve an international element that needs to be studied under the applicable treaties and international legislation, which exceeds the boundaries of the present work. However, given the importance that this has to environmental law in Colombia, this section will deal with the case of aerial herbicide spraying, whereby the Republic of Ecuador seeks to obtain damage compensation from the Colombian State for transboundary pollution.

605. On 31 March 2008, Ecuador instituted proceedings against Colombia before the ICJ concerning *Colombia's aerial spraying of toxic herbicides at locations near, at and across its border with Ecuador* which *has already caused serious damage to people, crops, animals, and the natural environment on the Ecuadorian side of the frontier.*[62] Ecuador opposes the Colombian aerial spraying programme given the harmful effects on Ecuadorian people and the environment. In recent years, Colombia has emphasized the aerial spraying programme as a necessary means for meeting its illicit crop eradication targets, as it constitutes an issue of national security. In spite of Ecuadorian protests, Colombia has offered to pay damages to Ecuadorian citizens affected by the glyphosate aspersion according to Colombian laws, increasing manual eradication of illicit crops, or negotiating a 10-kilometre strip for no herbicide spraying under well-detailed conditions. Since Ecuador grounds its pleadings on State liability and the breach of the precautionary principle, the ICJ will have to consider principles of international environmental law in order to weigh up the national interests of both countries.

62. International Court of Justice. Order of 30 May 2008. Case Concerning Aerial Herbicide Spraying.

§3. CIVIL LIABILITY

606. Colombia follows the Roman-Germanic law or continental law, evidenced in the Civil Code, which provides the legal basis to make individuals and companies accountable under civil law. This chapter will present the features of civil liability for environmental damage by reviewing the civil liability system in Colombia and the application of the civil liability principles to environmental pollution.

I. Civil Liability in Colombia

607. Traditionally, Colombian jurisprudence and authors have distinguished two sources of civil liability: contractual and extra-contractual liability. Contractual liability arises whenever a contractual provision or a rule coming from an agreement is breached. In this case, the contract is the source of liability that obliges the infringer to compensate the other contractor for damages. The breach of contractual provisions consists of not complying with the obligations agreed in the contract, wrong compliance or late compliance. According to some authors, there could be a third system of civil liability named pre-contractual liability, for those damages that are caused within the negotiations prior to the contract. In this respect, the Colombian Commercial Code sets forth the rules on offers and binding proposals, the requirements negotiators shall meet and the consequences of not behaving in good faith when making negotiations before the contract. Any other source of liability leading to damage compensation is covered by extra-contractual liability.

608. In Colombia, extra-contractual liability emerges from an act that injures someone and allows the injured person to claim damages. Extra-contractual liability, also known as civil tort, requires that the negligent or intentional tort results in damage triggering the obligation to compensate for such damage. The source of the obligation to repair or compensate damages, hence, is the wrongful act that results in damage. Likewise, the same tort can give rise to criminal and civil liability, in which case, the civil judge and the criminal judge will establish the applicable penalties according to each system, and will ensure that overlapping rules do not violate wrongdoers' rights to due process.

609. The aim of extra-contractual liability is the economic reparation of damages. Civil liability for tort does not seek to sanction the offender, but to make him responsible for the economic costs of the damage and ensure compensation for the victim. The victim has to demonstrate the existence of three elements: damage, tort and cause link. Damage, understood as the loss suffered by the victim, must be direct, certain and existing at the time of the lawsuit. Tort, referred to as the act that resulted in the victim's damage, is the objective or subjective factor triggering the illicit act, either intentionally or negligently. Finally, causation is defined as the causal relationship between the tort and the damage.

610. Notably, the physical nature of the damage will determine the subsystem of liability under which the wrongdoer will be judged, and the defence arguments the defendant will be enabled to bring up. Some authors refer to this classification as simple and complex liability. Simple liability is the one where the damage is caused by the actions of the wrongdoer itself, whereas complex liability is the one where the damage is external to the wrongdoer, such as in the performance of dangerous activities, the possession of animals or the employer for its employees.

611. The first subsystem of extra-contractual liability is known as subjective liability, while the second one is known as objective or strict liability. The main differences of each subsystem are evidenced in the aspects that the judge analyses when establishing the wrongdoer's liability, such as the standard of care or the activity risk; the available defence mechanisms, like the victim's consent or the duty of care; and the burden of proof.

612. Subjective liability is regulated in the Civil Code in Article 2341, establishing that the one who has caused damage to another must indemnify him, without prejudice to the penalty that other laws may establish. Subjective liability looks at the conduct of the wrongdoer by assessing how diligent or prudent the wrongdoer was supposed to be in relation to the standard of care. Accordingly, the defendant can prove he acted diligently and carefully by fulfilling the duty of care, which will break the fault presumption of his behaviour and thus will destroy one of the civil liability elements. This subsystem of liability requires the victim to prove the breach of the duty of care, by negligence or intentional tort, the damage and the causation link.

613. Liability for the facts of third parties' facts is known as indirect liability or vicarious liability and seeks to make a person liable for the damage caused by another, pursuant to Articles 2347 and 2349. Indirect liability emerges from a legal relationship between the actual responsible for the damage and the person or entity who is actually responsible for damage compensation. The legal relationship involves an individual or company who, according to law, is responsible for the acts of another person, such as employer and employee, parent and child, tutor and pupil. Therefore, the law establishes a duty of care for the responsible person and presumes his fault when the person under his surveillance or care has directly caused harm.

614. Finally, objective or strict liability creates a fault presumption on those carrying out dangerous activities. As regulated in Article 2356 of the Civil Code, liability for dangerous activities occurs for the performance of legal activities that pose risks of such nature that the causation of damage is imminent. In this case, the victim only has to prove the damage, the risky activity of the operator, and the causal link between the damage and the activity. The defendant could only argue as exculpatory factors the exclusive fault of the victim, exclusive fact of a third party and force majeure. In order to accurately establish who is liable, the judge will establish whether the activity causing damage was risky or not, and who was profiting from such activity.

II. Civil Liability Applied to Environmental Matters

615. Having reviewed the regulation of civil liability in Colombia, the elements integrating this system, and the subsystems that jurisprudence and authors have created, it is worth studying how this liability system can be applied in environmental matters. Certainly, the traditional categories of civil liability and more specifically tort liability find conceptual obstacles when trying to provide legal solutions to environmental pollution. This complexity encourages civil law to resort to environmental law tools and definitions so that judges are not trapped in rigid concepts that may hinder meaningful rulings. This section, then, will study the cases where civil liability for environmental damage arises, and the actual tools that judges have at hand to rule such cases.

616. Colombian jurisprudence and academics have identified two classes of environmental damage: pure environmental damage and consecutive environmental damage: the first one, protected by administrative and criminal law, is that kind of damage that affects the community as a whole, and, therefore, the State has to intervene using its enforcement powers to protect citizens' rights and achieve the ends of the State. The second type, consecutive environmental damage, is harm that affects the individual interests of citizens. The case where this difference was made concerns a contaminated lake, where the State sanctioned the lake polluter and required him to adopt compensatory measures, while the fisherman who had suffered economic loss sued the polluter for civil damage to protect their economic interests affected by the pollution of the lake. The sphere of protection where civil liability takes place is, therefore, the one where consecutive environmental damage occurs, in other words, to protect individual interests affected by pollution.

617. Civil liability for environmental damage enables natural and legal persons to seek damage compensation from the polluter. The substantive and procedural rules of this action are in the Civil Code, as explained above, and require the three elements of strict liability to be demonstrated: damage, conduct and causation. However, environmental damage hardly fulfils the certainty, actuality and damage criteria required by the Civil Code on damages; and the causal link becomes even harder to prove given the multiple actors involved in contamination episodes.

§4. Criminal Liability

I. Introduction

618. Colombia has a system of criminal liability for environmental matters established in the Penal Code of 2000. Criminal liability is regulated in the Penal Code in two parts, the general one, which provides for the elements of a crime and the incrimination modalities, and the specific part, which deals with every type of crime. To establish the applicability of criminal liability in environmental protection, this section will analyse the basic notions of criminal law, how they are applied to environmental matters, and the types of conduct considered environmental crimes.

II. General Part

619. The application of criminal law to environmental crimes is seen in Colombia as an additional layer of environmental protection. Criminal liability for environmental damage helps bridge the gaps of administrative environmental liability and prevents others from committing crimes against ecology. Criminal law seeks to protect the goods and interests established in the Constitution, which make life in society possible. Certainly, criminal law does not sanction any violation of the Constitution, but it does seek to ensure the maintenance and respect of the rules guaranteeing the expectations and conditions of society, like a pollution-free environment. In this context, criminal law emerges as a guarantor of a healthy environment that allows the very existence of society by punishing ecological or environmental crimes. It is important to mention that the terms 'ecological' and 'environmental crimes' are used in Colombian legislation indistinctively.

620. Pursuant to the Penal Code, wrongful conducts are deemed crimes whenever they are previously established in the law, harm or threaten a protected interest, and are imputable to the offender. The crime is therefore composed of a factual description and a consequence so that all the crime elements are expressly established in the crime description. In Colombia, environmental crimes involve the breach of an administrative rule which results in the penalization of the conduct. Criminal liability is the *ultima ratio* of an environmental liability system that responds to different levels of environmental protection, and which leaves the last protection layer to those conducts that entail serious offences to the environment and therefore require stricter sanctions. The manner in which the system is structured, though, opens the possibility of applying two sanctions to the same conduct, administrative and criminal. This possibility sets academic and practical questions on the breach of the constitutional principle of *non bis in idem.*

621. Criminal law defines its own concepts to accurately identify and punish ecologic crimes. Criminal law has understood the environment as everything that surrounds man, including air, water, soil, landscape, flora and fauna. This concept does not require threats or harms to human life as necessary elements to punish ecologic crimes and allows autonomous protection of the environment via criminal liability. What is more, the autonomous protection of the environment under criminal law allows differentiating environmental interests from other protected interests of criminal law, such as the economic and social order.

622. Following the lines of the Penal Code, one of the main elements triggering criminal liability is the material unlawfulness of the conduct. In other words, the conduct has to be such that the interest protected under criminal law is effectively endangered or harmed. Pursuant to Article 11 of the Penal Code, the protected interest must be determined or determinable. This notion can be challenging given the nature of environmental damage, since damages cannot be fully quantified at the moment of the criminal conduct, and its harmful effects can have late manifestation, which hinders a thorough determination of the material unlawfulness in ecologic crimes. Criminal law must assess the cases where the environment is effectively harmed or endangered to apply the corresponding provision

623. Colombian Penal Code establishes criminal liability for action and omission. Criminal liability for action refers to the positive conduct of the offender that is punishable by the Criminal Code. Criminal liability is triggered when pursuant to the law a person is supposed to act in a certain manner and that person fails to do so. Whenever the Penal Code establishes the obligation to act in a certain way, it is said that it creates a 'guarantor position'. The guarantor position and the consequent duty to act emerge from formal sources like the law or the contract, as established in Article 10; or from material sources, understood as certain situations, like the joint performance of risky activities or the voluntary assumption of protection, that make a person responsible for the risks posed to the people with whom the risk is shared, as established in Article 25. The guarantor position based on material sources is only established for crimes against life, sexual integrity or personal freedom, which leaves environmental crimes aside and does not allow allocating criminal environmental liability for omission. Consequently, environmental crimes only admit active conducts, meaning criminal liability for action.

624. Due to the nature of certain illicit conducts, the Penal Code provides for blank penal norms. Blank penal norms are crime types in which one of their elements is regulated by an administrative provision. The administrative provision fills out a blank of the crime concerning any of the elements of the fact description, such as the crime subjects, objects, conduct and illicit result. The remission to the administrative provision must be specific and unequivocal. This figure, often used in economic, and increasingly, in environmental crimes, allows the Penal Code to be constantly updated in matters like contamination definition or thresholds that otherwise would require a lengthy amendment to the Penal Code every time a new definition or threshold limit is adopted.

625. Another concern on criminal liability for environmental matters relates to the two types of crime modalities: crimes of danger and crimes of result.[63] Regarding crimes of danger, the lawmaker anticipates the protection barriers and sanctions the conduct at the moment the conduct poses an actual danger to the protected interest. Crimes of danger are subdivided into abstract danger and concrete danger. Abstract danger crimes are those where the action itself is presumed unlawful and therefore sanctioned, whereas in concrete danger, the conduct is assessed by the judge in order to establish whether it really endangers the protected interest or not. Concerning crimes of result, they refer to crimes where an illicit result is necessary

63. Francisco Bernate Ochoa, 'El delito ambiental', Perspectivas del Derecho Ambiental en Colombia, Universidad del Rosario Editorial, November 2006.

to charge criminal liability to the offender, like in homicides. In Colombia, environmental crimes are established as crimes of danger, meaning that the mere threat to protected interests, such as the environment, natural resources, flora and fauna, etc., is punished with criminal sanctions. No harmful results are required to charge criminal liability in environmental offences, with the exception of the environmental contamination crime.

626. Lastly, it is worth noting that, pursuant to the Colombian Penal Code, companies or entities cannot be held liable under criminal liability. This approach has been backed by the Constitutional Court and some authors who have pointed out the difficulties in charging criminal liability to corporate entities due to the innocuous sanctions companies would be exposed to and the limited defence instruments within proceedings. Notably, directors of companies are not exempted from being charged with criminal liability, provided that the Penal Code establishes sanctions when companies' directors use the corporate veil to carry out illicit actions. Companies and entities are autonomous entities, and therefore they can only be held liable under civil or administrative systems of liability for environmental infractions.

III. Specific Part

627. The second part of the Penal Code contains the conducts considered environmental crimes. Each kind of crime is said to be typified in the Penal Code, meaning that all the elements are established in the law and that such law precedes any punishable conduct. The fact of having all the crime elements in the law and having them prior to the punishable conduct translates into constitutional guarantees of the right to a due process, which enables the accused to exercise their defence rights in a timely manner. The crimes established in the special part develop the underpinning principles established in the general part of the Penal Code. The specific part establishes the cases where the mere attempt is punishable, the crimes admitting omission conducts, the crimes that need to resort to administrative laws in order to fill out one of the crime elements, and the cases of co-authority or complicity. In this context, this section will devote the following lines to illustrate what conducts involving environmental liability are considered crimes.

628. Title XI of the Penal Code regulates crimes against the environment and natural resources. This title has been revamped by Law 2011/2021 adopted on 29 July 2021 and is commonly known as the Environmental Crimes Law. The law introduces new crimes and increases the penalties and fines for the crimes already contemplated in the Penal Code. The new crimes added by Law 2011/2021 include deforestation, promotion and financing of deforestation, ecocide, fauna trafficking, illegal appropriation of national wastelands, financing of illegal appropriation of national wastelands and financing of invasion of areas of special ecological importance. One of the crimes that was eliminated with the issuance of the Environmental Crimes Law was the crime of violation of borders for the exploitation of natural resources.

629. Crimes against the environment and natural resources include illicit use of natural resources (Article 328), illicit handling of noxious microorganisms (Article 331), causation of damage to natural resources (Article 333), environmental contamination (Article 334), illegal experimentations with animal or vegetable species (Article 335), illegal fishing (Article 328C), invasion of areas of ecological importance (Article 336), illegal hunting (Article 328B), and illegal exploitation of mines or other materials (Article 332). Each one of the mentioned crimes has a number of elements, variations, modalities, subjects and verbs that deserve a special analysis. In the procedural field, the prosecutor formulates the accusation establishing the type of crime in which a presumed illicit conduct is subsumed. The judge assesses the facts of the case, the accusation and the defence, and decides whether the alleged conduct is punishable or not within the crime type proposed. In case the conduct fits in the proposed crime type, the judge analyses that all elements of the criminal type are fulfilled and proceeds to establish the sanction, in accordance with the Penal Code.

Part V. Juridical Actions of Individuals

Chapter 1. Administrative Remedies

630. In the previous parts, this work has discussed substantive rules of environmental law. This last part will focus on the existing procedural rules and possibilities to achieve environmental protection. The main aim is to analyse the position of individuals and groups from a legal perspective, and their right to participate in the adoption of public decisions, the possibility to challenge decisions from authorities concerning environmental issues and the mechanisms to access judicial remedies for the accomplishment of environmental goals. This part will therefore address administrative and judicial remedies in the environmental field.

631. Administrative remedies refer to the possibilities of individuals and groups to provide an input in the decision-making, as well as the mechanisms to challenge those government decisions affecting the environment. This chapter is divided into two categories: participation mechanisms and remedies to challenge the lawfulness of administrative decisions.

§1. Public Participation Mechanisms

632. Colombian environmental law provides for different mechanisms to assure public participation in decision-making processes that follow international principles. Pursuant to principle 10 of the Rio Declaration in 1992, public participation implies granting access to information about the environment and opportunities for participating in decision-making processes. In Colombia, the 1991 Constitution enables citizens to achieve the protection of their right to a healthy environment, by resorting to public participation mechanisms. Prior to 1991, Law 23/1973 and the NCNRN did not address public participation, and citizen participation was limited to water-user communities. The 1991 Constitution changes these conditions by establishing the right to a healthy environment in Article 79 and requiring the law to guarantee participation mechanisms so that the constitutional right is protected.

633. Public participation is a constitutional principle and a right. As a principle, authorities must carry out their activities by granting citizens the possibility to participate in the decision-making; as a right, authorities must ensure that communities have the possibility to participate in public decisions that may affect them. Public participation is developed in different pieces of legislation, such as Law 134/1994,

Law 99/1993 and Law 472/1998, among others. Public participation mechanisms can be grouped into three categories: legislative and normative; administrative control and management; and judiciary control.

634. Legislative and normative mechanisms of participation refer to those mechanisms that allow citizens to propose regulations or regulate aspects concerning the environment and natural resources, such as the popular legislative initiative, referendum, removal of governors from public office and programmatic vote. Administrative control and management mechanisms seek to involve citizens in the decision-making. For example, hearings taking place within the environmental licence-granting procedure are spaces where affected citizens can voice their opinions on the proposed projects. Finally, participation mechanisms include juridical control mechanisms aimed at challenging the decisions adopted by public authorities. The petition right, the popular legislative initiative and the public hearings in licensing procedures are the main participation mechanisms used by citizens to achieve environmental goals, and therefore they will be studied in the following paragraphs.

635. The petition right is a fundamental right consecrated in Article 23 of the Constitution and developed in Article 74 of Law 99/1993 for environmental issues. Any legal or natural person has the right to submit a petition requesting information on the elements that may cause contamination and the hazards that the use of such elements can pose to human health, in accordance with Article 16 of Law 23/1973. The petition right on environmental issues also involves the right of people to be informed on the use of economic resources that are designated for the preservation of the environment. Petitions grounded on Law 99/1993 must address the specific environmental issues established in the law, such as information requests on the elements that cause pollution, hazards to human health derived from the use of polluting elements and the destination of economic recourses in environmental preservation. The petition can be addressed to public and private entities and must be replied to within ten business days. The petition right empowers communities that may be impacted by certain projects to access technical, legal and procedural information on the project development and licensing stages.

636. The people's legislative initiative (referred to as popular initiative) is a participation mechanism regulated in Law 134/1994 that allows citizens, groups and different entities to propose regulatory instruments. Depending on the type of the regulatory instrument to be proposed, the competent public authority for its discussion and approval will be the Congress of the Republic, in case of laws; departmental assemblies, in case of departmental ordinances; and municipal or district councils, for agreement proposals. The minimum requirements to promote a popular legislative initiative include being a citizen in accordance with the National Constitution and having the signatures of 5% of the total population of Colombia supporting the initiative. The initiative is discussed and approved within the competent public authority and allows the initiative promoter to be present at the debates and the different approval stages.

637. The public hearing is a mechanism that allows people, social organizations, civil society and project stakeholders to participate in the environmental decision-making process. According to Article 72 of Law 99/1993, the entities with legal standing to request a public hearing include the General Attorney of the Nation, the Ombudsman of the People, the MASD, governmental environmental authorities, governors and majors, at least one hundred people, and/or three non-profit organizations. The authority responsible for assessing the environmental viability of the project can also call for public hearings when it deems it convenient, due to the importance of the project or the impact it can have on the community and the environment. Any projects requiring an environmental licence or permit can be subject to public hearings.

638. Public hearings can be requested before the project licence is granted, modified or revoked, in which case it will be named prior hearing. Public hearings can also take place once the project has been authorized with the purpose of raising concerns about the project's non-compliance with the conditions established in the licence. In this case, the authority verifies the evidence supporting non-compliance and establishes the applicable sanctions accordingly. The procedure for carrying out public hearings includes a formal request, submitted by those with legal standing to request public hearings; a public convocation called up by the competent authority, which involves the posting up of a public edict for ten days at the authority's offices, and the publication in a local newspaper. The public edict contains the time and place of the public hearing so that interested parties can prepare their queries and arguments. The public hearing is recorded in an act containing: the project identification, place and time of the hearing, the main discussed issues, the documents presented during the hearing and the interventions of the hearing participants. The hearing act is later considered in the Administrative Act that grants or rejects the environmental licence.

§2. Recourses Against Administrative Decisions

639. Citizens may challenge the decisions adopted by public authorities through legal actions before administrative courts, like the action of nullity, or the action of nullity and reestablishment of the right. Administrative remedies must be exercised prior to resorting to the courts. Once the administrative remedies have been exhausted and the answer has not been favourable to the petitioner, it can file a claim in court and exercise the corresponding actions. The action of nullity seeks to demonstrate the legal flaws of administrative decisions when an administrative decision contravenes the law and therefore affects collective and/or individual interests. In this action, the petitioner asks the administrative court to void the challenged decision and remove it from the legal framework. The action of nullity and reestablishment follows the aims of the action of nullity but goes further in the petition of the claimer by asking the administrative court to compensate damages caused by the adoption of the administrative decision. Administrative remedies as well as judiciary actions before administrative courts are regulated in the Code of Administrative Contentious Procedure.

640. Law 99/1993 establishes a special type of nullity actions in environmental matters. The nullity action provided for in Article 73 allows any citizen to challenge administrative decisions granting, modifying or revoking permits, authorizations, concessions or environmental licences from activities that may affect the environment. The particular feature of this action lies in the possibility of all individuals and groups to challenge decisions that would initially concern the permit, concession, authorization or licence holder. Remarkably, this action gives legal standing to any person to controvert the lawfulness of administrative decisions authorizing the construction or operation of projects that have impacts on the environment.

641. Provided that environmental sanctions are imposed through administrative acts, legal and natural persons can challenge such decisions by using any of the actions aforementioned. For example, the public authority imposed a sanction on a company for sea contamination due to the introduction of toxic and poisoning substances in marine water. The company argued that such sanction was imposed by infringing its right to due process, and challenged it before the administrative court by using the action of nullity and reestablishment of the right. The administrative court, Council of State, ruled against the company arguing that the technical studies demonstrating the death of fish in the affected area did not violate the company's right to due process, and consequently, the sanction imposed by the environmental authority was lawful, and therefore ratified.[64]

64. Council of State, Sentence of 29 Mar. 1989, Open Court of the Administrative Contentious Section, Magistrate Clara Forero de Castro.

Chapter 2. Judicial Remedies

642. This chapter will discuss the procedures to implement substantive rules of environmental law through the court system. Colombia has a rich array of procedures to enforce and remediate substantive law through legal actions. Legal actions can directly emerge from the Constitution, in which case the rules of procedure pursue quicker trials and judgments, or from the General Code of Procedure, Code of Administrative Contentious Procedure and the Code of Criminal Procedure. Concerning environmental issues, the possibility to exercise one or another legal action depends on the substantive rule and the strategy to protect environmental interests. Depending on the type of legal action, the effects of the judgments can be different: effects to everyone (*erga omnes*) or effects to the concerned party. Hence, this chapter will divide the available legal environmental actions according to the nature of the protected interest: collective or individual rights.

§1. Actions for the Protection of Collective Rights

I. Popular Actions

643. Popular actions, known in Spanish as '*acciones populares*', are regulated in Law 472/1998 and seek the protection of collective rights. Law 472/1998 develops Article 88 of the National Constitution, which establishes some of the collective rights or diffuse interests protected by this action, including the right to a healthy environment, administrative morality, public space, cultural heritage, security, public sanitation, public services, consumers and users, and free economic competition. Popular actions have a preventive and restoring character, as they are exercised in order to avoid contingent damages; stop the threat, danger, infringement or offence to collective rights and interests; or restore things to their previous state when possible. Although popular actions were early provided for in the Colombian Civil Code, it was not until 1998 with the adoption of Law 472 that these actions became a widespread instrument for the protection of collective rights.

644. As a public action, the popular action can be initiated by any natural or legal person; non-governmental organizations, including popular, civic or similar organizations; public entities with surveillance, intervention or control competences; the Attorney General of the Nation; the Ombudsman of the People; the district and municipal representatives, depending on geographical competences; and the major or public servants responsible for the protection and defence of collective rights. Popular actions can be addressed against public authorities or privates vested with public powers, and citizens and companies, depending on the presumed offender of collective rights. If the lawsuit is addressed against public authorities, the competent judge is the administrative court, while if it goes against citizens or companies, the competent judge will be the Civil Circuit Court. No attorney is required for filing popular action lawsuits.

645. The lawsuit for a popular action has to comply with certain requirements to be considered by the competent judge. It must indicate the collective right endangered or violated; the facts, acts, actions and omissions motivating the petition; the pleadings; the indication of the presumed responsible for the collective right threat or violation; the evidence; the addresses for notifications; and the identification of the plaintiff. The Council of State has said that notwithstanding the procedural conditions of the lawsuit are met, the lawsuit must also fulfil substantive requirements, including the demonstration of the legal source establishing a legal duty to the offender for which it is presumably liable; the concept of violation or threat to the collective right; and the causal link between the infringement and the offender's conduct. The judge will admit or reject the lawsuit within a three-day term.

646. The procedure of popular actions must be quick and expedited; therefore, they have priority over other legal actions. Although the judiciary procedure of popular actions resembles the standard procedure on stages and requirements, it has some peculiarities concerning injunctions and the compliance agreement (*pacto de cumplimiento*). Injunctions (*medidas cautelares*) are court orders aimed at ensuring compliance with legal duties or obligations. Particularly, Law 472/1998 establishes a set of injunctions that judges can take within the popular action procedure, including: ordering to stop activities generating damage, or that have caused damage; ordering the implementation of necessary actions when the presumed harmful conduct is the result of the defendant's lack of action; compelling the defendant to undertake a guarantee to ensure compliance with the aforementioned injunctions; or ordering the performance of technical studies to establish the nature and extent of the damage, and the measures to mitigate it.

647. An interesting topic has emerged from the application of injunctions in popular actions, relating to cases where the violation or threat to the collective right comes from an Administrative Act issued by public authorities.[65] Under this scenario, the courts have been asked to order the suspension and even the elimination of an Administrative Act in order to stop or remediate the harm to the collective right. In this respect, the jurisprudence of the Council of State has suffered significant changes as to whether it is possible or not to challenge the lawfulness of an Administrative Act via popular actions. In the beginning, the Council of State held that the courts were only empowered to order the suspension of an Administrative Act threatening or violating a collective right, but not to decide on its lawfulness.[66] Later on, the considerations of the Constitutional Court on the possibility of protecting collective rights by invalidating administrative acts[67] influenced the new jurisprudence of the Council of State, resulting in a judgment of 2009 which allowed the courts in popular actions to nullify administrative acts in the following circumstances: when the Administrative Act is a breach of superior hierarchy

---

65. Luis Felipe Botero, 'La anulación de actos administrativeos en la acción popular ¿es un ejercicio de una competencia implícita que viola el drecho fundamental al debido proceso?', Justiciabilidad de los Derechos Colectivos, Universidad del Rosario Editorial, 2009.
66. Council of State, Sentence of 6 Oct. 2005, Third Section, Magistrate Ruth Stella Correa Palacio.
67. Constitutional Court, Sentence No. SU-713 of 23 Aug. 2006, Magistrate Rodrigo Escobar.

norms; when the harmful conduct of public authorities is demonstrated; and when the collective right is threatened or violated.

648. Law 472/1998 provides for the compliance agreement. The compliance agreement is a negotiated settlement mechanism that takes place after the notification of the lawsuit to the defendant and during the special hearing, where all the involved parties are heard and manifest their views on the action. The judge or court proposes a compliance agreement to the parties whereby it establishes the manner in which the collective right has to be protected and the necessary measures to accomplish such protection. If the parties agree on the compliance agreement, the judge renders its judgment approving the said agreement, and requiring the involved parties to regard and comply with the obligations agreed thereupon.

649. Regarding the applicability of popular action in environmental matters, some authors affirm that this action is by far the most common mechanism for the protection of environmental rights. Although popular actions do not allow plaintiffs to seek damages, it does aim to prevent environmental damage and require the offender to adopt the necessary measures to restore things to their former state. When the violation of collective rights involves deterioration of natural resources, the Judge is enabled to fix a compensatory amount to restore the affected area. Popular actions, thus, can be used to prevent and repair environmental damage affecting the collective rights of the community.

650. This environmental nature of popular actions has been pointed out by Colombian case law. The case refers to a popular action where the plaintiff asked the judge to declare the existence of contamination in the river and in the sewerage system caused by the operation of a neighbouring asphalt plant, condemn the responsible for carrying out the necessary works to stop the contamination, pay damages to the municipality for the loss suffered in the sewerage system, and pay damages to the riverside dwellers for the river pollution. The judge accepted the pretensions of the plaintiff, except the one concerning damage compensation of riverside dwellers, based on the fact that such a petition had to be addressed through a civil liability action.

651. Articles 39 and 40 of Law 472/1998 used to incentivize the use of popular actions by granting claimants an incentive between 10 and 150 minimum monthly wages or 15% of the proceeds, when the action was against governmental authorities. Law 1425/2010 repealed these two articles following a ruling of the Constitutional Court thus repealing the economic incentive for claimants.

II. Unconstitutionality Action

652. The Unconstitutionality Action, named in Spanish '*acción de inconstitucionalidad*', is a legal action that seeks to exclude an alleged unconstitutional provision from the legal system. According to Article 241 of the National Constitution, the Unconstitutionality Action can challenge acts modifying the Constitution, laws, decrees with the standing of laws, and other special decrees, for considering that such instruments contravene the Constitution. The Unconstitutionality Action is public, can be exercised by any citizen and aims for the protection of the public interest. Bearing in mind that the Constitutional Court does not control the constitutionality of laws by default, the Unconstitutionality Action is required to be initiated by the public at any time, unless the Constitutional Court has already decided on the challenged provision, or the unconstitutionality vice refers to procedural faults, for which a term of one year is foreseen. The Unconstitutionality Action is regulated in Decree 2067/1991 laying down the requirements for the procedures before the Constitutional Court.

653. The Unconstitutionality Action is submitted through a lawsuit of unconstitutionality. The lawsuit must describe the laws and provisions considered unconstitutional, the constitutional provisions considered violated by the challenged law, the arguments on which the concept of violation is based, the legal grounds for the competence of the Constitutional Court, and if the alleged violation concerns a procedural vice, the description of the legislative procedure established in the Constitution for the adoption of the challenged law. However, the Constitutional Court has been narrowing the criteria to admit unconstitutionality lawsuits by ruling that although the Unconstitutionality Action is a public action, it has to fulfil minimum procedural requirements that allow the Court to render meaningful sentences, instead of inhibitory decisions.[68] The Constitutional Court assesses the constitutionality of the alleged provision by confronting it with the text of the National Constitution. If the Constitutional Court finds that the provision is indeed unconstitutional, the Court orders to exclude it from the legal framework, the sentence becomes res judicata, and the sentence has effects not only on the plaintiff but also on all the citizens. The Court has interpreted that it is competent to establish the effect of its own sentences; therefore, it establishes whether the decision on the constitutionality of a certain provision has retroactive effects or only affects future situations.

654. Concerning environmental matters, the Unconstitutionality Action is often used to challenge the constitutionality of laws considering that they violate environmental-related constitutional rights. The number of provisions deemed in violation of constitutional environmental rights is considerable; yet, the Constitutional Court tends to maintain legal security in this field and rarely rules the unconstitutionality of challenged provisions. Some of the most relevant pieces of legislation that have been sued for unconstitutionality include the Mining Code, Law 1333/2009 establishing the environmental enforcement procedure, and Law 357/1007 adopting the Ramsar Convention. An example of the Unconstitutionality Action in environmental matters concerned the provision establishing that the prescriptive period for imposing administrative sanctions for environmental infractions was twenty years.

68. Constitutional Court, Sentence No. C-652 of 21 Jun. 2001, Magistrate Jaime Córdoba Triviño.

655. A citizen challenged the constitutionality of Article 10 of Law 1333/2009, as he considered that the prescriptive term of twenty years was a breach of the Constitution by impeding an effective environmental protection and by denying access to justice for environmental damage victims. In addition, the plaintiff argued that twenty years was not enough time to start a legal action for environmental infractions, given the nature of environmental damages and their late effects. The Constitutional Court estimated that setting a term to initiate legal actions for environmental protection does not contravene the constitutional provision. Regarding the effective protection of the environment, the Court considered that sanctions are not the only mechanism that the State has to protect the environment, but also preventive measures, corrective measures and environmental management plans. Concerning the victims' access to justice, the Court found that mechanisms such as the popular action or collective action, whereby victims demand environmental protection and eventual damage compensation, allow victims of environmental damages to obtain economic compensation from the offender at any time. Finally, as to the charge of whether twenty years was enough or not to protect the environment, the Court argued that lawmakers deemed this term to be appropriate for pursuing offenders and imposing sanctions, under the current economic, social and political circumstances.[69] The application of Article 10 of Law 1333/2009 over time will shed light on the fitness and efficiency of the prescriptive action foreseen by the lawmaker to protect the environment.

III. Action of Compliance

656. The Action of Compliance, named in Spanish as '*acción de cumplimiento*', is regulated in Law 393/1997 and seeks to compel the authority to comply with their duties established in laws or administrative acts. The Action of Compliance proceeds against any action or omission of public authorities evidencing non-compliance with laws or administrative acts. For example, if there is a piece of legislation requiring a specific authority to regulate certain matters and the authority fails to do so, the authority is failing to comply with its legal duties. Pursuant to Article 8 of Law 393/1997, the Action of Compliance requires the plaintiff to previously request the authority to comply with its legal or administrative duty, and the authority to reply to the petition by justifying its non-compliance, or not reply within a ten-day term. The plaintiff cannot seek damages or the establishment of public expenditures through the Action of Compliance.

657. The Action of Compliance provides citizens with an additional mechanism to seek environmental protection through compliance assurance. Although the first aim of the Action of Compliance is to make the authority comply with a certain duty, there is no limitation for asking the authority to comply with legal duties relating to the protection of collective rights, such as the right to a healthy environment.

69. Constitutional Court, Sentence C-401 of 26 Mar. 2021, Magistrate Gabriel Eduardo Mendoza Martelo.

By means of an Action of Compliance, the Council of State ordered an environmental authority, the CAR of Santander, to suspend the execution of a cement project that was operating without the required atmospheric permit.[70] According to Law 99/1993, environmental authorities have to take preventive measures such as ordering the suspension of projects or activities whenever they are carried out without the required permits, licences, concessions or authorizations.

§2. Actions for the Protection of Individual Rights

I. Protection Action

658. The protection action, named in Spanish '*acción de tutela*', is a legal action that seeks to protect a fundamental right. The protection action is regulated in Law-Decree 2591/1991 which develops Article 86 of the National Constitution consecrating the right of every person to claim the protection of their fundamental rights before the courts. Although the 1991 Constitution lists a number of fundamental rights, this listing is merely enumerative, since fundamental rights are determined on a case-by-case basis.[71] Due to the importance of the matters being discussed in protection actions and the need to have a quick and efficient settlement, the protection action has a more expedite procedure than other legal actions and has priority over other legal matters submitted to the Court. Some of the main features of the protection action include its specificity, as it only concerns fundamental rights; immediateness, provided the need to protect the endangered right; and subsidiary, as it only proceeds when there is no other available judiciary remedy to solve the issue.

659. According to Decree-Law 2591/1991, the protection action is to be initiated by any natural or legal person seeking the protection of its fundamental rights and can be brought up against public authorities and private entities. The protection action does not require an attorney, it must be decided in ten days by the competent court and its ruling must be executed immediately. Pursuant to Decree-Law 2591/1991, any court of the place where fundamental rights are violated or endangered is competent to decide on the protection action. In order to protect the violated or endangered right, the judge is empowered to order provisional measures when it deems it necessary and urgent.

660. At first sight, the use of the protection action in environmental matters would not proceed given that collective rights, such as the right to a healthy environment, are not considered fundamental.[72] Nonetheless, there is a relationship between fundamental rights and the right to a healthy environment, as the protection of the latter assures the conditions for the realization of the former. In other

70. Council of State, Sentence of 23 Sep. 1999, Third Section, Magistrate Germán Rodriguez Villamizar.
71. Constitutional Court, Sentence No. T-451 of 10 Jul. 1992, Magistrate Ciro Angarita Barón.
72. Constitutional Court, Sentence No. T-315 of 12 Jul. 1994, Magistrate Fabio Morón Díaz.

words, the affection to the environment may cause the violation of a fundamental right, such as life and integrity. Grounded on this argumentative line, the protection action is commonly used for the protection of the environment, by enabling the plaintiff to demand the halt of polluting activities causing environmental damage.

661. In practice, the protection action has served to suspend projects lacking the necessary environmental studies, and projects causing major contamination. The first case is illustrated by a sentence of the Constitutional Court ordering the suspension of construction works in a highway project and conditioning it to the performance of an EIA establishing the necessary preventive measures in order not to cause additional harm to the plaintiffs.[73] Regarding projects causing major contamination, the Constitutional Court has deemed that whenever a polluting activity endangers fundamental rights, the judge is enabled to order public entities to adopt all the necessary measures to protect such rights. This situation has been evidenced in coal exploitation projects where, despite having the necessary permits and having adopted preventive measures to mitigate negative environmental impacts, the Court has demonstrated the existence of noxious factors threatening people's lives and has ordered the coal project suspension until friendlier environmental conditions are guaranteed.[74]

662. The protection action is also frequently used in projects requiring prior consultation with affected communities. For example, plaintiffs in a protection action argued being recognized as members of the Venado indigenous community, belonging to the Zenú people of the municipality of Ciénaga de Oro, in the department of Cordoba, and considered that the defendant entities violated their fundamental rights as a result of the failure to consult them before starting the construction of the Cantagallo landfill, as well as the impacts of Cantagallo and the environmental and social impacts that have been generated.[75]

II. Civil Liability Action

663. The civil liability action is the basic mechanism by virtue of which a legal or natural person can seek damages. The elements of this action have already been discussed in the civil liability section of this work, explaining the need to demonstrate the conduct, the damage and the causal link between them. Depending on the subjects involved and the nature of the contentious matter, the civil liability action is called direct reparation (*reparación directa*) when pursuing damages from the State, ordinary civil action (*acción ordinaria civil*) when the controversy involves private parties, and the establishment of the civil party (*constitución de la parte civil*) when the matter involves ecologic crimes. Regarding the environment, the civil liability action allows victims to obtain compensation for environmental damages.

73. Constitutional Court, Sentence No. T-428 of 24 Jun. 1992, Magistrate Ciro Angarita Barón.
74. Constitutional Court, Sentence No. T-528 of 18 Sep. 1992, Magistrate Fabio Morón Díaz.
75. Constitutional Court, Sentence No. T-294, 2014, Magistrate Maria Victoria Calle Correa.

664. One of the cases that best illustrates the applicability of this action concerns a ruling of the Supreme Court of Justice ordering an industrial facility to pay damages for contamination. Under this case, the Court found that a fixed source of Sulphur Acid released more than 1 tonne of Sulphur Dioxide (SO_2) per day, exceeding the maximum allowable limits. According to the plaintiff, the SO_2 emissions from the industrial facility caused oxidation in the plaintiff's equipment and installations leading to their deterioration. The Court established the causal link between the operation of the Sulphur Acid fixed source and the damage suffered by the plaintiff and condemned the industrial facility to pay for the damaged equipment and installations.

III. Group Actions

665. Group actions, also known as '*acciones de grupo*', are provided for in Article 88 of the Constitution as a mechanism to remediate individual damage suffered by a plural number of people. Group actions are regulated in Law 472/1998, resembling the structure of class actions provided for in Anglo-Saxon legislation, with the aim to protect a group of people that have been affected by the same cause, for example, the victims of defective products. The people integrating the group have to have uniform characteristics with respect to the cause of the damage. The group must be integrated by more than twenty people. Any person belonging to the affected group can initiate a group action through an attorney.

666. The main difference with popular actions is that group actions seek compensation for individual damages. Law 472/1998 sought to avoid addressing the same issue through different lawsuits and devoted only one specific action to address damages. Group actions can be brought against the State and citizens depending on who is presumed responsible for the damage. Likewise, in case the defendant is the State, the lawsuit has to be filed before the administrative court, whereas if it is an individual or company, the competent judge is the Civil Circuit Court. The term to start a group action is two years starting from the day the damage was caused or the action causing such damage was finished. The group action judgment establishes the compensation in favour of the affected group and the manner in which each beneficiary can claim its compensation portion.

667. The procedure of the group action follows the ordinary procedure for regular legal actions, including lawsuit admission, notifications, evidence checking, allegations and judgment. However, the procedure of group actions has two peculiarities: the exclusion from the group and the group integration. People integrating the group can ask to be excluded from it after the notification to the defendant. Likewise, the group integration takes place after the conciliatory hearing between plaintiffs and defendants. The judgment establishes the compensatory sum for all the members of the group.

668. The group action has not been used quite as much as popular actions in environmental matters. Group actions are often used on claims related to consumer rights or for damages in cases of tort.

Selected Bibliography

§1. Books

Aboul-Kassim, T. *Environmental Consequences of War and Aftermath* (Heidelberg 2009).

Amaya Navas, O. Nuevo Régimen Sancionatorio Ambiental. Bogotá: Universidad Externado de Colombia, 2010.

Atwood, D. *Radionuclides in the Environment* (Wiley 2010).

Bermúdez Muñoz, M. Responsabilidad de los jueces y del Estado. Bogotá: Librería del Profesional, 1998.

Colombia. Código de Recursos Naturales y del Medio Ambiente Anotado. Bogotá: Leyer, 2010.

Galindo, G. Planificación Ecorregional para la Conservación de la Biodiversidad. Bogotá: Instituto de Investigación de Recursos Biológicos Alexander Von Humboldt, 2009.

García Martínez, M. Principales Escenarios Internacionales de protección ambiental y del Conocimiento Tradicional para los Pueblos Indígenas. Bogotá: Universidad del rosario, 2009.

Gudynas, E. El mandato Ecológico: Derechos de la Naturaleza y Políticas Ambientales en la Nueva Constitución. Quito: Abya Yala, 2009.

Guzmán Hannessey, M. La Generación del Cambio Climático: Una Aproximación desde el Enfoque del Caos. Bogotá: Editorial Universidad del Rosario, 2010.

Le Prestre, P. Protection de l'environnement et relations internationales: les défis de l'écopolitique mondiale. Paris: Armand Colin, 2005.

López, C. Diálogos ente Saberes, Ciencias e Ideologías en Torno a lo Ambiental. Pereira: Universidad Tecnológica de Pereira, 2009.

Mengech, A. *Integrated Pest Management in the Tropics: Current Status and Future Prospects* (UNEP 1995).

Movimiento Político, Mira. Contaminación Ambiental en Colombia I. Problemas Ambientales Globales y Nacionales. Bogotá, 2010.

Motta González, N. Historia Ambiental del Valle del Cauca, Geoespacialidad, Cultura y Género. Cali: Universidad del Valle, 2010.

NATO. *The Role of Ecological Chemistry in Pollution Research and Sustainable Development* (Springer 2009).

Navarro, G. Delitos Contra la Salud y el Medio Ambiente. Buenos Aires: Hammurabi, 2009.

Pardavé Livia, W. Envases y Medio ambiente. Bogotá: Norma, 2004.

Pereira, M. Síndrome Holandés, Regalías Mineras y Políticas de Gobierno para un País Dependiente de Recursos Naturales: El Cobre en Chile. Santiago de Chile: CEPAL, 2009.
Pérez Rincón, M. Desarrollo Sostenible: Principios, Aplicaciones y Lineamientos de Política para Colombia. Cali: Universidad del Valle, 2010.
Rodríguez, G. La Participación en la Gestión Ambiental: Un Reto para el Nuevo Milenio. Bogotá: Universidad del Rosario, 2010.
Tolba, M. Environment, *Health, and Sustainable Development* (Hogrefe 2010).
Torgler, B. *Participation in Environmental Organizations* (Routledge 2010).
Uribe Vargas, D. Derecho Internacional Ambiental. Bogotá: Universidad de Bogotá Jorge Tadeo Lozano, 2010.

§2. Case Law

Council of State. Sentence of 29 March 1989. Open Court of the Administrative Contentious Section. Magistrate Clara Forero de Castro.
Constitutional Court. Sentence No. T-428 of 24 June 1992. Magistrate Ciro Angarita Barón.
Constitutional Court. Sentence No. T-451 of 10 July 1992. Magistrate Ciro Angarita Barón.
Constitutional Court. Sentence No. T-528 of 18 September 1992. Magistrate Fabio Morón Díaz.
Constitutional Court. Sentence No. T-092 of 19 February 1993. Magistrate, Simon Rodriguez.
Constitutional Court. Sentence No. T-315 of 12 July 1994. Magistrate Morón Díaz.
Constitutional Court. Sentence No. C-528 of 24 November 1994. Magistrate, Alejandro Martinez Caballero.
Council of State. Sentence of 23 September 1999. Third Section, Magistrate Germán Rodriguez Villamizar.
Constitutional Court. Sentence No. 795 of 29 November 2000. Magistrate Eduardo Cifuentes Muñoz.
Constitutional Court. Sentence No. C-652 of 21 June 2001; Magistrate Jaime Córdoba Triviño.
Constitutional Court. Sentence No. T-1263 of 29 November 2001. Magistrate Jaime Córdoba Triviño.
Constitutional Court. Sentence No. C-293 of 23 April 2002. Magistrate, Alfredo Beltran Sierra.
Council of State. Sentence of 6 October 2005. Third Section, Magistrate Ruth Stella Correa Palacio.
Constitutional Court. Sentence No. C-30 of 23 January 2008. Magistrate Rodrigo Escobar Gil.
Council of State. Sentence of 24 September 2009. First Section, Magistrate, Rafael E. Ostau de Lafont Pianeta.
Constitutional Court. Sentence No. C-595 of 27 July 2010. Magistrate Jorge Iván Palacio Palacio.
Superior Tribunal of Judicial District. Sentence of 15 September 2004. Civil Section, Magistrate Pedro Pablo Torres Beltrán.

Constitutional Court, Sentence C-401 of 26 March 2021, Magistrate Gabriel Eduardo Mendoza Martelo.

Constitutional Court, Sentence No. T-294, 2014, Magistrate Maria Victoria Calle Correa.

Constitutional Court, Sentence T-622, 2016. Magistrate Jorge Iván Palacio Palacio.

§3. Articles

Agricultura Sensitiva. 'La problemática Ambiental del Sector Agropecuario en Colombia'. www.angelfire.com/ia2/ingenieriaagricola/sectoragropecuario.htm, 14 Septiembre 2007.

Convention on Biological Diversity. 'Country profile-Colombia'. www.cbd.int/countries/?country=co.

Convention on Biological Diversity. 'Protected Area on Provisions in CBD'. www.cbd.int/protected-old/background.shtml, 25 May 2007.

Eugenia Ponce de León Chaux. 'Estudio jurídico sobre categorías regionales de áreas protegidas'. Presentado al Instituto Alexander Von Humbolt, Octubre 2003.

FAO. 'Visión General del Sector Agrícola Nacional. Colombia'. www.fao.org/fishery/countrysector/naso_colombia/es#tcNA009C, 1 Febrero 2005.

Francisco Bernate Ochoa. 'El delito ambiental'. Perspectivas del Derecho Ambiental en Colombia, Universidad del Rosario Editorial, November 2006.

Germán Márquez Calle. 'Ecosistemas Estratégicos de Colombia'. www.sogeocol.edu.co/documentos/07ecos.pdf, 15 Julio 2003.

International Atomic Energy Agency. 'Categorization of Radioactive sources'. www.hps.org/documents/IAEATecDoc1344.pdf, Julio 2003.

Juan Carlos Henao. 'Responsabilidad del Estado Colombiano por Daño Ambiental'. www.mamacoca.org/FSMT_sept_2003/es/doc/henao_responsabilidad_ambiental_es.htm.

Javier Gonzaga Valencia Hernandez. 'Los Medios de Defensa de la Comunidad para Garantizar el Derecho a un Ambiente Sano'. https://revistasojs.ucaldas.edu.co/index.php/lunazul/article/view/1483/1403.

Luis Felipe Botero. 'La anulación de actos administrativos en la acción popular ¿es un ejercicio de una competencia implícita que viola el derecho fundamental al debido proceso?'. Justiciabilidad de los Derechos Colectivos, Universidad del Rosario Editorial, 2009.

The World Fact Book. 'Colombia'. https://www.cia.gov/the-world-factbook/countries/colombia/, 1 December 2021.

United States Environmental Protection Agency. 'Ionizing Radiation'. https://www.epa.gov/sites/default/files/2015-05/documents/402-k-10-008.pdf, April 2012.

Index

The numbers here refer to paragraph numbers.

Index

www.ingramcontent.com/pod-product-compliance
Lightning Source LLC
Chambersburg PA
CBHW071444230926
51846CB00001B/332
9789403512181